Fathers in Work Organizations

Brigitte Liebig
Mechtild Oechsle (eds.)

Fathers in Work Organizations

Inequalities and Capabilities, Rationalities
and Politics

Content

1. Introduction

2. Life Conduct, Strategies and Capabilities

3. Cultures, Rationalities and Management

4. Policies and Politics of Fatherhood

5. Issues and Challenges in Research

6. Authors and Editors

1. Introduction

Fathers in Work Organizations: Introduction and Overview

Brigitte Liebig and Mechtild Oechsle

Fathers today are increasingly looking to be involved in the domestic events of the family as active, involved fathers (Lamb 2000). However, current research suggests that actual fatherly engagement depends on complex causal relations. Apart from welfare-state framework conditions, work organizations especially influence the lifestyle and engagement of a father. They are considered as constitutive of the production of asynchronicities between new cultural representations of fatherliness and observable traditional practices of fatherhood (Oechsle et al. 2012). Modified normative ideas of fatherhood encountered in work organizations are almost always hegemonic ideas of masculinity and the provider role associated with it (Smith 2008; Connell et al. 2005). Institutionalized behaviour and routines permit only a few men and fathers to attempt alternative professional paths and orientations. Empirical studies show that the gender connotation of family-friendliness in companies generally tends to be relatively one-sided, and family-friendly measures have so far hardly been used by men. This applies especially to parental leave by fathers (OECD 2016).

At the same time, work organizations are increasingly confronted with the demands of socially responsible actions today. These actions are of central importance for organizations, not only with regards to social legitimacy but also increasingly in view of the optimization of market opportunities. Organizational and business administration theories have attempted to create an empirically-founded explanation of the economic advantages of socially responsible action, drawing on examples of numerous fields of action, among them family-friendly measures and personal versatility. However, the prerequisites and effects of organizational activities which integrate fatherhood as an expression of social development and mutually negotiate with internal/external stakeholders remain largely unknown. This is the reason why problems remain unseen, which organizations with an engagement in the areas of family-friendliness and fatherhood face on their way to become a *corporate citizen*.

Important for the design and realization of active fatherhood are the *cultural aspects of the organization:* organizational and working cultures subtly but effectively control the use and/or the demand of family-friendly measures by fathers. In their overlap with gender cultures, cultural dimension create a hardly-resolvable referential connection. At the same time as a social-political restructuring and reconfiguration of masculinity occurs, hegemonic masculinity frequently finds itself deeply embedded in work organizations (comp. Connell and Messerschmidt 2005). As such, an involved fatherhood often stands in diametric opposition to a working culture dominated by hegemonic masculinity. Apart from a culture of presence and overtime, it also includes a lack of understanding regarding duties outside of work on the part of management or employees (Allard et al. 2011). Men's studies show that active fathers receive very little support in companies: instead, they are supposed to be oriented towards work, career and performance (Puchert et al. 2005). However, while the significance of these cultural aspects of organizations is undisputed, there are important differences, and sometimes even a vagueness, in the conceptualization of an organizational and gender culture (Liebig 2014; Alvesson 2013), especially in light of the analysis of compatibility with fatherhood.

On the level of those people involved, *motives, identities, lifestyle models and action strategies* contribute to a reproduction (or transformation) of hegemonic masculine structures or cultural representations of masculinity/fatherhood within organizations. Men who are fathers are increasingly looking to be involved in the domestic events of the family (BMFSFJ 2015, Lück 2015). However, the current state of research suggests that fatherly engagement depends on complex causal relations. Current studies find a wide range of quotidian reconciliation arrangements, strategies and subjective concepts of fatherhood within different organizational contexts (Halrynjo 2009; Gärtner 2012; Possinger 2013). In general, conflicts of compatibility and the desire for more time for the family seem to be addressed more frequently, even though the effects of such an approach are hardly visible in new and changed practices. The selection of an alternative lifestyle as a man is not only associated with a "readjustment of masculine identity" (Meuser 2007:64), but also frequently with a conscious decision against a professional career. The interplay between social structures, symbolic representation and constructs of identity causes fatherhood to become a social category of inequality, as research on intersectionality suggests. In addition, there are habitual dispositions of men towards being 'providers' which can also be defined as an expression of 'institutional rationalities'. However, men who combine a professional career path with family duties also demonstrate considerable changes in the definition of masculinity in society. It should be expected that they increasingly influence organizational life, and contribute to a shift in organizations when handling requests of compatibility on the part of fathers.

Due to demographic changes, a lack of qualified employees and new discourses about familiy policies, many companies have installed family-friendly measures. The challenges of institutional welfare-state emancipation and reconciliation policies, and their implementation and management, have gained more and more attention. In the last few years, business administration studies and research into organizational structures have reflected on group processes, management practices or processes of the formation of stereotypes and their consequences for conditions of inequality within organizations. In this context, fatherhood is recognized as a social category which is based on the social routines and practices within the every-day life of the organization and which includes a number of challenges. Not only managers, colleagues and the organization's workforce, but also father advocacy groups are becoming relevant players. However, on an organizational level, the politics of fatherhood have hardly been investigated. To date, decision, negotiation and compromise processes in regards to fatherhood in organizations have hardly been addressed by women's and gender studies as well.

About this book

This book addresses the role of work organizations for the realization of active fatherhood. The starting point of the contributions compiled in this book is the assumption that companies, administration bodies and business organizations of any kind significantly determine the lifestyle of fathers. Organizational structures, decisions and processes and their entanglements with normative ideas of gender, career, work and performance contribute to a divergence between formal claims of equality and actual practice. The contributions analyze the *barriers* in work organizations for an involved fatherhood and the associated restrictions for fathers, and investigate mechanisms and influence factors of such processes which generate inequality. On the other hand, the *scope of action* within organizations on the part of fathers is also investigated, as well as the relevant players, and the influence of discourses and policies and any *modification and learning processes* by, and within organizations.

Three different levels are considered especially relevant for the chances of fulfillment of fathers in the context of work organizations, which constitute the inner structure of this book.

In the first part, the quotidian lifestyle of fathers and the associated *identities, practices and strategies of action,* as well as their perception and interpretations, will be the focus and interpreted in their ambivalences as resources but also as restrictions. How do men perceive possible discrimination and exclusion from career options? What role do judgment and decision processes play in the utilization of family-friendly measures? Which desires and demands of work-family compatibility do men believe they are able to formulate and to whom are they addressed? In the second part, the influence of *organizational cultures and rationalities will be discussed,* which characterize the utilization of offers and practices of compatibility (for mothers as well as fathers). Which mechanisms confront fathers when they want to assert their claim to fatherhood? What kind of organizational barriers do they encounter and who is the gatekeeper? The third part of the book will focus on the *political framework conditions and operational measures* which define the possibilities of an active fatherhood. Apart from analyses of the negotiation processes on organizational levels and various policies, the instruments and objectives related to family and possible equality will be investigated in their consequences for the realization of active fatherhood. In doing so, the contributions provide empirical findings from various fields of research, disciplines and countries. Further important objective is the discussion of theoretical concepts and methodological approaches which are suitable for analyzing the possibilities and limits of active fatherhood in their interplay, as well as at the intersection of organizations and the lifestyle of a father.

The contributions collected here trace back to a conference in the spring of 2015 which was organized by the Center for Interdisciplinary Research (Zentrum für interdisziplinäre Forschung – ZiF) in Bielefeld, Germany. We would like to warmly thank the ZiF for the organizational and financial support of this conference.

About the articles[1]

Annette von Alemann, Sandra Beaufaÿs and Mechtild Oechsle start from the fact that fathers increasingly desire to take an active part in family life, while they still tend to maintain their role as breadwinners today. The authors argue that organizational settings, working conditions and labor market opportunities influence fathers' capabilities to achieve the level of family involvement they aspire to. In addition, fathers' life conduct, cultural conceptions and self-concepts seem to entail both, options and obstacles for active fatherhood. Both life conduct and cultural models can interact with organizational and working conditions to shape fathers' practices of involvement. Based on empirical data from Germany, the authors' present typical constellations of fathers' organizational settings and life conduct/living arrangements that lead to either more or less involvement in family life.

---

1   The abstracts are based on texts provided by the respective authors.

Mary Blair-Loy and Stacy J. Williams' article focuses on the accounts that executive-level businessmen in the United States give of their fathering roles and experiences. The two authors examine the ways in which the understanding of their fatherhood obligations are informed by the "work devotion schema", a broad cultural structure which defines work as demanding and deserving single-minded dedication. Starting from in-depth interviews with seventy male senior managers of for-profit firms in the U.S, Blair-Loy and Williams show that executive men are not compelled by gender egalitarian ideals to spend more time with their children. Rather, their orientation toward work devotion justifies their absence from daily family caregiving and minimizes the sense of work-life conflict. The work devotion schema therefore seems to reinforce gender inequality in the workplace and at home.

Sigtona Halrynjo and Selma Therese Lyng explore the role of parental leave for later work-family dynamics among elite professionals in Norway. As they demonstrate, the *fathers' quota* has indeed increased fathers' leave use in elite professions; however, the leave uptake of mothers in the same professions are still many times as long. Moreover, fathers still work more, earn more and are far more likely to have what is regarded as the most important job – while taking less responsibility at home. The chapter illustrates how characteristics, logics and demands of career jobs contribute to these gendered patterns: when dual career couples embark on parenthood with a gender traditional division of parental leave, mothers are constructed as replaceable at work and irreplaceable at home – while the opposite is the case for fathers. Further, the continuous demands for intensive and unpredictable investments in "high commitment" career jobs contribute to a gendered polarization of roles and responsibilities – and thus reinforce an unequal investment in career vs. care work.

Benjamin Neumann and Michael Meuser's article looks at fathers in parental leave in German work organizations. Here, the rate of fathers taking parental leave increased from 3.5 percent to 32 percent within the last ten years. Nevertheless, fathers who claim for taking the leave often still face problems within the organization. Relying on current data, the authors analyze work organizations and show how organizations try to handle the temporary absence of male employees in such a way that organizational routines are not endangered. They identify several conducive factors that allow a higher rate of fathers taking parental leave, as well as obstructive factors which inhibit more fathers taking leave or taking more than the usual two months. Further, the authors explore how organizational rationales and couples' motives are related in a way that the usual duration of two months of additional parental leave meets the interests of both.

Brigitte Liebig and Christian Kron start from the fact that organizational benevolence shows considerable limitations with respect to their effects, especially when fathers as stakeholders are concerned: as data on part-time working men or the share of men in household labor show, the success of father-friendly programmes can be assessed as rather moderate. But why do fathers not make use of corporate family-friendliness in great numbers? Which are the factors for involved fatherhood on organizational levels, and how do these interact with individual decision making? Inspired by neo-institutional theory, the authors argue that fathers' decisions for involved fatherhood is strongly determined by organizational norms and rationales, and that these are the most important factors of the 'decoupling' between official claims and everyday action. Analysis is based on case studies of nine large and medium-sized public organizations and private-sector companies in Switzerland, of which most have been certified as family friendly.

Annalisa Murgia and Barbara Poggio's contribution is devoted to the stories recounted by fathers and their experiences in coping with gender cultures in Italian work organizations. In order to describe fathers' experiences with parental leave, they refer metaphorically to three mythological figures: the Titan brothers Atlas, Epimetheus and Prometheus. With respect to structural changes in the labor market, the authors analyse the consequences of non-standard employment relations for fathers' rights. Their research shows significant differences in the right to use parental leave between fathers in fixed-term and in self-employed work. To give an account of changing conditions in the labour market, Murgia and Poggio refer to a further mythological figure, Menoetius, the fourth brother of the Titans, and illustrate the manifold and ambivalent experiences of fathers deprived of their rights at work.

Christoph Schimkowsky and Florian Kohlbacher's chapter offers an introduction to Japan's 'new fathers'. As they show, the image of fathers in Japanese society has changed considerably within the last few years. *Ikumen* – a popular term used in Japan to describe fathers who are actively involved in child-rearing – have received widespread media attention as well as support from the Japanese government, which also hopes to use these "nurturing fathers" to counter declining birth rates. The text highlights a range of public and private campaigns that strive to make company policies and executive behavior more amenable to fathers, advancing their ability to integrate family and work life. As the authors make clear, companies' involvement with fathers is not only furthered by public and private campaigns, but also by business interests and the desire to be perceived as a modern company. Also in Japan, work environment and work culture are primary factors thwarting fathers' involvement in parenting and childcare practices.

As *Elin Kvande and Berit Brandth* argue, the introduction of a special non-transferable quota for fathers in the Norwegian parental leave system represents a rupture with disembodied thinking about gender in organizations. The article explores how the introduction of the fathers' quota in the Norwegian parental leave system has been received in different work organizations. The analysis confirms that father's care obligations seem to be accepted in working life today. Making use of the father's quota has become normative and supports the dual-carer model in the family, as well as in working life. The findings of Kvande and Brandth also show that the fathers' quota – as a statutory right which is paid by the state and not dependant on the employers' good will - constructs the leave as a universal right. The principle of earmarking and non-transferability is very important since it relates fathers' care responsibility to their role as employees.

Johanna Possinger outlines the case of Germany, where breadwinning remains a key component of the concept of 'good fatherhood', although the majority of fathers strive to balance work and caring activities nowadays. This is partly due to fact that since 2007 German family policy has called on fathers to take parental leave and 'daddy months', which became very popular. However most men still do not claim their 'daddy months' and the gendered division of labor remains rather untouched. The article highlights the gap between fathers' ideals of 'active fatherhood' and the traditional practice of fathering, while drawing on interviews with fathers who are employed at a large heat and energy corporation. The author illustrates the barriers to paternal involvement, putting particular focus on work-related obstacles and outlining future policy steps that would strengthen fathers' participation in the caregiving process.

Stephan Höyng discusses the core issues of state family policy as a framework for balancing the interests of organizations, fathers, children and partners in Germany. As he outlines, parental leave regulations, the expansion of institutional childcare and tax splitting for married couples impact on the gender balance between couples. To support the reconciliation of work and family, work cultures must improve in different areas: in organizations, at home and in education and care facilities. In organizations, networking and performance definitions have to change. At home, work and responsibilities have to be shared in an egalitarian manner between partners. Education and care facilities have to leave behind the structures of the industrial age and seek closer ties with fathers. Overall, so the author argues, families would benefit most from a social policy which secures income and shortens work hours.

Finally, *Suzan Lewis and Bianca Stumbitz* outline the wider fields of work and family from the perspective of research, and consider implications for fathers. Four key challenges for future work-family research are drawn out:

the first refers to the ongoing need to better understand and confront deeply embedded and change-resistant gendered workplace practices and cultures that can undermine active fatherhood. Second, the impact of complex intersecting layers of societal, community, organizational and family contexts on experiences of work and family remain a research challenge. Thirdly, the range of contexts studied has to be broadened: most research takes place in large organizations within western, high income countries, neglecting other experiences in smaller organizations and in the developing world. Finally, the authors raise the question of how research can progress beyond describing and analyzing barriers to gender equity and involved fatherhood, towards contributing to systemic change in workplaces and families.

References

Allard, K. et al. (2011) 'Family-Supportive Organizational Culture and Fathers' Experiences of Work: family conflict in Sweden', *Gender, Work & Organization,* 18 (2), pp. 141–157

Alvesson, M. (2013) *Understanding Organizational Culture.* London: SAGE Publications

BMFSFJ (2015) *Dossier: Väter und Familie – erste Bilanz einer neuen Dynamik.* Available at: https://www.bmfsfj.de/blob/95454/54a00f4dd26664aae799f-76fcee1fd4e/vaeter-und-familie-dossier-data.pdf

Gärtner, M. (2012) *Männer und Familienvereinbarkeit. Betriebliche Personalpolitik, Akteurskonstellationen und Organisationskulturen.* Opladen: Verlag Barbara Budrich

Haas L. and Hwang, P. (2007) 'Gender and Organizational Culture: correlates of companies responsiveness to fathers in Sweden', *Gender & Society* 21 (1), pp. 52–79

Halrynjo, S. (2009) 'Men's Work Life-Conflict: career, care and self-realization; patterns of privileges and dilemmas', *Gender, Work & Organization* 16 (1), pp. 98–125

Hobson, B. (ed.) (2014) *Worklife Balance: The Agency and Capabilities Gap.* Oxford: Oxford University Press

Kapella, O. and Rille-Pfeiffer, Ch. (eds.) (2011) *Papa geht arbeiten. Vereinbarkeit aus Sicht von Männern.* Opladen: Verlag Barbara Budrich

Lamb, M. E. (2000) 'The History of Research on Father Involvement: an overview', *Marriage & Family Review,* 29 (2–3), pp. 23–42

Liebig, B. (2014) Zum ‚Cultural Turn' in der feministischen Organisationsforschung. Organisation und Geschlecht aus der Sicht von Organisationkulturkonzepten, in: Funder, M. (ed.) *The Gender Cage Revisited: Handbuch zur Organisations- und Geschlechterforschung.* Baden-Baden: Nomos, pp. 271–294

Lück, D. (2015) Vaterleitbilder: Ernährer und Erzieher?, in: Schneider, N.F., Diabate, S. and Ruckdeschel, K. (eds.) *Familienleitbilder in Deutschland: Kulturelle*

Vorstellungen zu Partnerschaft, Elternschaft und Familienleben. Opladen: Verlag Barbara Budrich

Meuser, M. (2007) Vom Ernährer der Familie zum involvierten Vater? Männlichkeitskonstruktionen und Vaterschaftskonzepte, in: Meuser, M. (ed.) *Herausforderungen: Männlichkeit im Wandel der Geschlechterverhältnisse.* Köln, Rüdiger Köppe Verlag, pp. 49–64

OECD (2016) *Parental leave: Where are the fathers? Men's uptake of parental leave is rising but still low,* Policy Brief, March 2016 Available at: https://www.oecd.org/policy-briefs/parental-leave-where-are-the-fathers.pdf

Oechsle, M. et al. (eds.) (2012) *Fatherhood in Late Modernity: cultural images, social practices, structural frames.* Opladen: Verlag Barbara Budrich

Possinger, J. (2013) *Vaterschaft im Spannungsfeld von Erwerbs- und Familienleben: „Neuen Vätern" auf der Spur.* Wiesbaden: Springer

Puchert, R. et al. (eds.) (2005) *Work Changes Gender: men and equality in the transition of labour forms.* Opladen: Verlag Barbara Budrich

Smith, A. (2008) 'Working Fathers as Providers and Carers: towards a new conceptualisation of fatherhood', *Social Policy Review* 20, pp. 279–296

# 2.	Life Conduct, Strategies and Capabilities

Work Organizations and Fathers' Lifestyles: Constraints and Capabilities

Annette von Alemann, Sandra Beaufaÿs and Mechtild Oechsle

1. Introduction

Research tells us that in Germany, as well as in many other countries, many fathers want to take a more active part in family life and childcare (Oechsle, Müller and Hess 2012). This runs counter to reports and assertions suggesting that gendered time use and a gendered division of paid and unpaid work are still prevalent. Research on fatherhood and fathers in late modernity indicates, on the one hand, that fathers today are experiencing a stronger desire to be involved in their children's upbringing and to take a more active part in family life. On the other hand, however, they still tend to maintain their role as breadwinners, and when children arrive, mechanisms of re-traditionalization begin to influence the division of labor between fathers and mothers (Schulz and Blossfeld 2006; Grunow 2014).

In our paper, we present findings from our research project "Work Organizations and Life Conduct of Fathers". The project was conducted from 2011 to 2015 at Bielefeld University, Germany, as part of the Collaborative Research Center 882 "From Heterogeneities to Inequalities" (funded by the Deutsche Forschungsgemeinschaft/German Research Foundation, DFG). In this project, we ask which factors lead to differences in capabilities (chances) between fathers in order to better understand what they perceive as an equal (or good) work-family balance (WFB). Thus, we focus not on gender inequalities but on differences between men. Contrary to classical inequality research, we pursue the holistic capability approach (Sen 1992, 1993), not considering earning capacities or career opportunities as primary but instead, the chances for achieving life goals.

In this paper, we will first outline our theoretical approach and the state of current research (section 2) as well as our methods and data (section 3). We will then present empirical insights about organizational constraints and capabilities and the impact of lifestyle on fathers' involvement in the family (section 4). In the conclusion (section 5), based on our results, we will discuss the impact of organizations on fathers' involvement in the family and the relevance of cultural models, self-concepts, and bargaining processes within the family. It is the interrelationships of structures, cultures, and actors that function as constraints or capabilities unequally allowing or preventing fathers in achieving their life goals.

2. Organizations and fathers' lifestyles: state of the art and theoretical framework

2.1. The capability approach

Following Sen's (1992, 1993) capability approach, we assume that individuals have different capabilities at their disposal to achieve what they consider a good life. Capabilities are "alternative combinations of functionings" (or goals) a person can achieve in life and "the ability to get access to these functionings" (1993: 31; cf. Zimmermann 2006). Capabilities denote a person's opportunity and ability to generate valuable outcomes, taking into account relevant personal characteristics and external factors. We understand social inequality, then, as unequal chances to achieve relevant life goals (Sen 1992, 1993). Following the approach of Hobson (2014: 14) who applied Sen's capability approach to the achievement of work-family balance, we analyze different factors that are influential for social inequalities among fathers. Hobson (Hobson 2014; Hobson and Fahlén 2009) proposes a multilevel approach with the levels (1) individual (e.g. resources, abilities, qualifications; social structures such as gender, class, age, etc.; private lifestyle; and individual preferences), (2) institution (with the levels welfare state, work organization, and working time regime), and (3) social and/or cultural factors (such as norms, social movements, politics, public discourses, etc.). In this paper, we will analyze the individual and the organizational side, a variety of cultural factors, and the mutual interplay of factors on all three of the aforementioned levels.

We are looking at the capability approach from a pragmatist perspective. That is, we understand what individuals do as a process of action shaped by values and environment as well as habits and multiple preferences (Oechsle and Reimer 2016). Following Zimmermann (2006), we combine a pragmatist perspective with configurational material and immaterial elements: objects, tools, and equipment, but also time and temporalities (2006: 479). Thus, Sen's capability approach as developed by Zimmermann (2006) and Hobson (2014) for the analysis of action (Zimmermann) and work-family balance (Hobson) sheds a new light on active involvement in the family as a life goal. Valuable concepts for our study on fathers and their capabilities are fathers' agency and their "sense of entitlement" (Lewis and Smithson 2001; Hobson et al. 2014), which refers to the demands fathers believe they can make because they are "entitled to" them legitimately.

2.2 Constraints and capabilities within organizations

In contemporary societies, reconciling family and working life is becoming increasingly important for men (Oechsle, Müller and Hess 2012; Possinger 2013). But for fathers, the desire to spend time and engage with children during the working week is still often outweighed by their role as the main breadwinner in the family (Grunow 2007). Hence, their time use is structured primarily by workplace requirements. Work organizations are therefore important agents in processes of traditionalization in family constellations (Klenner and Pfahl 2008; Possinger 2013) and may therefore contribute to persistent gender inequalities.

Work organizations are characterized by very specific constellations of factors within organizations that interact either to create constraints on fathers or to foster their ability to conduct their everyday lives in line with their own desires and priorities. Following Stainback, Tomaskovic-Devey and Shaggs (2010), we assume that there are generic organizational mechanisms which generate inequalities in access to respect, resources, and rewards. Organizational processes are influenced by inertial tendencies of organizational structure, logic, and practice, the relative power of actors within the organization and the specific contexts, i.e. cultural models and discourses, politics, social movements, and organizational fields.

Structural changes in the organization of work over the last few decades have significantly altered relationships between work organizations and their employees. Employers now offer employees more autonomy and broader scheduling options (Kossek and Lambert 2005), yet they also expect more in terms of employee availability and are increasingly becoming "greedy organizations" (Kvande 2009; Hearn and Pringle 2006). Neo-institutionalist scholars have interpreted the increased focus on family-friendly policies in companies' promotional statements and their implementation of family-friendly programs in the workplace as reactions to a changing environment (Müller 2010; Scott 1995). In Germany as well as in other OECD countries, the topic of a family-friendly workplace has become a subject of public discourse. As a family-friendly work environment is seen by employers as an important means of attracting qualified employees, companies try to meet such expectations by releasing mission statements that emphasize their family-friendly policies, and by making considerable efforts to present themselves as family-friendly employers. However, many studies have identified problems in the uptake of family-friendly programs (Kodz, Harper and Dench 2002); here it is evident that fathers often do not even attempt to make use of existing programs out of fear of negative reactions (OECD 2016; Possinger 2013). The neo-institutional approach describes the widespread underuse of the family-friendly programs (Müller 2010) that are offered in many workplaces as "decoupling" (i.e. the separation of talk and action, cf. Meyer and Rowan 1992). From a neo-institutional perspective, expectations in the institutional environment often contravene intra-organizational necessities, strategies, and practices.

The concept of organizational culture (Alvesson 2013; Haas and Hwang 2007; Kvande 2007; Smircich 1983; Schein 1990) is useful in understanding decoupling processes as well as the gap between formal family-friendly policies and the limited use thereof. Organizational culture plays a significant role in how an organization deals with employees' problems and desires for compatibility between work and family life (Hochschild 1997; Haas and Hwang 2007). According to Schreyögg (1999: 438), organizational culture can be seen as a collective phenomenon based on tacit values and assumptions representing the conceptual world of the organization.[1]

Organizational cultures contain assumptions about the relationship between the organization and private life, and about how (and to whom) responsibility is assigned for achieving work-life balance. Thus, they create implicit standards for employees' behavior. As research on gender and organization has shown, social norms about working hours and employee availability have gender connotations, and they are interwoven with constructions of masculinity (Meuser and Scholz 2012; Collinson and Hearn 2004; Hofbauer 2006; Halrynjo 2009).

Such constructions may be linked to "hidden rules" (Payne 2005) in organizations. Hidden rules are based on organizationally established assumptions about the employees' behavior, suggesting how to behave or not to behave and legitimizing the behavior deemed appropriate (Oechsle and Beaufaÿs 2016). Thus, they may contradict values espoused by the organization, such as the value of work-life balance as a source of productivity and official programs of family-friendliness. Whenever they are in direct contrast to an organization's official statements and programs, they are able to prevent the use of family-friendly programs and state-sanctioned rights and thus reduce fathers' "sense of entitlement" (Lewis and Smithson 2001; Hobson 2014).

---

1   See also Schein's (1990) model of organizational culture, which distinguishes between visible and less visible facets of organizational culture, as well as between more and less conscious aspects. Schein (1990) differentiates three levels: artifacts, expressed values, and basic assumptions, most of the latter being unconscious and ineffable.

Organizational cultures are not always consistent (Alvesson 2013) and thus may not only produce ambivalence and fear but also provide windows of opportunity for resourceful actors who use them to pursue their goals. This perspective leads us to take into account micro-political negotiation processes that people use to achieve their aspired level of work-family compatibility. Studies show that, in these negotiation processes, direct supervisors have an important gatekeeper function (Hochschild 1997). Sensitivity towards needs and specific problems of fathers and families plays a key role in the working group context (Jurczyk and Lange 2010; Possinger 2013).

2.3 Constraints and capabilities within lifestyle and everyday life

Fathers' capabilities to take on an active role in family life are not only shaped by organizations and their structures and cultures, they are also influenced by patterns of lifestyle and different employment constellations (e.g. labor market chances).

When analyzing fathers' lifestyle, we use the concept of everyday life conduct[2] as a form of individual attainment (Jurczyk, Lange and Thiessen 2014; Jurczyk, Voß and Weihrich 2015; Weihrich and Voß 2002). This concept is founded on the idea that the complex effort required to mediate between different life areas and to balance the specific demands arising from each is "a performance of the individual[s]" (Voß 1991). Its focus on everyday practical activity also implies an inequality perspective (Jürgens 2002). Different patterns of lifestyle and the respective risks they entail can be interpreted as expressions of structurally determined inequalities in living situations, but they can also be understood as a means of overcoming social inequality and as resources for achieving life goals.

How fathers conduct their lives is shaped by complex constellations of factors such as fathers' work contexts, their partners' work and personal situations (e.g. occupation, employment, cultural models), children (number and age, availability of childcare), financial situation (family income, property, mortgages), geographic location (e.g. local surroundings, distance to workplace and childcare), and social and regional backgrounds (Alemann and Beaufaÿs 2015). Furthermore, it is influenced by fathers' cultural models, i.e. social assumptions of normality, which express socially accepted ideals and

---

2   In this paper, we prefer the term "lifestyle" because it is more common in the English speaking world (and allows highlighting the difference between our theoretical perspective and the philosophical meaning of "conduct of life" as proposed by Emerson 1860). We understand "lifestyle" in the sense of "conduct of life" referring to the term as it has been developed in the research group around Voß (1991). Thus, lifestyle does not only refer to an expressive or aesthetic style of life but designates the individual's active, integrative part in constructing one's own way of living within specific social conditions.

life goals (Alemann and Beaufaÿs 2015; Possinger 2013). Cultural models can be seen as a link between institutions and individual action, and individuals have to select and adopt them in an active way (Oechsle 1998). Models of fatherhood and fatherliness play an important role in the fathers' lifestyle, and they interact with their partners' models of motherhood and motherliness and with both partners' cultural models of partnership and family life (Schneider et al. 2015). Cultural models operate on the level of cultural representations, as institutional models for welfare state institutions, as social discourses, and as individual orientations and attitudes. Between the various levels, asynchronies can be found (Oechsle et al. 2006; Oechsle and Reimer 2016; Oechsle and Beaufaÿs 2016). Everyday life is the place where fathers experience ambivalent or contradictory cultural models of family, gender, and work commitment, and the place where they have to cope with these contradictions.

3. Methods and Data

For our study, we recruited a sample of seven companies, both public and private, of different sizes and sectors (insurance, financial services, retail trade, high technology, telecommunication, and logistics), located throughout Germany. Most of them are certified as family-friendly. We gathered data on their organizational contexts by analyzing company homepages and documents and conducted expert interviews with heads of human resources, gender affairs, and diversity managers, as well as staff council and executive board members. The data consist of 110 problem-centered interviews (Witzel 2000) with fathers at different levels and in various areas of each organization. The fathers had to have at least one child under the age of six in the household. Additionally, we conducted 16 problem-centered interviews with selected partners of the interviewed fathers.

The respondents' ages are between 26 and 52 years (ø 39 years of age). The large majority were born between 1965 and 1976, 83% in western Germany, 14% in eastern Germany, and 2.7% outside Germany. The number of children varies between one and five (ø 1.8 children). Most of the fathers (almost 80%) are employed full-time which means, in Germany, that approximately 40 hours per week are contractually agreed. However, 57% of the fathers work between 41 and 60 hours per week. Qualified professionals in leadership positions are overrepresented in our sample. Fathers who took significantly more than two months of parental leave are an exception. The partner's working hours range between 0 and 60 per week, with very few of these women working full-time or more.

The empirical material was analyzed in three steps on three levels: organization, lifestyle, and interdependencies between organizations and lifestyle. In order to examine the organizational level, we used a range of data from different sources to reconstruct both the corporate image and the internal perspective. The corporate image was studied on the basis of the companies' homepages, while organizational beliefs and values were analyzed through expert interviews and the company culture as seen by the interviewed staff members. For the analysis of the level of paternal lifestyle, we coded the interviews with fathers and mothers according to a deductively-inductively developed categorical scheme using the qualitative data analysis software MaxQDA. For each father interviewed, we created a brief structured portrait. Based on the interviews with selected fathers and their partners, we then created structured portraits of couples, which were analyzed comparatively. Based on Zimmermann's concept of configurational approaches (Zimmermann 2006), we analyzed, in a third step, typical configurations of organizational contexts and fathers' lifestyles from a comparative perspective. The result is a typology of concepts of fatherhood and their chances of realization.

4. Empirical Findings

In the following sections, we present the cases of two fathers who work in different organizations. Their cases are exemplary for contrasting configurations of constraints and capabilities for fathers who want to be involved in family life.

Mr. Smith is thirty-four years old and has a two-year-old son. He works about 50 hours per week, and his wife works part-time. He holds a position as a senior consultant at "Consumer Goods", an international retail company in the private sector. The company has more than 100,000 employees worldwide, including more than 2,000 in Germany. 82% of the employees are female, but only 20% of the women hold leadership positions. Working time arrangements are flextime, trusted flextime, part-time, jobsharing, and home office. The company is certified as a family-friendly employer.

Mr. Roberts is thirty-nine years old and has two children aged four and seven. He works 30 hours per week, as does his wife. Mr. Roberts holds a position as a senior expert at "Communication Systems", an international telecommunications company in the private sector. The company has more than 100,000 employees worldwide, including more than 60,000 in Germany.

30% of the employees are female, and about 20% of the women obtain leadership positions. Working time arrangements are flextime, trusted flextime, part time, shift work, jobsharing, and home office. The company is also certified as a family-friendly employer.

Mr. Smith and Mr. Roberts appear to share many close similarities in terms of their overall situation. They differ slightly in age, but both hold senior positions in their companies, and their family incomes are equal. Both men have a wife who is equally highly qualified, and both work at the level of their qualifications. But the men differ substantially as fathers in their working and childcare practices. Whereas Mr. Roberts works part-time and took several parental leave months for his two children, Mr. Smith tends to work overtime, has never taken leave, and does not plan to do so – despite claiming not to be career-oriented. In the interview, Mr. Smith and Mr. Roberts both profess their willingness and desire to be involved in family life. But Mr. Smith indicates that he feels unable to achieve his goal, whereas Mr. Roberts reports to be fully satisfied with his situation. We want to know, then, which factors discourage Mr. Smith and encourage Mr. Roberts to be involved in their children's upbringing. To answer this question, in the following we look at the organizations where they work. Each of the organizations involved in our study is shaped by structural and cultural factors and constellations of organizational actors. The interrelations among these factors lead to a set of constraints and capabilities.

4.1 The impact of work organizations

"Consumer Goods", Mr. Smith's organization, sells interchangeable products in a highly competitive market. Therefore, the organizational structure is subject to constant change, job insecurity, and a constant scarcity of staff. As part of the German private sector, working conditions are, to a certain extent, subject to individual negotiations between employee and employer or direct supervisor. The organizational culture is highly competitive. It is common to work long hours and to hide family commitments from superiors. The culture is characterized by presenteeism and hidden rules. These hidden rules prevent the use of the manifold family-friendly programs and of state-sanctioned rights such as parental leave, and they are in direct contrast to the organization's family-friendly self-presentation. Examples of such hidden rules are: "Family-friendliness is an issue (mostly) affecting women"; "Be grateful for any goodwill shown by supervisors and the company in general"; "You are responsible for making enough family time and for your performance as a father. Don't blame your employer". Although the organization offers time flexibility for employees on all company levels, this has more to do with the demands of the market than with the demands of the fathers. Mr. Smith describes how he sees the chances of his CEO understanding his situation:

> I don't expect too much understanding for my urge to get home in the evening, or for me arriving late because I had to drop off my child at daycare or something like that. I don't mention these things in that context. I try to avoid that, since I don't want him [the CEO] to view me as unsuitable, because I have a strong hunch he won't agree and he won't understand.

In this organization, the supervisors have significant power as gatekeepers. Just as supervisors are expected to show total commitment and availability to the company, they expect the same from their subordinates. The HR department, which considers itself an agent of family-friendliness, has relatively low bargaining power in the organizational setting.

Among the fathers in this organization, we observe processes of self-exclusion. They anticipate implicit expectations of availability and behave accordingly: either they adapt to these anticipated expectations, renouncing their desires for active fatherhood, or they self-exclude from career positions. This is due to the fathers' relatively weak bargaining power. Mr. Smith is especially dependent on his organization because of his weak position in the labor market. As a social scientist, his chances to earn a good income outside this organization are relatively low. However, Mr. Smith is not the only father whose sense of entitlement is reduced by the organizational culture. It is the totality of all of the working conditions in the organization that leads to a low sense of entitlement in employees who want to reconcile work and family life.

"Communication Systems", Mr. Roberts' employer, is a market leader in telecommunication systems. Parts of the organizational structure are highly regulated, stemming from a history as public-service organization, and there are varied family-friendly programs. The job security is quite high.

The culture is characterized by a high level of co-operation and output orientation with a low level of social control among employees. Talking about family commitments is widely accepted within the organization. Especially in positions for highly qualified staff at company headquarters, a flexible schedule is possible, and using it for family matters is accepted within the organizational culture. Mr. Roberts feels accepted and supported by his supervisor in his way of life.

> I can imagine that he [my supervisor] wasn't happy when I came to him with my request to take leave. But he didn't let me sense that, for example, when I returned to work part-time. (...) Or in matters of career development, I don't feel overlooked, although I have taken a lot of liberties, so to speak, for the sake of my family.

Mr. Roberts envisions himself as a pioneer in the use of flexible working time arrangements, and as an agent of change, and he hopes to function as a model for other fathers.[3] Within his organization, Mr. Roberts has significant bargaining power because, as an engineer, his chances on the labor market are quite high. In addition, the employees' sense of entitlement in the company is high.

4.2 The impact of lifestyle

It is not only the organizational setting and the chances on the labor market that influence fathers' capabilities to achieve the level of fatherly involvement they aspire to. Fathers' lifestyle also entails both chances and obstacles for active fatherhood. Mr. Smith and Mr. Roberts both present themselves as fathers who would like to be active fathers and to be involved in their children's lives. But whereas Mr. Roberts actually does feel involved and openly displays his involvement in the work context, Mr. Smith expresses fears of losing contact with his child and still keeps up with the expectations imposed on him in his workplace. How can we explain the difference between them in their everyday practices apart from organizational preconditions? When asking the two fathers how their individual living arrangements evolved, we learn a great deal about Mr. Smith's and Mr. Roberts' general orientations in life.

Mr. Smith recalls the family situation when his son was born:

Some things were just set. So it was clear that I'd work more (...) I mean, that I'd have to continue working 100%. And otherwise, I tried to meet her expectations as far as possible. (...) But somehow there are no traditional reasons for our arrangement. We just decided on the basis of what each of us felt comfortable with – as well as the facts.

Mr. Roberts tells a quite different story:

My initial goal, or our goal, was to have an equal relationship with each of us bearing 50% of the workload, including gainful work and housework. And on the whole – from my perspective – things have worked out pretty well. And in that sense, we have stuck with our plan. The only thing is that it's more work than I expected.

Mr. Smith's orientation is clearly geared toward the things that were set and given, as he sees it. In particular, his full-time job cannot be called into question. Otherwise, he tries to meet his wife's expectations. Although this attitude

---

3   In other organizations, we observed powerful actors such as CEOs changing organizational cultures into more family-friendly cultures for fathers because they believed this would be a "win-win" situation for both the fathers and the company.

may not be rooted in traditional values, it is still embedded in traditional practices. Mr. Smith sees his impact as small.

In contrast, Mr. Roberts interprets his arrangement as based on practices that were consciously established from the very beginning. He, too, refers to his partner when expressing the couple's shared values regarding equality. "Doing family" this way means following a schedule. It is exhausting, but it works. Judging from his point of view, things seem to be quite simple. His message is: just do it.

As we analyze the interactions between organizations (structures, cultures and policies), and fathers' lifestyles (their personal ideals and self-concepts of fatherhood as well as their everyday fathering practices), we observe in particular that the negotiation processes between couples concerning the division of labor play an important role. Besides the organizational impact, there are barriers due to the couple and their images of family life and childhood. There are expectations on the mothers' side that the fathers would like to meet. To understand the degree of the fathers' involvement, we have to consider the perspective of their partners as well.

Mrs. Smith recalls her early career orientation and life plans:

> *Well, actually I always had been toying with the idea of working half-days by the time I had kids. Back then, I thought that dentistry would be very convenient for that because you earn quite a bit. So I had the attitude that if I study dentistry and then work half-days, I'll earn as much as a teacher.*

Mrs. Roberts had very different plans for her life:

> *To stay home three years with your child and then have the <u>right</u> to return to your job – this is how <u>I</u> interpret it – that's something I cannot imagine for my own life. You know, I never planned on staying home for the kids until they're allowed to go to kindergarten, and then probably only work from 8 to 12, which is still common in rural areas.*

In the paradigmatic cases of Mr. Roberts and Mr. Smith, we find typical constellations and living arrangements that lead to either more or less involvement in family life. In the case of Mr. Smith, both parents favor a lifestyle as homeowners in the suburbs, implying a commuting working father and a mother managing the household. Mr. Smith's parents lived according to this same model. He grew up in a small town in western Germany, and his mother stayed home to take care of the children. Mr. and Mrs. Smith's self-concepts reflect this cultural model. Although both of them are highly qualified, Mr. Smith sees himself as the (main) breadwinner, and Mrs. Smith pictures herself mainly as a mother. Fathering in this family is practiced mainly as support to the mother. The father puts his own desires for a close relationship to his child on hold, looking forward to spending more time with his child when the child is older.

The Roberts follow the cultural model of total equality and self-realization in the job and in the family. This is also rooted in Mr. and Mrs. Robert's social background: Both were born in eastern Germany. Mr. Robert's parents are highly qualified and both still work. They, too, support the idea of equal opportunities in the family. The Roberts picture themselves as a caring father and a working mother. This is reflected in their family practices: The father takes the opportunity to be actively involved in his children's upbringing, and he is doing more than just supporting the mother.

So, although both fathers vary little in the facts of their respective situations (especially regarding qualifications, position, and income) and although they both wish to be active fathers, Mr. Smith and Mr. Roberts lead completely different lives. This may partly derive from their own and their partners' heritage, but that is not the point we want to make here. Rather, we would like to stress that, in any case, practices evolve into obstacles or capabilities and can reinforce constraints or capabilities at the workplace.

4.3 Configurations of constraints and capabilities

In our study, we have found that father's cultural models and self-concepts, plus those of their partners, shape their practices of involvement. We reconstructed three types of fatherly self-conceptions: the *(main) breadwinner* (inclusion in family activities mostly on weekends: leisure activities, play, sports, and fun); the *companion* (inclusion in family activities during the week as well: getting the children off to bed, bathing, taking children to daycare; but main responsibility for care rests with the mother); and the *caring father* (inclusion in family activities since early childhood, participation in care on a regular basis from the very beginning, egalitarian division of labor). Two thirds of the fathers interviewed live (more or less) according to one of these self-conceptions as fathers, and, all in all, they feel satisfied with their lives as fathers. One third are struggling with their own ideals of being a good father but cannot realize them in everyday life. These fathers feel uncomfortable with their situation: The breadwinner feels marginalized in the family; the father who wants to spend more time with his children as they are growing up is more a "would-be companion" and has limited capabilities to fulfill this self-conception, and the caring father experiences conflicts with his wife as well as with supervisors or colleagues. Furthermore, it is important to see the differences behind similar wishes of fathers to be involved in their children's lives. The wish to be an active father does not necessarily mean seeking or striving for an egalitarian division of labor. We therefore differentiate between the caring father and the father as companion.

Mr. Smith is a very good example for the *would-be companion* father. Analyzing the case of Mr. Smith and his wife, we can see that the couple's cultural model, self-conceptions, and practices increase the implicit expectations of the organization. The organizational conditions of Mr. Smith and the couple's way of "doing family" mutually compound each other. In the interview, we hear Mr. Smith very clearly expressing his aspirations: He rejects the idea of being a weekend father and says he does not want to put his career first – and still we find him struggling with his situation because this is exactly what he is doing. If he does not pursue his career in his competitive working environment, he is putting his job at risk, and to prevent this, he has to give in to the presenteeism culture of his company.

Mr. Roberts is an example of the *caring father* who is able to realize his self-conception of being a good father. Here we have all the conditions that lead to equal involvement in the family – not only on the side of the organization, but also on that of lifestyle. These two aspects work together to enhance his involvement in his family. In the interview, Mr. Roberts says that he has postponed his career aspirations for a certain time. This is acceptable to his supervisor.

Mr. Smith's and Mr. Roberts' cases are extreme examples within a wider range of configurations. The family arrangements they have developed together with their partners are examples of very different configurations of constraints and capabilities. Mr. Smith represents a configuration of multiple constraints on being an involved father, both at work and within the family. These barriers mutually reinforce each other and they have led to an arrangement Mr. Smith never wanted to accept, even unintentionally, and as a father he feels quite uncomfortable with this situation. The case of Mr. Roberts shows a set of capabilities for active and involved fatherhood in the organizational context as well as in his family. These capabilities also reinforce each other. Mr. Roberts is quite satisfied with his life and the situation at work and within his family, and he is convinced that he is leading a life according to his values and preferred goals.

5. Conclusions

We chose the two cases presented here to show the impact of different configurations of constraints and capabilities for fathers' involvement in the family. Our sample includes other types of configurations of constraints and capabilities that work in other directions. For example, organizational constraints on involved fatherhood can be moderated by strong capabilities in the fathers' lifestyle, and vice versa. Yet these two to some extent polarized examples display the impact of organizational parameters as well as the influence of fathers' conduct of life on achieving involved fatherhood. In this last section, we refer back to our theoretical concepts to analyze constraints and capabilities for fathers' involvement more generally.

Beginning with the influence of organizational structure and culture, we can see some highly important parameters that make a difference for fathers who want to be involved in their children's lives. Of course, the sector and the market position of the company as well as the organization of work and the working conditions play a crucial role in fathers' capabilities. We can see great differences in the regulation of working conditions and time arrangements. Organizations that occupy a role as a market leader and/or are subject to a stronger regulation of working conditions allow fathers to develop a set of capabilities for fatherhood, whereas organizations in a competitive market position, and with low regulation of working conditions, build up a set of constraints for fathers who are trying to achieve involved fatherhood. In sum, the structure of an organization has an important impact on fathers' capabilities, and our data show a clear profile of corresponding features.

But the impact of organizational culture should not be underestimated. In our study, we found strong evidence that cultural factors have a great impact on fathers' capabilities, too. Even though six out of seven companies in our sample are certificated as family-friendly and offer programs to promote work-family balance, the use of such programs is often restricted by hidden rules.[4] We reconstructed these hidden rules in our interviews with fathers when they told us their stories about their decisions to take parental leave, or about their trying to use flextime for family needs (Oechsle and Beaufaÿs 2016). The narratives and reflections of the interviewed fathers show clearly the decoupling of "talk" and "action" in some companies as described by the neo-institutional approach. An important part of these hidden rules is the issue of responsibility for work-family compatibility: It is often seen more as an individual responsibility of the employee than as a responsibility of the employer.

The attribution of responsibility (e.g. for the reconciliation of work and family life) is part of the construction of normality in organizations: what is taken for granted and seen as normal, and what is contested in the organization when dealing with issues of work-family compatibility for fathers. For many fathers, minimizing the visibility of involved fatherhood and preventing themselves from being assigned a status as "tokens" are crucial problems.

---

4   One company in our sample had neither formal certifications nor family-friendly programs. However, we identified numerous practices there that support fathers' wishes to be more actively involved in everyday family life.

Young fathers with career aspirations in particular tend to take less parental leave, take leave in smaller chunks, or even not take any leave at all due to concerns about how this will affect their career, their supervisors, or their colleagues. Other fathers who do not want to offer the level of availability they think is expected of them tacitly reduce their career aspirations in advance. We can analyze this as a kind of self-exclusion, which makes the conflicts fathers face in trying to achieve work-family balance invisible as well. The decision to work overtime versus part-time or full-time can also be seen as an important aspect of practices that make involved fatherhood more or less visible. The underlying perception is that care and career are mutually exclusive. This is usually directed mainly at women, but it also applies to men if they are care-oriented in practice. Thus, we are dealing with a mechanism of social inequality that is linked to care rather than to gender.

Among the fathers interviewed, most have a limited sense of entitlement (cf. Lewis and Smithson 2001) and conceive of the use of family-friendly programs not as a right but as a "give-and-take"-reciprocity. In the interviews, they express feelings of gratitude and loyalty towards their employer for allowing them to take their legally guaranteed rights (such as taking fatherhood leave). All in all, the fathers' sense of entitlement is moderated by (different) layers of social comparison with other welfare states, other generations, and other gender norms. As, in general, family-friendliness is seen more as an issue for mothers than for fathers, the fathers' sense of entitlement to work-family compatibility is very weak, and it is also limited by gender norms. However, we observe a desire among fathers to increase the normality of paternal care beyond traditional gender norms (Oechsle and Beaufaÿs 2016).

Constructions of normality are not stable; they are changing over time. Powerful actors in organizations can promote cultural change or they can set barriers for it. Our analysis shows the crucial role of supervisors as gatekeepers and role models, and also the important role of other organizational actors who push forward issues of work-life balance on behalf of fathers (owner-managers, works council members, human resources departments, etc.).

However, organizational structure and culture are not the only factors that affect fathers' capabilities to be involved in family life. Fathers' self-conceptions and cultural models, as well as those of their partners, are important impact factors as well. It is important to keep in mind that organizational settings are interpreted by individuals, and they matter to different degrees for different fathers according to their individual configurations of constraints and capabilities. As we have seen in the cases of Mr. Smith and Mr. Roberts presented here, implicit cultural models and social backgrounds have an impact on fathers' capabilities. For Mr. Roberts, being an involved father necessarily implies an egalitarian gender arrangement and an equal division of labor in the couple, and this is also true for his wife. In the case of Mr. Smith, we can see ambivalences and asynchronicities in cultural models and self-conceptions. Throughout the entire interview, Mr. Smith never makes reference to traditional gender roles to explain the gender arrangement in his family. But we can see that he and his wife do refer in a certain way to traditional models of family and childhood that are, in fact, strongly gendered.

It is interesting that most of the *caring fathers* in our sample have been able to realize their self-concept, whereas the majority of fathers who see themselves as *companions* fail to achieve their ideal of being good fathers. On the other hand, most fathers with a self-conception as the *(main) breadwinner* are able to realize their ideals of being good fathers and husbands. These differences indicate the impact of cultural models and the relevance of institutions for everyday life. The male breadwinner model, especially in more rural areas, has strong support from local institutions and prevailing values. As a result, the majority of the interviewed fathers who see themselves as *breadwinners* are living in line with their self-concept. *Caring fathers,* on the other hand, regard themselves as pioneers: They know that they have to actively develop a new type of lifestyle and everyday practices that are partially in opposition to institutional settings and cultural expectations. Mr. Roberts is a good example of this configuration. Fathers who want to be *companions* of their children primarily experience ambivalences in their everyday lives. Caught between traditional and modernized images of fatherhood, between the demands of greedy work organizations and their own desires to be involved fathers, they often fail to develop new and resilient practices in their everyday conduct of life (see Oechsle and Reimer 2016). Mr. Smith is a paradigmatic example of this configuration.

Fathers' self-conceptions and the underlying cultural models play an important role. Still, as we have shown in the examples of Mr. Smith and Mr. Roberts, organizations and lifestyles work together to create sets of constraints and capabilities for fathers' involvement. Organizational factors – structures, cultures, and constellations of actors – lower or enhance fathers' sense of entitlement. Patterns of lifestyle, as results of biographical choices as well as of contingent constellations, also have a great impact on fathers' capabilities for involvement. Thus, organizational factors and aspects of everyday conduct of life mutually reinforce each other's discouraging and encouraging effects.

References

Alemann, A. von and Beaufaÿs, S. (2015) Die Verteilung von Care und Karriere bei Vätern: Reproduktionsarbeit als Ungleichheitsdimension zwischen Männern?, in: Lessenich, S. (ed.) *Routinen der Krise – Krisen der Routinen. Verhandlungen des 37. Kongresses der Deutschen Gesellschaft für Soziologie in Trier 2014.* Available at: http://publikationen.soziologie.de/index.php/kongressband/article/view/282

Alvesson, M. (2013) *Understanding Organizational Culture.* London: Sage Publications

Collinson, D. L. and Hearn, J. (2006) Men, Masculinites and Workplace Diversity/Diversion: power, intersections and contradiction, in: Konrad, A. M., Pringle, J. K. and Prasad, P. (eds.): *Handbook of Workplace Diversity.* London: Sage, pp. 299–322

Emerson, R. W. (1860) The Conduct of Life. Boston: Ticknor and Fields.

Grunow, D. (2014) Aufteilung von Erwerbs-, Haus- und Familienarbeit in Partnerschaften im Beziehungsverlauf. Der Einfluss von Sozialpolitik in Europa, in: Lück, D. and Cornelißen, W. (eds.) *Geschlechterunterschiede und Geschlechterunterscheidungen in Europa.* Stuttgart: Lucius & Lucius, pp. 237–263

Grunow, D. (2007) Wandel der Geschlechterrollen und Vaterhandeln im Alltag, in: Mühling, T. and Rost, H. (eds.) *Väter im Blickpunkt. Perspektiven der Familienforschung.* Opladen: Verlag Barbara Budrich, pp. 49–76

Haas, L. and Hwang, P. C (2007) 'Gender and Organizational Culture: correlates of companies' responsiveness to fathers in Sweden', *Gender & Society,* 21(1) pp. 52–79

Halrynjo, S. (2009) 'Men's Work-Life Conflict: career, care and self-realization: Patterns of privileges and dilemmas', *Gender, Work & Organization,* 16(1) pp. 98–125

Hearn, J. and Pringle, K. (2009) *European Perspectives on Men and Masculinities: national and transnational approaches.* Basingstoke: Palgrave Macmillan

Hobson, B. (ed.) (2014) *Work-Life Balance: the agency and capabilities gap.* Oxford: Oxford University Press

Hobson, B. and Fahlén, S. (2009) 'Competing Scenarios for European Fathers: applying Sen's capabilities and agency framework to work family balance', *The Annals of the American Academy of Political and Social Science;* 624, pp. 214–33

Hochschild, A. R. (1997): The Time Bind: When work becomes home and home becomes work. New York: Metropolitan Books

Jurczyk, K., Lange, A. and Thiessen, B. (eds.) (2014) *Doing Family – Familienalltag heute. Warum Familienleben nicht mehr selbstverständlich ist.* Weinheim: Beltz/Juventa

Jurczyk, K. and Lange, A. (eds.) (2010) *Vaterwerden und Vatersein heute. Neue Wege – neue Chancen!* Gütersloh: Verlag Bertelsmann Stiftung

Jurczyk, K., Voß, G. G. and Weihrich, M. (2015) Conduct of Everyday Life in Subject-Oriented Sociology. Concept and Empirical Research, in: Schraube, E. and Højholt, C. (eds.) *Psychology and the Conduct of Everyday Life.* London: Routledge, pp. 34–64

Jürgens, K. (2002) Lebensführung als Dimension sozialer Ungleichheit?, in: Weihrich, M. and Voß, G. G. (eds.) *Tag für Tag. Alltag als Problem – Lebensführung als Lösung?* München: Hampp, pp. 71–94

Klenner, C. and Pfahl, S. (2008) *Jenseits von Zeitnot und Karriereverzicht – Wege aus dem Arbeitszeitdilemma. Arbeitszeiten von Müttern, Vätern und Pflegenden und Umrisse eines Konzepts.* Wirtschafts- und Sozialwissenschaftliches Institut in der Hans-Böckler-Stiftung. Düsseldorf (WSI-Diskussionspapier 158)

Kodz, J., Harper, H. and Dench, S. (2002) *Work-Life Balance: beyond the rhetoric.* Brighton: Institute for Employment Studies

Konrad, A. M., Pringle, J. K. and Prasad, P. (eds.) (2006) *Handbook of Workplace Diversity.* London: Sage

Kossek, E. E. and Lambert, S. J. (eds.) (2005) *Work and Life Integration: organizational, cultural, and individual perspectives.* London: Lawrence Erlbaum Associates

Kvande, E. (2009) 'Work-Life Balance for Fathers in Globalized Knowledge Work: some insights from the Norwegian context', *Gender, Work & Organization,* 16(1)pp. 58–72

Lewis, S. and Smithson, J. (2001) 'Sense of Entitlement to Support for the Reconciliation of Employment and Family Life', *Human Relations,* 55(11) pp. 1455–1481

Meuser, M. and Scholz, S. (2012) Herausgeforderte Männlichkeiten. Männlichkeitskonstruktionen im Wandel von Erwerbsarbeit und Familie, in: Baader, M. S. et al. (eds.) *Erziehung, Bildung und Geschlecht. Männlichkeiten im Fokus der Gender-Studies.* Wiesbaden: Springer VS, pp. 23–40

Meyer, J. W. and Rowan, B. (1992) The Structure of Educational Organization, in: Meyer, J. W. and Scott, R. W. (eds.) *Organizational Environments: ritual and rationality.* Newbury Park/London/NewDelhi: Sage Publications, pp. 71–97

Mühling, T. and Rost, H. (eds.) (2007) *Väter im Blickpunkt. Perspektiven der Familienforschung.* Opladen: Verlag Barbara Budrich

Müller, U. (2010) 'Organisation und Geschlecht aus neoinstitutionalistischer Sicht. Betrachtungen am Beispiel von Entwicklungen in der Polizei', *Feministische Studien,* 28(1) pp: 40–56

O'Brien, M., Brandth, B. and Kvande, E. (2007) 'Fathers, Work and Family Life: global perspectives and new insights', *Community, Work and Family,* 10(4) pp 375–386

OECD (2016) *Parental Leave: Where are the fathers?* Policy Brief, March 2016. Available at: https://www.oecd.org/gender/parental-leave-where-are-the-fathers.pdf

Oechsle, M. (1998) Ungelöste Widersprüche. Leitbilder für die Lebensführung junger Frauen, in: Oechsle, M. and Geissler, B. (eds.) *Die ungleiche Gleichheit. Junge Frauen und der Wandel im Geschlechterverhältnis.* Opladen: Leske + Budrich, pp. 185–200

Oechsle, M. and Beaufaÿs, S. (2015) Hidden Rules and Competing Logics in Germany, in: Brandth, B., Kvande, E. and Halrynjo, S. (eds.) *Work-Family Dynamics: competing logics of regulation, economy and morals.* London: Routledge

Oechsle, M., Müller, U. and Hess, S. (eds.) (2012) *Fatherhood in Late Modernity: cultural images, social practices, structural frames.* Opladen: Verlag Barbara Budrich

Oechsle, M. and Reimer, T. (2016) ‚Väter zwischen Beruf und Familie: Handlungskrisen, Bewältigungsstrategien und gesellschaftliche Transformationsprozesse‘. Österreichische Zeitschrift für Soziologie 41(1 Supplement), pp. 213–237

Payne, R. K. and Krabill, D. L. (2002) Hidden Rules of Class at Work. Aha! Process, in:Peukert, A. (2015) *Aushandlungen von Paaren zur Elternzeit. Arbeitsteilung unter neuen Vorzeichen?* Wiesbaden: Springer VS

Possinger, J. (2013) *Vaterschaft im Spannungsfeld von Erwerbs- und Familienleben. „Neuen Vätern" auf der Spur,* Wiesbaden: Springer VS

Schein, E. H. (1990) ‚Organizational Culture‘, *American Psychologist,* 45(2) pp. 109–119

Schneider, N. F, Diabaté, S. and Ruckdeschel, K. (eds.) (2015) *Familienleitbilder in Deutschland: Kulturelle Vorstellungen zu Partnerschaft, Elternschaft und Familienleben.* Opladen: Verlag Barbara Budrich

Schreyögg, G. (1999) *Organisation. Grundlagen moderner Organisationsgestaltung.* Wiesbaden: Gabler

Schulz, F. and Blossfeld, H-P. (2006) Wie verändert sich die häusliche Arbeitsteilung im Eheverlauf? Eine Längsschnittstudie der ersten 14 Ehejahre in Westdeutschland. *Kölner Zeitschrift für Soziologie und Sozialpsychologie,* 58 (1) pp. 23–49

Scott, R. W. (1995) *Institutions and Organizations: ideas, interests and identities.* Los Angeles: Sage Publications

Sen, A. (1992) *Inequality Reexamined.* Oxford: Oxford University Press

Sen, A. (1993) Capability and Well-being, in: Nussbaum, M. and Sen, A. (eds.) *The Quality of Life.* Oxford: Clarendon Press, pp. 30–53

Smircich, L. (1983) ‘Concepts of Culture and Organizational Analysis’, *Administrative Science Quarterly* 28(3) pp. 339–358

Stainback, K., Tomaskovic-Devey, D. and Shaggs, S. (2010) ‘Organizational Approaches to Inequality: inertia, relative power, and environments’. *Annual Review of Sociology,* 36, pp. 225–247

Voß, G. G. (1991) *Lebensführung als Arbeit.* Über die Autonomie der Person im Alltag der Gesellschaft. Stuttgart: Enke

Weihrich, M. and Voß, G. G. (eds.) (2002) *Tag für Tag. Alltag als Problem – Lebensführung als Lösung?* München: Hampp

Witzel, A. and Reiter, H. (2000) *The Problem-Centred Interview.* London: Sage Publications

Zimmermann, B. (2006) ‘Pragmatism and the Capability Approach: challenges in social theory and empirical research’, *European Journal of Social Theory,* 9, pp. 467–484

Devoted Workers, Breadwinning Fathers: The Case of Executive Men in the United States

Mary Blair-Loy and Stacy J. Williams[1]

1. Introduction

Cultural expectations for involved, caregiving fatherhood are rising in the United States (Aumann, Galinsky, and Matos 2011; Kaufman 2013) and in Europe (Oechsle, Müller, and Hess 2013). However, despite these expectations, fathers still generally devote less time than mothers to parenting and housework. This is particularly the case for men who work long hours and provide the sole or primary financial support for the family (Blair-Loy et al. 2015; Cha 2013).

This article analyzes the accounts that executive-level businessmen in the United States give of their fathering roles and experiences. We examine the ways in which their understanding of their fatherhood obligations are informed by the "work devotion schema", a broad cultural structure, which defines work as demanding and deserving single-minded dedication.

Our respondents are leaders among the share of male managers in the United States who spend long hours at work.[2] Their experiences are important because they establish and reinforce cultural expectations for their subordinates. Executives help determine whether workplaces stigmatize, tolerate, or penalize employees seeking to reign in their work commitments in order to attend to caregiving responsibilities.

The next section briefly locates our study within the literature by combining insights from previous research on the gendered division of labor, perceived work-family conflict for men, and the schema of work devotion. After that, we present our interview data and analysis plan. We then present

1   Mary Blair-Loy (mblairloy@ucsd.edu) and Stacy J. Williams (sjw006@ucsd.edu), Department of Sociology, UC San Diego, La Jolla, CA, U.S.A. http://sociology.ucsd.edu. We acknowledge the expert research assistance of Tom Waidzunas and Devon Smith. We thank Brigitte Liebig and Mechtild Oechsle for insightful comments.

2   Thirty-eight percent of managerial and professional men in the United States work 50 or more hours per week (Aumann, Galinsky, and Matos 2011; Kuhn and Lozano 2005; Williams and Boushey 2010).

our findings. In contrast to Aumann et al.'s (2011) nationally representative survey of employed American men with families, our executive respondents are not compelled by gender egalitarian ideals to spend more time with their children. We find that their orientation toward work devotion justifies their absence from daily family caregiving and minimizes the sense of work-life conflict. Moreover, this pattern persists whether or not their wives are employed full-time. In conclusion, we note how the work devotion schema reinforces gender inequality in the workplace and at home. We encourage more cross-national research on the cultural possibilities for combining careers and involved caregiving.

2. Theoretical Framework

In the United States, fathers continue to work longer hours than mothers, on average, and women still do most of the childcare and housework (Bureau of Labor Statistics 2015; Sayer 2016). In part as a response to gender egalitarian ideals and to rising work hours among women, the time men spend on housework and childcare has increased over the past thirty years. The average time per day that fathers report spending on child care has increased from only 13 minutes in 1965 to 32 minutes in 2012. During this same period, men's housework hours have increased from 36 minutes to 83 minutes per day (Sayer 2016). However, mothers spend nearly double the time that fathers do on housework. Each day, mothers also spend twice as much time caring for their children (Blair-Loy et al. 2015; Sayer 2016).[3]

Scholars usually argue that fathers' increasing family involvement is related to their growing perception of work-life conflict, especially for fathers who work long hours. Within a comprehensive meta-analysis of organizational policies, culture, work-hours, and work-family conflict, Kelly et al. (2008: 320) find that longer work hours and the sense of work overload are linked to work-life conflict for employees. Consistent with those results, a nationally representative survey finds that about half of employed men with families in the United States experience a sense of work-family conflict and that about half would prefer to work fewer hours (Galinsky, Aumann, and Bond 2011). Aumann et al. (2011) interpret these results by pointing to pressure from egalitarian ideals on men to become more involved fathers:

---

3   In these studies, child care is defined as activities in which the parent is primarily interacting with the child: bathing, dressing, feeding infants, supervising older children, organizing events for children, teaching children activities, reading to children, or playing.

"Men today view the "ideal" man as someone who is not only successful as a financial provider, but is also involved as a father, husband/partner and son. Yet flat earnings, long hours and increasing job demands contribute to the pressures men face to succeed at work and at home, and thus to work-family conflict." (Aumann 2011: 2)

Thus, Aumann et al. (2011) and others (Kelly et al. 2008) find that in broader samples, work-family conflict generally increases with longer work hours. These researchers measure survey responses of typical employed fathers, which may not capture the experiences of those organizational leaders most influential in creating and maintaining organizational culture, including the expectations of work hours and work-life balance. Our study turns the spotlight on one influential segment of the workforce working long hours: executive men. We assess whether perceived work-family conflict remains low for the executive men in our sample. Aumann et al. (2011: 9) find that men's work-family conflict does not vary by the employment status of their spouse or cohabiting partner. Therefore, we also examine whether an executive man's orientation to work and family responsibilities depends substantially on whether his wife is employed full-time.

In previous research focusing on senior managers and professionals, scholars have found that executives' long work hours are not solely due to the desire for career advancement or financial success. Their orientation toward work is organized, inspired, and coerced by "the work devotion schema" (Blair-Loy 2003), which defines and justifies executives' single-minded allegiance to their employers and careers. The schema induces the cognitive, emotional, and moral understanding that work is a vocation, which demands and deserves single-minded dedication.[4]

Researchers have stated that the work devotion schema exists at different levels of analysis. Blair-Loy and colleagues have emphasized its presence at the organizational level, specifically as a coercive, cultural-structural feature of the capitalist firm for men and for women (Blair-Loy 2003; Wharton, Chivers, and Blair-Loy 2008; Blair-Loy and Williams Forthcoming). The schema also exists at the level of individual employees, as a set of expectations subjectively embraced by many, but not all, workers (Blair-Loy 2003; Blair-Loy and Cech 2016). Other literature has argued that the work devotion schema is also a feature of other particular industries. These include the specialized financial industry of leveraged buy-out firms (Turco 2010), as well as the sci-

---

4   In contrast to social psychological definitions of schema to denote a cognitive map (DiMaggio 1997), we analyze schemas as the virtual dimension of social structure (Sewell 1992). Further, these "schemas are frameworks for viewing, filtering, understanding, and evaluating what we know as reality. Constructed by societies over time, they gradually become largely unquestioned. Schemas are objective in the sense of being shared, publicly available understandings .... with real consequences" (Blair-Loy 2003: 5).

ence and technology industry (Greenman 2011) and academia (Blair-Loy and Cech 2016; Fox, Fonseca, and Bao 2011). Researchers using broad national data sets have used the work devotion schema to make sense of trends characterizing the labor market sector of managers and professionals in the U.S. (Schieman, Milkie, and Glavin 2009; Williams, Blair-Loy, and Berdahl 2013; Davies and Frink 2014).

Further, some (Blair-Loy 2003; Fox et al. 2011) have argued that the work devotion they see in particular organizations or professions is linked to the broader national culture influenced by the Protestant Ethic, identified by Max Weber (Weber 1958a, 1958b). The systematic, methodical, dedication to a vocation urged by Puritanism is echoed in the single-minded, methodical dedication to a secular career, now expected within many organizations, professions and industries. Even more broadly, as companies, industries, and professional socialization transcend national borders, the work devotion schema does as well. For example, Halrynjo and Lyng (2009) argue that the work devotion schema defines work as all-consuming for professionals in the private sector of Norway, which helps explain the withdrawal of many mothers from these demanding careers after they have children.

Thus, the work devotion schema is a broad cultural understanding that pervades many levels of social analysis. The current study addresses the analytical levels of work organizations and the work orientations and family commitments of individual leaders.

Our chapter on executive men's orientation toward fatherhood has implications for understanding the work-family climate of employer organizations more broadly. As Kelly et al. (2008: 318) conclude: "The evidence clearly indicates the important impact of perceived support – from supervisors and in the broader organizational culture – on [reducing] work-family conflict." Aumann et al. (2011) also find that supportive work-life cultures and supervisors reduce the sense of work-life conflict. We argue that if the company's executives personally feel little sense of work-family conflict or no obligation to increase their daily caregiving, they will likely be less supportive of their subordinates who may be struggling to juggle their paid work and family responsibilities.

3. Data and Methods

Our data derive from semi-structured, in-depth interviews that the first author conducted with seventy male senior managers of for-profit firms in the U.S. These respondents navigate financial markets, either as high-ranking professionals in financial or related business services firms or as among the top operational managers (e.g. CEO, President, General Manager) or financial managers (e.g. CFO, Treasurer) in companies in other industries. Almost half of the respondents hold the company's top job or report directly to the CEO. Fifty-three respondents work in publicly traded or large privately held companies, while seventeen are leaders in entrepreneurial or family-controlled firms. The first author conducted these interviews during three different economic contexts: growth (1998-2000); relative stagnation (2004-05); and the fragile aftermath of the Great Recession (2011). The last set of interviews is comprised of men who were also interviewed in 2004-05. Thus, while we have longitudinal data for some of our respondents, in this chapter we do not focus on changes over time; instead, we examine how executive men's dedication to their work justifies their absence from their families.

At the time of their interview, most of the respondents were married fathers and sole or primary breadwinners. Sixty-four of the seventy were fathers (with an average of 2.67 children), while an additional man was raising a stepchild and another's wife was expecting. These children ranged in age, from quite young to being grown adults themselves. Sixty-two men (89%) were married at the time of the interview. Of the eight men who were not currently married, two were widowed, four were currently divorced, and two had always been single. Sixty-five men (93%) earned two-thirds or more of the family income. In every firm type, respondents worked long hours. At the time of the interview, men ranged from their mid-thirties to mid-sixties. Thus, when we asked these men about the relationship between work and fatherhood, some men were reporting on current issues, while others were recalling an earlier time when their children were young. Therefore, regardless of their children's ages, all men discussed the same point in the lifecycle of the work-life conflict – when their children are young. Retrospective interview data needs to be interpreted cautiously, since individuals may recall and refashion past events to fit their current understandings (Blair-Loy 2003). We did not find that the age of the respondent, or whether they were reporting on past or current fatherhood experiences, systematically affected the experiences that were reported.

Interviews were audio-recorded and transcribed. We coded the transcripts in NVivo10, software for qualitative data analysis. We discovered empirical patterns in the data and then used NVivo to code and organize these concepts into first- and second-order concepts and relationships. At the same time, we assessed these emerging inductive patterns in relation to deductive categories, which had emerged in earlier research. Thus, we used a reiterative process of inductive and deductive reasoning to construct coding categories related to the work devotion schema. All names are pseudonyms.

The men in our study are predominantly white and upper-middle- to upper-class, and therefore not typical of the average U.S. worker. However, they are important to study to help us understand workplace culture.

4. Findings

Our respondents work long hours and are proud to ensure security and wealth for their families. Most of our respondents are the sole breadwinners for their families. Many of them had married professional peers, who then left full-time careers after marriage and motherhood; this pattern has also been described in other studies (e.g. Cha 2013).

We explored whether, for married fathers, wives' employment status affects their orientation to work and fatherhood. Consistent with other research on high-earning managerial and professional men (Hochschild 1989; Shows and Gerstel 2009), most respondents had wives who were full-time homemakers or who were only employed part-time. Only eleven of the sixty-two married men had wives who worked full-time at the time of the interview, and only eight of these wives worked full-time when their children were in preschool. Some of these wives who worked full-time were professional peers; others had less time-intensive, female-dominated jobs in education or retail.

Our respondents largely subscribe to the work devotion schema, which draws them into long hours at work instead of being involved in the daily care of their children. Their primary contribution to their families was breadwinning. However, the generous financial compensation is only one factor that shapes men's decisions to spend almost all of their waking hours with their co-workers instead of their families. We find that men are also pulled out of the family and into the workplace by their embrace of the work devotion schema. Adhering to this cultural mandate, these men see their jobs as intrinsically interesting, seductive, and morally rewarding. Most of our respondents find it inconceivable that they would be any less dedicated to their careers.

4.1 Traditional division of labor, supported by a wife at home

The majority of our respondents had wives at home when their children were young. These wives devoted themselves to the daily caregiving of their children. In contrast, our respondents worked such long hours that they had little time spend with their children, prohibiting them from being involved in the day-to-day childcare. If these men participated in weekly activities with their children at all, they were likely to exhibit "public fatherhood", in which they attended their child's sporting events or concerts, but were not substantially involved in daily care at home (Shows and Gerstel 2009).

Many respondents spend so much time traveling or at the office that they miss a large portion of their children's lives and forgo even public fatherhood. These men often left the house for work before their children were awake and returned after their bedtimes.

They described hearing complaints from family members that they were rarely home, but most of our respondents did not report a personal sense of conflict between work and family. Most accepted their work demands as legitimate. For example, Ben, a Chief Financial Officer, said that his wife and son complained that *"you're married to your job."* However, he personally felt *"that was just the way it was, you know, you had to have a job. It was also something I enjoy."*

Moreover, for many, their orientation toward – and rewards from – work devotion made their jobs so seductive that they justified spending little time with their wives and children. For example, Kirk, a partner in an accounting firm, explained that his wife wanted him to be more involved at home. However, he found that impossible because he was addicted to his work. He explained

> *It's probably kinda' like how a junkie works. You get mainlined into the system and that becomes really important, and then after a while all of a sudden you go, 'this is nuts,' and something breaks. And [for me] personally, it was the marriage.*

Kirk was so committed to his job that he did not recognize that he was neglecting his family.

We see this pattern in many respondents. The work devotion schema justifies the minimizing of family time. As another example, Jason, who was recently promoted to Chief Financial Officer for a large company, calls on the intrinsic enjoyment and meaningfulness of his work to explain why he works long hours, even on weekends.

> *But the last year and a half it's just been so fascinating – it's been so much fun – that my wife has said she doesn't like the hours because I work more hours than ever… I get up and go to work on Saturdays generally because I love it. I like it. Is it hard? Yeah… That's okay. It's meaningful work.*[5]

The work devotion schema also demands single-minded dedication to one's work. This prevents most of our respondents from even recognizing the possibility of becoming more involved fathers. Toward the end of the interviews with men whose wives were not employed full-time, the first author urged

---

5   In quotes from the executive men, ellipses mark that we have eliminated small pieces of their response that were tangential to the point at hand.

them to consider a counter-factual. What would life be like if their wives were employed?

Although our respondents' wives were deeply important to them, some of the respondents were so astounded by this counter-factual that they stated their marriages would never work if their wives had paid jobs rather than being full-time mothers and household managers. These men explained that if their wives were employed, their family would fall to pieces or they would not be married in the first place; they did not engage with the possibility that they could scale back at work to help with the children. For example, Keith, a senior finance manager in a large corporation, explains, *"Well, if my wife was working we wouldn't be married, clearly, I think; it just wouldn't happen."* This sentiment is echoed by Haru, an executive in an energy company. He stated, *"Yeah, if you do not have a supportive spouse then your family would be in shambles, because I'm just not around."*

By demanding single-minded dedication to one's job, the work devotion schema makes it inconceivable for many of these men to spend a significant amount of time and energy on raising children. Faced with a hypothetical situation in which their wives were employed full-time, these men imagine divorce or a breakdown of the family a more likely possibility than scaling back the hours they spent on the job.

There is some variation within our sample – a few men did not take it for granted that they had to focus on their careers at the expense of spending time with their children. For instance, Reuben, a managing director for an investment bank, desperately wanted to be a more involved father. In fact, he took nine months off of work when his first child was born. He hoped that he could be the parent to stay home, but his wife ended up being the homemaker because his career was more financially lucrative. Although he questioned the notion that he should be primarily committed to his career, various elements of the work devotion schema still helped him justify why he spends so much time away from his children. Rather than resenting his job for pulling him away from his children, he explains that he finds great fulfillment in his career. *"I derive a significant amount of satisfaction out of my career. And that makes it easier [to spend time away from my children]."*

In addition, Reuben calls upon other tenets of the work devotion schema to explain why he is able to cope with being away from his family so often. The work devotion schema frames work as exciting, engaging, and challenging. In accordance, he explains that he enjoys solving the problems that he faces in his job.

> But I really do enjoy it [my work]. At times it's somewhat of a mystery to me. I wonder how I can enjoy something that can demand so much. But it is satisfying at a sort of visceral level – the solving of problems, the figuring out how

to do something... So those type of things have like – you almost hesitate to call it professional appeal because it doesn't seem that way to me. I just like doing what I do and dealing with the people I deal with, to solve problems like that. (emphasis added)

The work devotion schema frames work as exciting and engaging, and accordingly, he reports that he finds his work intrinsically interesting despite the long hours. This dimension of the work devotion schema helps him remain dedicated to his job, even though he would also like to spend more time with his children.

Reuben also justifies his lack of time with his children by pointing to the ways in which the investment bank financed projects that benefit the community. He is proud of his role in bank projects that helped the city improve environmental impact and public transportation.

I like the fact that we have water that gets cleaned up before it's dumped... I like the fact that, through the efforts of a number of individuals, we're gonna' have mass transit. I like the fact that if no one ever thanks me now or thanks me within my lifetime, that 100 years from now... the quality of life is just incrementally a little bit better because day to day life is a little bit easier. And the air isn't as polluted, and it's just a more efficient way to live.

The work devotion schema helps Reuben explain – to himself, as much as to others – why he continues to work in a job that prevents him from being a more involved father. In addition to enjoying the stimulating challenges of problem solving that comes with his work, he finds moral satisfaction in financing social wellbeing. In a sense, Reuben and other executive men "provide" improvements for their communities in a similar manner to how they provide for their families. Yet, serving the community gives these men a moral justification for being away from their families for much of the week.

Most of the men in our sample were the primary breadwinners for the family. However, the financial rewards were not the sole reason why many of our respondents committed so much of their time to their jobs and so little time to their families. These men also reported being engaged by and committed to the intrinsically interesting work and to the moral contributions they believed they were making. This demonstrates the power of the work devotion schema in shaping the taken-for-granted understanding that these men must dedicate long hours to their careers, preventing them from participating in the daily caretaking of their children.

4.2 Public fatherhood

The work devotion schema pulls our respondents out of the home, justifying long hours at work and little time with their families. Because the work devotion schema requires its adherents' undivided attention, any family responsibilities are seen as detrimental to one's commitment to work. However, some respondents want to take part in some aspects of their children's lives and find the best way to negotiate this is by enacting "public fatherhood" (Shows and Gerstel 2009). By attending their children's sporting, Scout, and musical events, these men are able to participate in one part of their children's lives. Our respondents reported sacrificing time at work to participate in these activities, but these sacrifices are much smaller than they would be if these men were involved in the daily tasks of childrearing.

Most of our respondents reported attending or participating in some of their children's extracurricular activities. While these activities add responsibilities to these men's already busy lives, they require less time and energy than the daily tasks that accompany raising a child.

Attending their children's events often require reorganizing work schedules, but many of these men can do this and are proud of this display of fatherly involvement. For example, Darrell, a senior manager in an investment bank, explained the tradeoffs between work and attending his children's activities:

> *Yeah, there are times when I have to make a decision between this appointment or this evening function with either the client or just a work related deal versus something with the family. And if the kids have a concert or something going on, then I'm there. That's always first. And I just have to re-adjust my appointments with my clients.*

Darrell describes his children's occasional public events as "coming first", ahead of his work schedule. Other respondents reported a similar prioritization. For example, Quinn, the president of a financial services company, is an assistant coach to his child's soccer team. Likewise, Derek, a senior manager of a financial services firm, explained: *"I was involved with their sports, with Scouts. I still worked nights for a few years after they were born. But they were my top priority, and I worked my schedule around theirs."*

Similarly, Kenneth took weekend time and one week every summer off work to co-lead the scouts on backpacking trips:

> *We had a great scout master who liked to do overnight hikes on weekends, and so I would do a number of those. And he liked these 50 mile hikes during the summer and so I, the last week in July, I set aside each year there about five years, I guess. He and I took 20 to 30 boy scouts on a 50 mile hike through the [mountains].*

Kenneth, Darrell, Derek and others had the autonomy at work to rearrange their work schedules to accommodate their children's extracurricular activities. These events are usually planned well in advance and require a few hours a week. In Kenneth's case, the backpacking trips he helped lead required him to take vacation for one week per year. The predictable and limited nature of these events make them easier for men to attend. Unpredictable tasks or routine, daily child care would be much more difficult to accomplish while continuing to perform at the same level at work.

Other men reported that their jobs kept them from attending many of their children's events. For example, Casey, who was the division head of a large corporation, traveled about 75% of the time. He tried to prioritize his children's public events, but that was not always possible. Casey was unable to attend his daughter's high school graduation. He explains,

> Their school events, I tried to always be involved in... And I tried not to miss key events. The only key event I missed was my daughter's high school graduation because a [work] crisis came up, but I did make her college graduation. Made everything else.

For many of these men, their allegiance to work devotion precluded their involvement in children's day-to-day care. Instead, attending games, concerts, Scout events, and graduations was seen as the highest level of accepted involvement – and even this was not possible for some men. Therefore, the work-family struggle for these men was not framed as a problem of childcare, but of attending public events.

For example, Lonnie said that he struggled to "*just fit everything in.*" By "everything", he meant his job and his children's extracurricular events. He explained, "*I'd fit everything in from coaching soccer to coaching basketball.*" However, he was not attempting to "fit in" the childcare, preparing his children for school, transporting them between their various activities, grocery shopping, cooking, or any other daily tasks that went along with raising children. These daily actions of caretaking were incompatible with the full dedication to work required by the work devotion schema.

In fact, public fatherhood was generally seen as the only acceptable form of involvement with one's children. This idea was so ingrained in these men that many of them viewed attending public events as the only thing that they needed to do with their children. If their children did not have games, concerts, or other public events, these men did not believe their children needed their presence. For example, Tyler, divisional head of a large bank, explained that he did not experience any conflict when he was traveling for work and spending large amounts of time away from his family. When asked about the conflict between work and his family, he responded, "*I never thought about it.*

There was never any problem… And I was gone only during the week, and they [my children] go to school anyway." Because his fatherhood responsibilities did not include the daily care of his children, he believed that it made no difference if he was traveling or home. From his perspective, traveling during the week did not detract from any of his fatherhood responsibilities.

Similarly, Bret explains that his long working hours do not detract from his fatherhood responsibilities to his young children: *"The kids are really young, anyway. Under age two, there's not much you can do with them. I can see it with my oldest child, though, he is now able to do more things."* Bret views "what you can do with them" as his main parenting task – not the time-intensive childcare that young children require. He understands that there will be more conflicts as his children grow older and begin participating in events that he might like to attend. However, he reveals the strength of the work devotion schema by arguing, *"But I won't put in less time at work. I suppose there is a law of diminishing returns. But would you put in less time than was necessary to excel at your work?"* He argues that he will continue to devote as much work as is needed to excel in his career, which he expects will mean he will not spend much time with his children.

In sum, the work devotion schema allows its devotees to engage in limited versions of "public fatherhood." While rearranging meetings to take a couple of hours to attend a game is acceptable, the more time-intensive and unpredictable tasks that come with raising children are outside of the realm of possibility. These tasks would betray men as having competing commitments and therefore failing to be fully committed to their work.

4.3 Respondents with full-time employed wives are also fully oriented toward career

Above, we showed how some respondents, particularly Keith and Haru, relied heavily on their wives who were full-time homemakers. Keith and Haru imagined that having a wife who worked would result in a divorce or breakdown of the family; these men did not even consider the possibility that they themselves could scale back at work. Other respondents (eight out of the seventy) had wives who were employed full-time when their children were young. Contrary to Keith and Haru's predictions, these men do not report large family crises that are caused by their wives working. One might think that these crises are averted because the men scale back at work and take on more of the child care responsibilities that their employed spouses cannot complete. However, the men with employed wives are no more involved in the day-to-day childcare than the men whose wives stay at home. These men also exhibit a limited public fatherhood. We argue this pattern is due to the strength of the work devotion schema, which pervades their workplaces regardless of their wives' employment status.

For example, Shawn is the CEO of a health services company, whose wife worked full-time even when their children were small. He explains that he rarely saw his children when they were growing up due to his career focus. He only feels as if he were putting in the time his work deserved if he worked well over 60 hours a week: *"I feel like if I have had [just a] 60-hour week, that I haven't given my full measure."* He believes that he better serves his children by funding their advanced education than by spending time with them. He explains, *"I think my kids have benefitted more from my success in being able to fund their education and making sure that they have a good start... So I, uh, I was not around very much. I worked all the time."* This understanding of fatherhood as being a good provider complements the work devotion schema. One could be a good provider while also being fully dedicated to work and logging long weeks.

Evan, a regional director for a large financial services company, also has a wife who worked full-time while their children were young. However, his wife's career per se did not create pressure for him to be more involved in daily caregiving. He expressed many of the tenets of the work devotion schema, which prevented him from spending time with his children. He believes his work served his family as a strong breadwinner, but this role prevented him from giving time to his family, and his absence from home created marital difficulties. When asked what it is about the job that makes family relationships difficult to maintain, he replies that his job is just too much fun.

> It's just great fun. This is — you know, I think it's the greatest job there ever was. You never have a dull day hardly. You are constantly barraged with news about companies and markets and, I mean, just every kind of news event there ever was. You don't ever have to drag yourself out of bed to come to work. You really wanna go. You have to... As much as you love your family, you have to drag yourself home in a sense because you could be doing something every single night with clients and people that are related to the industry or all kinds of things. And you'd be having fun doing it.

Although Evan's wife is employed full-time, he does not take on more of the daily parenting tasks. Instead, he echoes the sentiments that the husbands of men whose wives are homemakers or only work part-time, such as Jason and Ben, expressed. All these men find an intrinsic enjoyment in their work and relish their relationships with co-workers and clients.

When explaining why he found it hard to spend time with his family, Evan also cited a sense of camaraderie with his work colleagues. He says he jumps out of bed to go to work every morning, but he feels almost like he has to drag himself home at the end of the day. His orientation toward work and family aligns with the work devotion schema, which promises financial, moral, and social rewards to its devotees. He reports feeling like he belonged to a tight-knit "tribe" at work and refers to his colleagues, not his family, as the people that he "gels with." In her study of the eroding divide between work and home, Hochschild (1997) also finds that men form a sense of community with their co-workers. We agree with Hochschild that this camaraderie gives men emotional fulfillment that ordinarily is provided by one's family. This is a major piece of the work devotion schema, which continues to draw executive men into their careers and away from spending time with their families, even if their wives are also employed full-time.

However, a terrible family tragedy prompted Evan to realize that he needed to cut back on work and spend more time with his family. His baby boy died of sudden infant death syndrome (SIDS), and his wife filed divorce papers shortly thereafter. He explained,

> *That whole thing kind of made me realize in a sense how important family really is, and even though I thought I was paying attention to them, somebody else had different ideas about all of that, so I cut back [at work] considerably.*

It took the death of a child, followed by divorce, to shake his automatic and unquestioned commitment to his career. At the time of his interview, Evan explained that he is concentrating on spending more time with his children. However, like many of the other men in our sample, he modeled public fatherhood by attending his children's events. *"I never missed a single game of theirs, of which the boys were heavily involved in athletics. My daughter is now involved with all that."* Yet, he admits that work still manages to get in the way from time to time: *"I did miss one of her games last year."*

In sum, the working status of our respondents' wives does not appear to affect how these men engage in fatherhood. The work devotion schema justifies these men's absence from their families by framing work as a moral calling that deserves their undivided attention. Similar to other executive men in our study, men with wives who work full-time also report that they find work exciting and emotionally fulfilling. Even though the potential for work-family conflict may be greater for men whose wives are employed, the work devotion schema continues to reconcile this conflict. The work devotion schema excuses most of the men in our study from participating in the day-to-day care of their children, whether their wives work full-time or not.

5. Conclusion and Implications

Situated in high-ranking positions or on express tracks to the top, the executive men we study largely subscribe to the taken-for-granted understandings within the work devotion schema. The work devotion schema frames careers as seductive, engaging, and interesting, and provides its devotees with moral, social, and financial rewards. We find that the work devotion schema provides a powerful pull for these men out of day-to-day family life, regardless of their wives' employment status.

In contrast to Aumann et al.'s (2011) analysis of typical male workers in the U.S., the executive men in our sample do not seem to feel compelled by egalitarian gender ideals to spend more time with involved fathering. Our respondents do report complaints from their wives about spending little time at home. However, they generally defend their work commitments as legitimate, engaging, and meaningful. For most, their fathering revolves around breadwinning and attending their children's public programs (cf. Shows and Gerstel 2009). The work devotion schema glorifies their breadwinning role and justifies their time away from families as service to their company and to broader society. Rather than giving at least lip service to egalitarian gender roles, many could not even engage with the possibility that they could scale back at work to help with the children.

Again, in contrast to Aumann et al.'s study, most of our respondents do not express a personal sense of work-family conflict other than regret about missing out on their children's public events (such as a daughter's high school graduation). Even those who are notable exceptions to this pattern continue to subscribe to work devotion. For example, Reuben, the managing director for an investment bank who had wished to take more time at home with his new baby, continues to find work viscerally satisfying and morally meaningful. And even Evan, who faced a massive family tragedy, continues to find work interpersonally engaging.

We have seen how the work devotion schema justifies fathers' lack of daily caretaking. Breadwinning and public fatherhood fit best with the demands of the work devotion schema; other models of more involved fatherhood violate the work devotion schema. These findings have many implications for working parents in the United States. One implication of this finding is that the work devotion schema justifies the penalizationof workers who engage in family caregiving responsibilities (Williams et al. 2013). Another implication is that, by rewarding long workweeks with handsome salaries, the work devotion schema supports the traditional gendered division of labor at home. According to the literature, high-earning men have more marital power and do less routine family caregiving (Hochschild 1989). Further, the wives of men working long hours (60 or more hours a week) are much more likely to leave their jobs, compared to wives of men who work less than 50 hours per week (Cha 2010). Researchers also have argued that the overwhelming demands of the work devotion schema help push professional women with children out of intensive careers (Stone 2007; Halrynjo and Lyng 2009).

We find that the work devotion schema continues to be powerful for executive men, despite egalitarian ideals of involved fathering that may be growing in other contexts (Aumann et al. 2011; Kaufman 2013). We expect that the resilience of the work devotion schema is in part due to the schema's presence at multiple levels of social analysis (e.g. individual, organizational, industry-level, national, or cross-national). We encourage future research to consider how the work devotion schema shapes social life within and across varying levels of analysis.

Our findings on a sample of executive men in the United States shed light on research on other national contexts. The work devotion schema justifies the cultural understanding of the "ideal worker" (Acker 1990), who is constantly available for paid work (Williams et al. 2013). Similar cultural models underlie professional work in other national contexts. For example, in von Alemann, Beaufaÿs, and Reimer's (2012) study of German firms and managers, most companies in the sample did not prioritize work-family balance for men and actively discouraged parental leaves for fathers. In the words of one respondent, "There is still the dominant concept that the easiest way to do things is with all of the [managers] being always available, preferably from eight a.m. to eight p.m." (von Alemann et al. 2012: 19).

Likewise, research on managers and professionals in Norway find that many professional mothers in for-profit organizations feel unable to compete with the full-time, full-commitment demands of the work devotion schema (Halrynjo and Lyng 2009). At the same time, professional fathers feel pressured to limit their parental leave, in order to avoid losing "career momentum" (Halrynjo and Lyng 2013). We encourage more cross-national research on the relationships among societal expectations, organizational culture, and executives' work orientation. We expect that if male executives personally feel little sense of work-family conflict or accountability to provide their daily caregiving, they will likely be less supportive of employees who have significant family responsibilities in addition to workplace obligations. Broadly, we encourage more research on the ways in which cultural understandings of work and of family enable and constrain the possibilities for combining careers with family care.

References

Acker, J. (1990) Hierarchies, Jobs, Bodies: A Theory of Gendered Organizations, *Gender & Society,* 4(2) pp. 139–158

von Alemann, A., Beaufaÿs, S. and Reimer, T. (2012) *Gaining Access to the Field of Work Organizations with the Issue of "Work-Family-Life Balance" for Fathers.* Bielefeld: DFG Research Center. Available at: https://sfb882.uni-bielefeld.de/en/publications Retrieved May 10, 2016

Aumann, K., Galinsky, E. and Matos, K. (2011) *The New Male Mystique.* New York: Families and Work Institute. Available at: http://familiesandwork.org/site/research/reports/newmalemystique.pdf) Retrieved November 22, 2015

Blair-Loy, M. (2003) *Competing Devotions: Career and Family Among Women Executives.* Cambridge, MA: Harvard University Press

Blair-Loy, M. and Cech, E. A. (2016) *Demands and Devotion: cultural meanings of (over)work among women researchers and professionals in science and technology industries.* University of California, San Diego/Department of Sociology. Research Report (unpubl.)

Blair-Loy, M, Hochschild, A., Pugh, A. J., Williams, J. C. and Hartmann, H. (2015) 'Stability and Transformation in Gender, Work, and Family: insights from the second shift for the next quarter century', *Community, Work & Family,* 18(4), pp. 435–454

Blair-Loy, M. and Williams, S. J. (Forthcoming) Long Hours and the Work Devotion Schema: the case of executive men in the United States, in: Brandth, B., Halrynjo, S. and Kvande, E. (eds.) *Work-Family Dynamics and the Competing Logics of Regulation, Economy, and Morals.* London: Routledge

Bureau of Labor Statistics (2015) *Charts by Topic: Household Activities.* Available at: http://www.bls.gov/TUS/CHARTS/HOUSEHOLD.HTM Retrieved May 9, 2016

Cha, Y. (2010) 'Reinforcing Separate Spheres: the effect of spousal overwork on men's and women's employment in dual-earner households, *American Sociological Review,* 75(2), pp. 303–329

Cha, Y. (2013) 'Overwork and the Persistence of Gender Segregation in Occupations', *Gender & Society,* 27(2), pp. 158–184

Davies, A. R. and Frink, B. D. (2014) 'The Origins of the Ideal Worker: the separation of work and home in the United States from the Market Revolution to 1950', *Work and Occupations,* 41, pp. 18–39

DiMaggio, P. (1997) 'Culture and Cognition'. *Annual Review of Sociology,* 23, pp. 263–287

Fox, M.F., Fonseca, C. and Bao, J. (2011) 'Work and Family Conflict in Academic Science: patterns and predictors among women and men in research universities, *Social Studies of Science,* 41, pp. 715–735

Galinsky, E., Aumann, K. and Bond, J. T. (2011) *Times Are Changing: gender and generation at work and home.* New York: Families and Work Institute. Available at: http://familiesandwork.org/downloads/TimesAreChanging.pdf. Retrieved May 3, 2016

Greenman, E. (2011) 'Asian American-White Differences in the Effect of Motherhood on Career Outcomes', *Work and Occupations,* 38(1) pp. 37–67

Halrynjo, S. and Lyng, S. T. (2009) 'Preferences, Constraints or Schemas of Devotion? Exploring Norwegian mothers' withdrawals from high-commitment', *The British Journal of Sociology,* 60(2) pp. 321–343

Halrynjo, S. and Lyng, S. T. (2013) Fedrepermisjon I Karriereyrker [Paternity Leave in Career Jobs], in: Brandth, B. and Kvande, E. (eds.) *Fedrekvoten og den farsvennlige velferdsstaten [The Fathers Quota and the Father Friendly Welfare State].* Oslo: Universitetsforlaget, pp. 222–236

Hochschild, A. (1989) *The Second Shift.* New York: Penguin Books

Hochschild, A. (1997) *The Time Bind: when work becomes home and home becomes work.* New York: Metropolitan Books

Kaufman, G. (2013) *Superdads: how fathers balance work and family in the 21st Century.* New York: NYU Press

Kelly, E. L. et al (2008) 'Getting There from Here: Research on the Effects of Work-Family Initiatives on Work-Family Conflict and Business Outcomes', *The Academy of Management Annals,* 2(1), pp. 305–349

Kuhn, P. and Lozano, F. (2005) *The Expanding Workweek? Understanding Trends in Long Work Hours Among U.S. Men, 1979–2004.* Cambridge, MA: National Bureau of Economic Research Working Paper Series. Available at: http://www.nber.org/papers/w11895. Retrieved November 22, 2015

Oechsle, M., Müller, U. and Hess, S. (2013) *Fatherhood in Late Modernity: Cultural Images, Social Practices, Structural Frames.* Opladen: Verlag Barbara Budrich

Sayer, L. C. (2016) Trends in Women's and Men's Time Use, 1965–2012: Back to the Future?, in: McHale, S. M., King, V.,Van Hook, J. and Booth, A. (eds.) *Gender and Couple Relationships.* Cham: Springer International Publishing, pp. 43–77

Schieman, S., Milkie, M. A. and Glavin, P. (2009) 'When Work Interferes with Life: work-nonwork interference and the influence of work-related demands and resources', *American Sociological Review,* 74(6), pp. 966–988

Sewell, W. H. Jr. (1992) 'A Theory of Structure: Duality, Agency, and Transformation', *American Journal of Sociology,* 98(10), pp. 1–29

Shows, C. and Gerstel, N. (2009) 'Fathering, Class, and Gender: a comparison of physicians and Emergency Medical Technicians, *Gender & Society,* 23(2), pp. 161–187

Stone, P. (2007) *Opting Out? Why Women Really Quit Careers and Head Home.* Berkeley, CA: University of California Press

Turco, C. J. (2010) 'Cultural Foundations of Tokenism: evidence from the leveraged buyout industry', *American Sociological Review,* 75(6) pp. 894–913

Weber, W. (1958a) Science as a Vocation, in: Gerth, H. H. and Mills, C. W. (eds.) *From Max Weber: Essays in Sociology.* New York: Oxford University Press, pp. 129–56

Weber, M. (1958b) *The Protestant Ethic and the Spirit of Capitalism.* New York: Charles Scribner & Sons

Wharton, A. S., Chivers, S. and Blair-Loy, M. (2008) 'Use of Formal and Informal Work-Family Policies on the Digital Assembly Line' *Work and Occupations,* 35(3), pp. 327–350.

Williams, J. C., Blair-Loy, M. and Berdahl, J. L. (2013) 'Cultural Schemas, Social Class, and the Flexibility Stigma', *Journal of Social Issues,* 69(2) pp. 209–234.

Williams, J. C. and Boushey, H. (2010) *The Three Faces of Work-Family Conflict: the poor, the professionals, and the missing middle.* Washington, DC: Center for American Progress and Center for WorkLife Law. Available at: http://papers.ssrn.com/sol3/papers.cfm?abstract_id=2126314. Retrieved November 22, 2015

Fathers' Parental Leave and Work-Family Division in Norwegian Elite Professions

Sigtona Halrynjo and Selma Therese Lyng

1. Introduction

Norway is regarded as an ideal society for combining work and family (Crompton et al. 2006; Gornick and Meyers 2009). The attitudes regarding the division of paid work and caring responsibilities between mother and father have radically changed towards broad support of a gender equal work-family division. From being an ideal for the minority in the 1980s, a large majority of Norwegian parents agree that the best thing for a family with children under school age is that both parents have equally demanding jobs and equally share housework and childcare (Hansen and Slagsvold 2012). The support is even higher among the elite educated (Halrynjo and Lyng 2010) and top managers (Halrynjo 2015). Furthermore, when it comes to practice, fathers increasingly participate in the family and in unpaid household work. Nevertheless, Norwegian fathers in average still spend an hour and a quarter more than mothers per day on paid work, while mothers spend on average just over an hour more than fathers on household work (Kitterød and Rønsen 2013). In time-demanding careers gender equal ideals and investment in work and family may be more difficult to reconcile. Time spent on work can be understood both as a burden and as a resource. In career jobs, available time is not necessarily a burden to be exchanged for a wage, but also a meaningful activity and an important investment in a future career (Halrynjo 2014). It has been argued that women are not interested in careers, management positions and high earnings, and that gender-based differences in preferences explain the gender gap in working life (Hakim 2011). However, mothers and fathers in Norwegian elite professions report equal preferences for career development, high wages and management positions. And they strongly support gender-equal attitudes. Despite this, the actual division of work and family responsibility is still gendered: While there are no gender differences in actual career realization among men and women without children, fathers in elite occupations work more and earn more than their partners. In addition, very few fathers have the main responsibility at home. In line with this pattern, fathers are much more likely than mothers to have reached higher career levels (Halrynjo and Lyng 2010).

This gender-traditional pattern is also found in a recent study among Norwegian top-managers, showing that male top-managers working in large companies typically have family and children, but their contribution of childcare during the entire childhood is meagre (Halrynjo 2015). This study shows the importance of career investment during the family-building years between the ages of thirty and forty in order to make it all the way to the top.

In this chapter we examine the role of parental leave for work-family adaptation. More specifically, we explore why and how parental leave may represent specific challenges in career jobs and how division of parental leave relates to later work-family dynamics among elite professionals in Norway.

2. Parental leave and later work-family adaptation

Norwegian family policies are increasingly based on an egalitarian family ideal in which both parents have paid work and take an active part in caring for their own children (Ellingsæter and Leira 2006). Paid parental leave was introduced in Norway as early as 1977, equally available for mothers and fathers. However, the "gender neutral" and "optional" leave schemes did not affect fathers' leave practice (Brandth and Kvande 2013). A more gender-equal uptake of parental leave is regarded as important for increased gender equality, both in family and working life. This has been one of the explicit rationales for the Norwegian fathers' quota; introduced in 1993 as four weeks non-transferable paid leave for fathers, and gradually extended in length until 2013 (Brandth and Kvande 2013)[1].

However, research findings point in opposite directions in terms of the impact of fathers leave on gender equality. Studies of the quota reform do find a significant negative relationship between leave and wages: the longer the leave, the lower the future wages (Cools and Strøm 2014; Evertsson 2015). Several studies also show that fathers who have taken long parental leave, work a little less when the children are growing up, than fathers who have

---

1 From 1977 to 1992, the total parental leave with full pay was extended from 18 to 35 weeks. When the four weeks fathers' quota was introduced in 1993, the total parental leave was increased from 35 to 42 weeks. In 2005 the fathers' quota was expanded to five weeks, in 2006 to six weeks, with an expansion of the total parental leave to 43 and 44 weeks, respectively. From 2009 to 2013 the non-transferable leave for fathers was further extended, first into 10, then gradually into 14 weeks. However, in 2014 the quota was reduced from 14 to 10 weeks, while the total leave was 49 weeks with 100% wage compensation.

taken less leave (Arnalds, Eydal and Gíslason 2013; Duvander and Jans 2009). In contrast, studies trying to isolate the direct effect of the introduction of the quota provide different conclusions: Some Nordic studies have produced evidence that the introduction of the quota helped change the specialization pattern within the family, identified through negative effect on fathers' future salary or income (Rege and Solli 2013), and positive impact on mothers' income (Kotsadam, Ugreninov and Finseraas 2011). Other studies find no effect on fathers' income and work involvement (Cools, Fiva and Kirkebøen 2015; Ekberg, Eriksson and Friebel 2013; Johansson and Duvander 2013).

Qualitative studies also point in opposite directions regarding the relation of parental leave to later work-family adaptation. On the one hand, studies have described how being "home alone" (Brandth and Kvande 2003), without a mother as a "facilitator" (Aarseth 2011), contributes to increased father involvement and feelings of responsibility for child care. On the other hand, other studies conclude that the expectations of the significance of fathers' parental leave on later family involvement need to be more modest, because the division of paid work and family work are shaped by deep-seated attitudes and orientations not necessarily affected by arrangements during the limited period of the parental leave (Doucet 2009; Farstad 2010).

2.1 Parental leave – specific challenges in career jobs?

The non-transferable father's quota has made infant care an acceptable reason for absence from work among the majority of Norwegian fathers. Most Norwegian fathers use some of the available parental leave (Brandth and Kvande 2009). Earlier research based on register data for all Norwegian parents finds that the most common practice among couples is that the father makes use of the earmarked father's quota, while the mother uses all common leave (Lappegård 2012). However, the costs of taking parental leave in different working life segments seem to affect the division of leave uptake: both mothers and fathers working in the public sector are more inclined to take longer leave than those working in the private sector. This may be explained by the fact that the public sector is not driven by profit, and absence from work has no direct consequences on economic productivity. Also, the direct costs of taking leave for parents with earnings exceeding the fixed ceiling for income replacement are lower, as public sector employers compensate for the discrepancy. However, fathers are much more likely to work in the private sector where the costs of using parental leave are higher (Lappegård 2012). Accordingly, the fact that fathers in elite professions typically have jobs where high costs are involved, would point towards lower uptake of parental leave.

Interestingly, high education level and high income level among these fathers may pull the anticipation of leave uptake – as well as work-family division – in opposite directions: On the one hand, highly educated fathers are known to have more gender-equality oriented attitudes, as well as practices, compared to other fathers (Wærness and Knudsen 2006; Halrynjo and Lyng, 2010). Further, highly educated fathers are more supportive towards the fathers' quota than other fathers (Bringedal and Lappegård 2012). Also the uptake of parental leave among fathers rises with increased education level for fathers. When mothers' education *and* income level increase, fathers' uptake of parental leave also rises (Grambo and Myklebø 2009). On the other hand, *fathers' income* pulls in the opposite direction: high income for fathers increases the probability of a gender-traditional work and family adaptation (Skrede and Wiik 2012), and fathers with high incomes are also those with the lowest uptake of the fathers' quota (Grambo and Myklebø 2009).

The introduction of the fathers' quota should make leave uptake among fathers in career professions easier. Existing schemes typically cover the direct costs of leave of absence, also for fathers in career jobs: in addition to statutory rights, many high-paid employees have contractual arrangements at work that compensate fully for loss of wages beyond the statutory amount that is reimbursed by the state. Moreover, non-transferable leave can reduce the immediate obstacles on leave negotiations with the employer. Previous studies have shown that the fathers' quota may have particular significance as a limit marker for fathers who work in knowledge occupations and "boundaryless" jobs. Firstly, the fathers' quota is a reserved right for fathers, and also perceived as such by employers. The leave does not have to be negotiated individually, and the institutionalized entitlement makes it easier to take the leave – even if the father should encounter resistance at work (Bloksgaard 2009). Second, it works as a "gentle coercion" since the quota cannot be transferred to the mother (see for example Brandth and Kvande 2009). This gentle coercion is emphasized as particularly important in parts of working life where greedy and seductive time cultures pull in the opposite direction of the political intentions of promoting gender equality and fathers increased involvement in caring for children (Brandth and Kvande 2005).

Family-friendly policies such as parental leave address the *formal rules* in working life. Laws, regulations and collective agreements between the trade unions and the employer's organizations are central factors to understand the positive significance of the development of family-friendly arrangements in Norwegian working life. However, mothers and fathers trying to reconcile career and family life also have to take into account the *informal rules* of the game based on the logic of competition. These rules reward some practices and performances and restrict others, and may conflict with the intensions of the formal rules (Halrynjo 2010; Hochschild 1997; Kanter 1977). The formal rules, based on the logic of regulation, can guarantee that you will not lose your current job or wage, but they cannot guarantee that you will not lose future career chances and salary increases. Within a segment of working life where employees do not climb a career ladder, but collectively trade their *time for a wage* – the formal rules and regulations are functional. In non-career jobs paid leave and reduction in working time are unconditional benefits that all workers gain from. Within segments based on *career logic,* on the other hand, individual employees 'sell' achievements, results and irreplaceability. Thus, reduction of this investment not only involves setting up boundaries against employers, coworkers or your own inner drive, but also negotiating against investment in a future career (Halrynjo 2010). Among highly educated women and men, childbirth and parental leaves typically occur in the years between ages thirty and forty, thus coinciding with the "make or break years" in competitive-intensive career jobs. During these crucial years the *pace* of career advancement is highly relevant for the prospects of making it to the top levels (Lyng 2010). Hence, the consequences of uptake and division of parental leave may be particularly accentuated within this segment.

Our earlier research has shown that women and men in Norwegian elite professions are equal in many respects (Halrynjo and Lyng 2010): the majority of both men and women have families; nine out of ten have a partner with high level of education, and they have an equal number of children. In addition the majority have a strong orientation towards gender-equal work-family ideals. The question is then how these similarities across gender relate to parental leave uptake and work-family adaptation.

In this chapter we draw on quantitative and qualitative data, in order to explore the role of parental leave in the gap between gender-equal work-family ideals and more gender-traditional practices among Norwegian elite professionals. Differences in attitudes may influence leave uptake as well as later work-family division. To focus attention on the significance of parental leave uptake, we will examine the association between fathers' use of parental leave and later work-family division among the most gender-equality prone fathers. Analyzing consequences, mechanisms and underlying notions of fathers' and mothers' parental leave and later work-family adaptation, we explore distinctive challenges that may arise from negotiating work and family demands within competitive elite professions.

3. Data and methods

The data consists of a survey among Norwegian elite educated women and men (economists/MBAs, lawyers and graduate civil engineers), and qualitative interviews with mothers and fathers with experience of "high commitment", labor-intensive career jobs. [2]The sample was limited to respondents between 30–50 years of age to get a sufficient number of parents with relatively recent experiences of caring responsibilities. 1309 fathers and 1534 mothers who had their first child in the period 1979–2007 were included in the quantitative sample.

The gender balance among lawyers and economists were initially relatively even. Among civil engineers however, we had to draw a stratified sample with a 50/50 gender distribution in order to get a sufficient number of women. The survey contains data about family career and professional career with detailed information on the use of parental leave, job level and the job held at the time of first, second and third child births, in addition to subjective data on career preferences and attitudes towards work and family adaptation. Survey data is used to examine the association between fathers' leave uptake and their later work-family adaptation in the family.

The qualitative data set consists of 38 semi-structured in-depth interviews (23 mothers and 15 fathers) conducted in the period 2005–2007. The age range is 30–50 years; most are in their thirties. They have from one to three children living at home, with a current partner, and with the exception of four interviewees they all have children of preschool age. All informants have invested in long educations and careers; most of them are economists/MBAs, lawyers and graduate civil engineers with experience from prestigious commercial law firms and management consulting companies. These businesses represent a type of competitive intensive work organizations that have traditionally been male-dominated, but now up to half of the employees in recruitment positions are women. The qualitative data includes mothers and fathers with experiences from various job levels, and informants were recruited both informally, through the "snowball method" from various separate social networks, and formally through firms. This dual selection strategy was chosen to avoid potential bias in the sample linked to specific social networks and companies' assessments of the employees who were concerned interviewees.

---

2   The survey on Gender, Career and Care Responsibilities was conducted in cooperation with the Norwegian Association of Lawyers, The Association for Technical and Scientific Professionals (Tekna) and Siviløkonomene (MBAs) in 2007. The online survey was sent to a random sample of working members aged 30-50 years in the three organizations. To ensure response from a minimum of 1,000 respondents from every profession, a random sample of +/- 3,000 women and men was drawn. Altogether 8836 received the form. 3924 responded, providing an overall response rate of 44%.

Some informants were interviewed at home, but most interviews took place at the informant's office or at a meeting room at their workplace. The interviews lasted between one and a half to two hours.

These data sets are the newest available data on work-family adaptations in Norwegian elite professions. Recent quantitative studies on the general population in the Nordic countries (Arnalds, Eydal and Gíslason 2013; Cools and Strøm 2014; Duvander and Johansson 2015; Evertsson, Boye and Erman 2015), a recent survey among Norwegian top managers in large firms conducted in 2014 (Halrynjo 2015), as well as a qualitative study of Norwegian fathers' use of the 10 weeks long quota (Smeby 2013), confirms the actuality of the work-family patterns described in this chapter.

4. Findings: father's quota in elite professions

We find that the father's quota has had a significant impact on fathers' uptake among fathers in elite professions. Before the introduction of the father's quota only 15% of the fathers in this sample took parental leave. After the quota 71% took parental leave. Thus, the fathers' quota has changed fathers' leave from being an exceptional phenomenon to a normal practice, even in elite professions. Fathers' average uptake of leave in these occupations has increased by about a month, from 0.3 months to 1.4 (see table 1). During this period, however, there has even been a significant extension in the *total* parental leave, which parents can choose how to divide between them. Parallel to fathers' one-month increase, mothers' average leave uptake increased from an average of 7.2 to 10 months. Consequently, the average uptake of leave among mothers is still more than seven times longer than the average uptake among fathers.

Table 1: Elite educated fathers' use of paid parental leave before/after the introduction of the fathers' quota

FATHERS' USE OF PARENTAL LEAVE: FIRST CHILD	Before Fathers' quota (1977–1992) N 274	After Fathers' quota (1993–2007) N 1016	After quota Gender equality prone fathers N 716	After quota Gender trad. prone fathers N 300
Uptake	15 %	81%	85%	76%
Average leave length	0.3 months	1.4 months	1.5 months	0.8 months

Research has shown that fathers working in the public sector in general take slightly more parental leave than fathers working in the private sector (Lappegård 2012). We find the same pattern among fathers in elite professions. Those who worked in the public sector at the time their first child was born, took a little longer leave (1.5 months), than fathers working in the private sector (1.3 months). The difference in uptake among fathers in public versus private sectors is small, but significant on a 0.05 level. Also in line with earlier research, fathers working in female-dominated or gender-balanced organizations took a somewhat longer leave than fathers working in male-dominated organizations. Nevertheless, the variation in leave uptake among fathers is limited compared to the variation between fathers versus mothers (see table 2.

Table 2: Variation in length of parental leave by sector and gender composition in the work place

WORK PLACE CHARACTERISTIC AT THE TIME THE FIRST CHILD ARRIVED	Fathers N 931 Average number of months (SD[*])	Mothers N 1101 Average number of months (SD)
Private sector	1.3 (1.4)	10.1 (2.0)
Public sector	1.5 (1.7)	10.3 (1.9)
Male-dominated	1.3 (1.4)	10.0 (2.0)
Gender-balanced	1.5 (1.5)	10.6 (1.9)
Female-dominated	1.5 (1.7)	10.4 (1.9)

* *SD = Standard deviation*

4.1 Parental leave and later work-family adaptation

The majority of the surveyed fathers had two or more children, a partner with a high level of education, and supported gender equality attitudes. However, fathers in elite professions work long hours. 69% of the fathers work 41–70 hours per week. We find a consistent pattern where fathers who have taken the shortest leave also continue with gender-traditional work-family patterns. Most of the fathers (64%) work more than their partner. The average leave uptake for the first child among these men is only one month of leave (see table 3). 28% of the fathers report that they spend the same amount of time on paid work as their partner. The average leave uptake among these fathers was 1.5 months. Only a minority of 8% report a non-traditional gender division of paid work. As the group of non-traditional fathers in elite professions is so limited, the relevant division is between the gender-traditional fathers on the one hand and the gender equal/non-traditional on the other.

The division of unpaid work at home follows the same pattern: Those with a gender-traditional division of responsibilities at home also had the shortest uptake of parental leave, less than a month. Those reporting equal sharing of responsibility took more leave (1.3 months), and those taking most responsibility at home took the longest leave, nearly the double length as the fathers who demonstrated gender-traditional practices. Half of the elite educated fathers report equal sharing at home. The gender atypical fathers are, however, very few. Thus, the empirical alternatives among fathers are basically either "equal sharing" or "partner does most". This pattern of the division of unpaid work at home is directly opposite to the pattern among mothers (not shown here). Roughly half of the mothers also report sharing equally; however their empirical alternative to equal sharing of unpaid work is "mostly me".

Table 3: Length of fathers leave (first child) and later division of paid and unpaid work, income and job-status in the family.

FATHERS N 1006–1213	DIVISION OF UNPAID WORK AT HOME		DIVISION OF PAID WORK		INCOME DIVISION		DIVISION OF JOB STATUS	
LATER WORK-FAMILY PRACTICE	All/gender equality prone fathers %	Months of parental leave Mean (SD)	All/gender equality prone fathers %	Months of parental leave Mean (SD)	All/gender equality prone fathers %	Months of parental leave Mean (SD)	All/gender equality prone fathers %	Months of parental leave Mean (SD)
Gender traditional practice	47 / 37 "Mostly partner"	0.88 (1.76)	64 / 54 "I work most"	1.0 (1.25)	84 / 78 "I earn most"	1.00 (1.25)	62 / 52 "My job most important"	1.00 (1.76)
Gender equal practice	50 / 60 "Equal sharing"	1.33 (1.23)	28 / 36 "Equal amount"	1.47 (1.60)	8 / 11 "Equal earnings"	1.47 (1.66)	33 / 41 "Jobs equally important"	1.38 (1.23)
Gender non-traditional practice	3 / 3 "Mostly me"	1.67 (1.76)	8 / 10 "Partner work most"	1.51 (1.92)	8 / 11 "Partner earns most"	1.51 (1.92)	5 / 7 "Partners job most important"	1.88 (1.76)

The division of income and job status follows the same pattern. Fathers with the shortest leave uptake display higher earnings and have a job with more responsibilities and status than their partner. Conversely, the more leave a father has taken, the more gender equal or non-traditional division we find later on. Only 3% of the elite educated fathers report taking most responsibility at home and having a partner with a more important and a higher-earning job than themselves (see table 2).

4.2 Parental leave uptake and work-family dynamics among the most gender-equality prone fathers

Even though we find a robust relationship between the length of fathers' parental leave and later work-family adaptations across different measures, other factors may also play an important part. Multivariate analyses suggest that the spouse's level of education and fathers' preferences for gender-equal vs. gender-traditional adaptation to work and family life contribute significantly to explain the current adaptation to work and family life. Thus, to further explore the association between the length of fathers' leave and their later work-family adaptations, we selected a subsample of gender-equality prone fathers: i.e. fathers with gender-equal work-family ideals, and highly educated spouses with children born after the introduction of the fathers' quota. Among these fathers (N=716), 85% took parental leave, and the average length of parental leave was 1.5 months, in comparison to more gender–traditional fathers where 76% took parental leave and those who used the leave, took less than a month (0.8) for their first child. The length of leave of their partners, however, does not vary significantly. Long paid leave among mothers in Norway is the norm regardless of other circumstances (Lappegård 2012).

We examined if the length of parental leave (for children born after the fathers' quota) among equality-prone fathers reduced the probability for gender-traditional divisions of 1) unpaid work (house and care work; 2) paid work; 3) income; 4) who has the most "important" job with highest level of responsibility. As expected, the equality-prone fathers report a higher degree of sharing the unpaid work at home than other fathers. 60% of these fathers report equal sharing and 3% "do the most", themselves. However, as many as 37% of the equality-prone fathers report that they actually have "ground crew" at home, as their spouse does the most of the unpaid work. Moreover, they also invest more in their job and career than their spouses: even in this equality-prone sub-sample, 54% of the fathers report that they spend more time in paid work than their partner. The fathers typically report that they have the job with the most responsibility. Only 36% say that they have an equal division of paid work in the couple, in line with the prevailing ideal of these fathers. Looking at income differences, the results are even more gender-traditional: 78% of the gender-equality prone fathers earn more than their spouse (table 3).

In sum, the equality-prone fathers report more gender-equal work-family adaptations than other fathers. Nevertheless, their practice cannot be considered as gender equal. There is still a gap between (gender equal) ideals and (gender traditional) practices.

4.3 Longer leave – reduction in gender-traditional patterns?

Is longer leave uptake among fathers associated with more gender-equal work-family practices among the most gender-equal oriented fathers? To examine this relation among fathers with highly educated spouses and gender-equality ideals, we apply binary logistic regression and use the four different measures of relative work-family adaptation as dependent variables. *Gender traditional division* is coded as 1, *gender equal or non-traditional* is coded as 0. We use the total months of paid parental leave during the fathers' careers, control for age, number of children and the fathers' preferences for career, and measure if the traditional division is reduced. The length of the spouse' leave uptake is not significantly related to any of the four measures of work-family division, and does not relate to fathers' leave uptake. Thus this variable is not included in the analyses.

Figure 1. Probability of gender-traditional division among gender-equality prone fathers by use of parental leave.

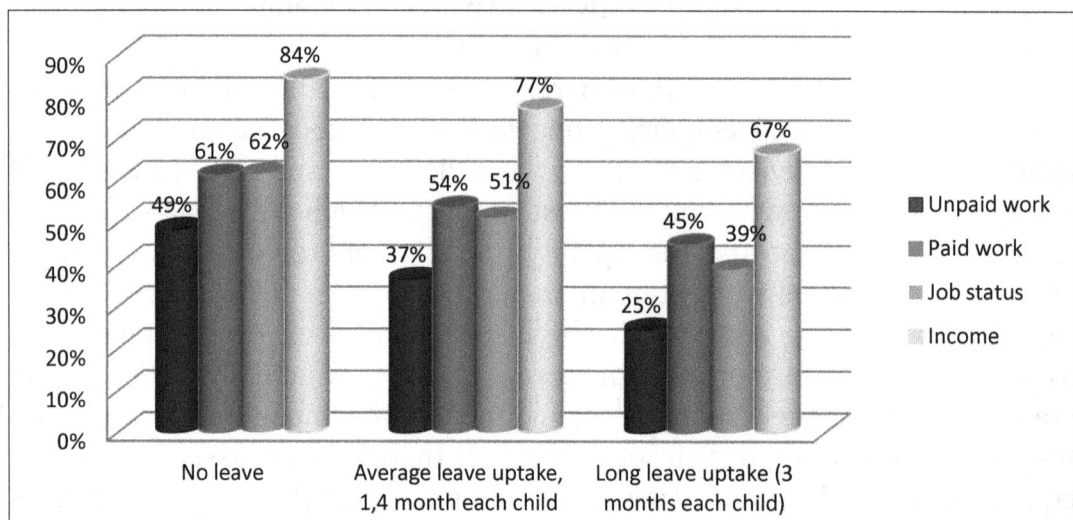

In the regression models we predict the probability of having a gender traditional division among fathers with gender-equal ideals, a highly educated partner, and children born after the introduction of the fathers' quota. We use the average characteristics for these fathers and estimate the probability for a thirty-nine year old father, with two children and an average level of career preferences[3] (see Appendix).

We find that the length of fathers' leave correlates significantly with a reduction in gender-traditional patterns on all four measures. The strongest correlation is found in a reduction of the traditional division of unpaid work at home and income. While a father who did not take any leave has a 49% probability of having a traditional division of unpaid work, a father who took three months' leave for each child has only a 25% probability for a traditional division later on. Furthermore, the probability of having a gender-traditional division of job status in the couple is strongly reduced. A father without any leave experience has a 62% probability of being in a relationship where he is considered to have "the most important job, with the highest degree of responsibility and career status". A father with long leave has a much higher probability for having a relationship where both partners have equally important job and career status. The weakest correlation of length of parental leave with reduction of the gender-traditional division is found for division of paid work, but the association is still significant on a 0.01 level.

We cannot exclude the possibility that there may be unobserved differences among fathers, explaining both the longer uptake of leave and the later equal gender division of paid work and family work. But on the other hand, we cannot exclude that fathers' uptake of parental leave may contribute to shaping the division of paid and unpaid work in the family, both in the short and the long run. In addition, there may be self-reinforcing patterns of work-family divisions that pull couples where fathers take more leave in an egalitarian direction, and couples where fathers limit their leave uptake in a more gender-traditional direction.

To sum up: we find that fathers with gender-equality oriented attitudes and highly educated partners take longer leaves than other fathers. Still, the uptake of parental leave is highly gendered, also among these fathers. A high share has gender-traditional work-family adaptations where the spouse serves as "ground crew" at home, thus making it easier for the father to fulfil the work demands in competitive careers. Nevertheless, the variation in leave uptake among gender-equality prone fathers is strongly linked to later work-family adaptation. Longer leave strongly predicts less gender-traditional work-family patterns later on.

How can we understand and interpret these patterns? In the following sections we turn to the qualitative data in order to first explore how the gendered uptake of parental leave contributes to a shift from gender equal

---

3   3.2 on a scale from 0 'not important at all' to 5 'very important'.

to gender traditional work-family adaptation among mothers and fathers in competitive intensive career jobs. And secondly: how and why a gendered uptake of parental leave may be the default option even among gender-equality oriented mothers and fathers.

4.4 Division of parental leave – shaping (ir)replaceability at work and at home

The parents in our qualitative data set represent career jobs where demands for investments are particularly pronounced and accentuated. Most of them are – or have until recently – pursued successful careers in prestigious corporate law firms or management consulting companies. These work organizations are perceived to be among the most attractive in their industries, recruiting top-level candidates. Moreover, these firms are characterized by a pyramidal "up-or-out" career structure and culture: you either go up fast – or you go out. Staying on the A-team, eligible for promotion, in these work organizations comes with an "up-and-go career contract" (Lyng 2010) implying high explicit and implicit expectations for "outputs" as well as "inputs". Demands for investments include extensive flexibility and availability for clients, superiors and colleagues. Average work weeks of 50–70 hours is regarded as necessary in order to produce the continuous dedication and achievements required to stay on the A-team and keep up in the competition for promotion (Lyng 2010). With particularly pronounced expectations for career investments, these work organizations provide an apt context for exploring the impact of parental leave on work-family adaptation and career realization among elite educated fathers in career jobs – where gender-equal ideals and investment in work and family may be difficult to reconcile.

Fathers, as well as mothers, describe how the gendered uptake of parental leave has contributed to a work-family adaptation that is more gender-traditional than they had pictured for themselves. Analyzing these accounts, we find that the division of parental leave has a twofold contribution in shaping later gender-traditional work-family adaptations. First, there are specific career costs related to taking parental leave in competitive intensive "up-or-out" organizations. These career costs are gender neutral per se, but with gender unequal uptake, parental leave has gendered consequences (Lyng 2010). Second, even among gender-equality oriented parents, who originally planned to share equally, the gendered division of work and family responsibilities during parental leave push and pull mothers and fathers in a gender-traditional direction.

The career costs of parental leave are closely related to what it takes to succeed in competitive career jobs. In jobs where you are never better than your last achievement (Sørensen et al. 2005), taking a break from career in order to invest in care implies a break with the continuous career investments needed to keep up when many highly qualified and "hungry" colleagues are competing for the same opportunities, projects and promotions. In the following interview extract, a female lawyer articulates the consequences of parental leave confronted with the logic of continuous investment and competition:

> Well, for me it's unthinkable that being away from work, then, be it nine months or a year, will not have any significance. For you are competing all the time with people, others, who are not on leave, so it is obvious that a year's more experience has significance.

> (Anna, female lawyer)

Hence, even if taking parental leave is accepted by employers and colleagues, and short-term, direct costs of being absent from work are compensated, taking parental leave implies the risk of being constituted as *replaceable* in these jobs where continuous *irreplaceability* is a core value and required in order to succeed (Halrynjo and Lyng 2009). Returning to work after parental leave, respondents describe being re-categorised as B-team members and lagging behind, watching their peers in their initial own heat of the A-team pulling away (Lyng 2010). This experience is also described by the few fathers who have actually taken somewhat longer leave than the fathers' quota. However, the dominant pattern of gendered division of parental leave produces a gendered division of career costs.

Also, fathers articulate the gender-unequal consequences of their gender-unequal uptake of parental leave. In the following interview extract, a male manager reflects on how and why he and his wife have ended up with a gender-traditional work-family adaptation, even if they graduated from the same elite education at the same time, and despite the fact that they were both highly and equally ambitious – and thought that when they got married they would "share fifty-fifty". He makes a point that illustrates how the gendered uptake of parental leave has consequences in terms of gender division in career and family investment: with two or three children, the time mothers and fathers invest in career in a crucial period of make-or-break years may in effect be substantially different:

> The fact that we have prioritized my career is not a result of me being more clever or competent than her, I'm not in any respect. It's due to the fact that I advanced faster, and that's in part a consequence of her taking those parental leaves. (...) After all, she has actually been absent from work for three years in total. For how long have we worked now? Twelve years. So in effect she's been on parental leave for 25 percent of her working years. Of course that will have consequences. (...) Well, at any rate it turns out like this [unequal].

So it may well be that the parental leave has led us into a pattern that we haven't gotten out of after she finished her leaves.

(Henrik, male manager/consultant)

This manager and father reflects on how the division of career costs related to parental leave has led him and his wife into a pattern of unequal work-family adaptation and relative career progression. However, the division of parental leave not only contributes to this unequal pattern through constituting mothers as replaceable, while fathers continue investing in their own irreplaceability – *at work*. It also plays a role in shaping parents (ir)replaceability *at home:*

Suddenly it's like you're in these gender role patterns, traditional ones. But it's also like me offering to do it, a little bit. Because I feel that to me it's meaningful to be there a lot [for the children] now. Because I don't think that anyone else could do it better for them. He [her partner] is very ambitious. And he thrives – I've always known that he would work a great deal. He is a very restless type, efficient and stuff. He is always doing something. He's got a lot of energy. (...) I guess he is more like staying the course and having his own – But he can also be a bit naïve, in my opinion, regarding – He is very ambitious on my behalf too, he is not at all the one who says "could you stay at home next year too?" I'm the one who said that. There are lots of men that appreciate a woman who stays at home and facilitates. But he is more like "If you look at your CV now, this is the perfect time for you to obtain that management position" and things like that. (...) [But] now he has felt and experienced that there has been a lot to do here at home also this last year [after having their second child], so now he is very supportive of me doing this [prolonging her one-year parental leave with a year of unpaid leave].

(Ellinor, female manager/consultant).

Taking an additional full year of unpaid parental leave is far from typical among Norwegian mothers in elite professions. However, with the gendered division of the generous paid leave, even highly gender-equality oriented parents embark on parenthood with a gender-traditional, complementary work-family arrangement, where mothers provide the flexibility for their partners to uphold their career investments after becoming fathers.

The characteristics, logic and demands of career jobs also contribute to *reinforce* the gendered polarization of roles, responsibilities and (ir)replaceabilities – and thus continued unequal investments in career vs. care work. In effect, the impossibility of combining child care with both parents investing what it takes to succeed in these competitive, "high commitment" career jobs, is articulated as a significant explanation for the parents making a shift to a gendered work-family adaptation where the father continues his career investment and progression, while the mother remains in, or shifts to, a position that allows her to take the main responsibility for unpaid family work – at the cost of career opportunities and income. More specifically, the demands for intensive and flexible investments implies that parents with a "ground crew" taking main responsibility for both predictable and unpredictable investments required at home, have a significant advantage in the competition for staying on the A-team and further promotion and career opportunities.

4.5 Gender traditional uptake: in conflict with ideals – but still taken for granted

The gender unequal leave uptake is presented as a "default" practice, with no need for explanation. In other words, even among highly educated mothers and fathers, with gender-equal work-family ideals and career preferences and ambitions, it seems to be "natural" and taken-for-granted that fathers take short leaves and mothers take long leaves. When asked directly why they divided the leave so unequally, neither mothers nor fathers expressed this as a matter of maternal gatekeeping (e.g. Allen and Hawkins 1999), or as traditional views implying that mothers provide better care for infants compared to fathers. Instead, their answers and explanations reflect gendered notions implying that their gender-equality ideals must give way when a more equal division of parental leave represents a risk to *fathers'* future career opportunities. In other words, there seems to be a gendered taken-for-granted notion that for *fathers* a conceived career risk justifies both opting out and limiting the length of parental leave as well as timing it in order to minimize its consequences for deliveries and demonstrating dedication at work:

> *I could – I would like to be home for six months, but it's like I feel that I can't. And I haven't got a good explanation for that.*

> Not even two [months]?

> *Well, I take six weeks actually, because the due date [for the delivery of the expected child] fits perfect with the summer. Because then I can go off work just when [high season with high production pressure] is over, then I take leave and then holiday. It will be a long vacation, sort of. And I read this in the newspaper, that it's typical for men to take such leave, that they are in reality long holidays. And that's what I do, really. And I'm not proud of it, but this is the way it is, kind of.*

> *(Philip, male manager/consultant)*

This gender bias is rarely commented on among our informants. In the following interview extract, however, the taken-for-grantedness is explicitly addressed by a female lawyer, sharing her frustration of the reality of inequality in competitive intensive career jobs:

> When a female junior associate is expecting a baby, everyone takes for granted that she'll be gone for a year. But male junior associates don't have the time, not even to take the one month daddy quota. And the reasoning just doesn't add up, because they actually do have time for the typical one-year leave being deputy judge or other career promoting assignments outside the firm. But they have no time for paternity leave, and no one challenges them on that. (...). I think that the underlying message is that his career is more important than hers. (...) And I don't think that many men would actually say "Yes, I really mean that". I think they will say "No, no, that's not what I mean". There is a mismatch between attitude and practice.

(Celine, female lawyer)

Hence, these gendered notions and taken-for-grantedness in effect provide fathers – in contrast to mothers – with the *flexibility* to take parental leave in a way that prevents it from jeopardizing his A-team membership and irreplaceability at work – both in the short and long run.

5. Conclusion

Among Norwegian elite professionals there is a gap between strong gender-equal work-family ideals and more gender traditional practices. In order to better understand this gap we have examined the role of division of parental leave and explored the specific challenges arising from manoeuvring within demanding career professions. The non-transferable fathers' quota has been of great importance in increasing fathers' leave use in Norway – also in elite professions. However, the distribution of parental leave between mothers and fathers in these occupations has not changed, as mothers' leave uptake has increased as well. Despite gender-equal attitudes and preferences, fathers work more, earn more and are far more likely to have "the most important job" – while taking less responsibility than mothers at home. Our analyses show that the uptake of leave is strongly linked to this pattern, with no or short parental leave predicting a higher probability of having a gender-traditional division later on, while longer leaves reduce the probability of having a gender-traditional division, on all four measures: unpaid work, paid work, income and work status. We find the strongest relation between leave use and later division of unpaid work. While there may be unobserved characteristics explaining fathers reluctance to take parental leave as well as later gender-equal divisions of work and family responsibility, the findings based on the selected sub-sample suggest that self-reinforcing patterns of work-family divisions are at play, drawing couples into an either egalitarian or gender-traditional direction – regardless of attitudes. Even among the most equality-prone fathers within these professions, the typically gendered division of parental leave seems to contribute to a gender-unequal work-family adaptation.

This interpretation is supported and amplified in the analysis of the qualitative data. We identify a twofold contribution of the gendered uptake of parental leave in shaping later gender-unequal work-family adaptation. First, when dual career couples embark on parenthood and the mother takes the typical long leave – implying up to one year of gender-traditional division of career and care work – mothers are constituted as replaceable at work and irreplaceable at home, and vice versa for fathers, despite gender-equal attitudes towards work-family adaptation. Second, the logic, characteristics and demands of career jobs in turn *reinforce* the gendered polarization of roles, responsibilities and (ir)replaceabilities – and thus continued unequal investments in career vs. care work after the parental leave period.

Not only does the logic of continuous investment and competition imply that taking parental leave represents a risk to career. The demands for intensive and flexible investments within these careers also implies that parents with a "ground crew", taking main responsibility for both predictable and unpredictable investments required at home, have a significant advantage in the competition for staying on the A-team and further promotion and career opportunities. In effect, the impossibility of combining childcare with both parents investing what it takes to succeed in these competitive, "high commitment" career jobs, is articulated as a significant explanation for the parents making a shift to gendered work-family adaptations. Thus, within competitive career jobs, the gendered leave uptake seem to contribute to a strong pull towards gender unequal investments in care and career: the father continues his career investment and progression, while the mother remains in or shifts to a position that allows her to take the main responsibility for the unpaid family work – at the cost of career opportunities and income.

The demands in career jobs are not gendered per se. However, combined with the taken-for-grantedness of mothers taking long leaves while fathers take short leaves, the demands for continuous and extensive investments in competition intensive career jobs have gendered consequences. While it is not impossible to change the gender traditional pattern established during the parental leave, the logic, characteristics and demands of career jobs make it difficult – even when the gender-unequal adaptation contradicts initial plans and preferences. Thus, challenging the "naturalness" of short parental leaves among fathers seems important in order to narrow the gap between work-family ideals and actual practices. Moreover, there is a need for leave policies that take into account the specific conditions and dynamics in competition intensive career jobs and work organizations.

References

Aarseth, H. (2011) *Moderne familieliv. Den likestilte familiens motivasjonsformer.* Oslo: Cappelen Damm Akademisk

Allen, S. M., and Hawkins, A. J. (1999) 'Maternal gatekeeping: Mother's beliefs and behavior that inhibit greater father involvement in family work' *Journal of Marriage and Family*, 61, pp. 199–212

Arnalds, Á. A., Eydal, G. B. and Gíslason, I. V. (2013) 'Equal Rights to Paid Parental Leave and Caring Fathers – the Case of Iceland', *Icelandic Review of Politics and Administration*, 9(2) pp. 323–44

Bloksgaard, L. (2009) *Arbejdsliv, forældreskab og køn – forhandlinger af løn og barsel i tre moderne virksomheder,* SPIRIT – Doctoral Programme Aalborg University Denmark. SPIRIT PhD Series

Brandth, B. and Kvande, E. (2003) *Fleksible fedre: maskulinitet, arbeid, velferdsstat.* Oslo: Universitetsforlaget

Brandth, B. and Kvande, E. (2005) 'Fedres valgfrihet og arbeidslivets tidskulturer', *Tidsskrift for samfunnsforskning*, 1/2005, pp. 35–54

Brandth, B. and Kvande, E. (2009) 'Gendered or Gender-Neutral Care Politics for Fathers?', *The Annals of the American Academy of Political and Social Science,* 624(1) pp. 177–189

Brandth, B. and Kvande, E (eds) (2013) *Fedrekvoten og den farsvennlige velferdsstaten [The fathers' quota and the father friendly welfare state],* Oslo, Universitetsforlaget

Bringedal, K. H. and Lappegård, T. (2012) 'Holdninger til fedrekvote: Småbarnsforeldre sier ja til fedrekvote', *Samfunnsspeilet*, 1/2012, Statistisk sentralbyrå

Cools, S. and Strøm M. (2014) 'Parenthood Wage Penalties in a Double Income Society', *Review of Economics of the Household.* 1–26. doi: 10.1007/s11150-014-9244-y

Cools, S., Fiva, J. H. and Kirkebøen, L. J. (2015) 'Causal Effects of Paternity Leave on Children and Parents,' *The Scandinavian Journal of Economics,* 117(3) pp. 801–28

Crompton, R., Lewis, S. and Lyonette, C. (eds.) (2006) *Women, Men, Work and Family in Europe.* New York: Palgrave Macmillan

Doucet, A. (2009) 'Dad and Baby in the First Year: Gendered Responsibilities and Embodiment', *The ANNALS of the American Academy of Political and Social Science* 624, pp. 78–98

Duvander, A. and Jans, A. (2009) 'Consequences of fathers' parental leave use: Evidence from Sweden', in: *Finnish Yearbook of Population Research,* Special Issue of the 16th Nordic Demographic Symposium in Helsinki 5–7 June 2008

Duvander, A-Z. and Johansson, M. (2015) 'Parental Leave Use for Different Fathers: A Study of the Impact of Three Swedish Parental Leave Reforms,' in: Eydal, G. B. and Eydal, T. R. (eds.) *Fatherhood in the Nordic Welfare States: Comparing Care Policies and Practice.* Bristol: Policy Press, pp. 347–69

Ekberg, J., Eriksson, R. and Friebel, G. (2013) 'Parental Leave – a Policy Evaluation of the Swedish "Daddy-Month" Reform.' *Journal of Public Economics,* 97(0) pp. 131–43

Ellingsæter, A. L. and Arnlaug, L. (2006) *Politicising Parenthood in Scandinavia: Gender relations in welfare states.* Bristol: Policy Press

Evertsson, M., Boye, K. and Erman, J. (2015) *Fathers on Call – a Study on the Sharing of Care Work among Parents in Sweden. A mixed method approach.* Families and Societies Working Paper Series 27

Farstad, G. R. (2010) 'Hva betyr det å ta pappaperm? Når fedrekvotens intensjoner møter menns ulike farskapsmodeller', *Sosiologi i dag,* 40(1-2) pp. 151–171

Grambo, A-C. and Myklebø, S. (2009) *Moderne Familier – Tradisjonelle Valg.* Oslo: Arneids- of velferdsdirektoratet

Gornick, J. C. and Meyers, M. (2009) 'Gender equality: transforming family divisions of labor', in: Wright, E. O (ed.) *The Real Utopias Project.* London and New York: Verso

Hakim, C. (2011) *Feminist Myths and Magic Medicine: the flawed thinking behind calls for further equality legislation.* London: Centre for Policy Studies. Available at: http://eprints.lse.ac.uk/36488/

Halrynjo, S. (2010) *Mødre og fedre i møte med karrierelogikkens spilleregler. [Mothers and fathers encountering the rules of the career game. How do elite educated men and women adapt to work and family when they have children?],* PhD-thesis, Dept. of Sociology, University of Oslo

Halrynjo, S. (2014) 'Arbeidsliv og familieliv – Klassedelt og kjønnsdelt', in: Reisel, L. and Teigen, M (eds.) *Kjønnsdeling og etniske skiller på arbeidsmarkedet.* Oslo: Gyldendal Akademisk, pp. 186–202

Halrynjo, S. (2015) 'Kjønn, topplederkarriere og familie', in: Teigen, M. (ed.) *Virkninger av kjønnskvotering i norsk næringsliv.* Oslo: Gyldendal, pp. 97–116

Halrynjo, S. and Lyng, S. T. (2009) 'Preferences, constraints or schemas of devotion? Exploring Norwegian mothers' withdrawal from high-commitment careers', *British Journal of Sociology,* 60(2) pp. 321–343

Halrynjo, S. and Lyng, S. T. (2010) 'Fars forkjørsrett – mors vikeplikt? Kjønn, karriere og omsorgsansvar i eliteprofesjoner' [Fathers' Priority – Mothers' Duty to Give Way? Gender, Career and Childcare in Elite Professions]. *Tidsskrift for samfunnsforskning, Journal of Social Research,* 51(2) pp. 249–275

Halrynjo, S. and Lyng, S. T. (2013) 'Fedrepermisjon i karriereyrker' [Paternity leave in career jobs], in: Brandth, B and Kvande, E. (eds.) *Fedrekvoten og den farsvennlige velferdsstaten [The fathers quota and the father friendly welfare state],* Oslo, Universitetsforlaget, pp 222–236

Hansen, T. and Slagsvold, B. (eds.) (2012) *Likestilling Hjemme.* Norsk institutt for forskning om oppvekst, velferd og aldring: NOVA-rapport 08/2012

Johansson, M. and Duvander, A-S (2013) *Effekter På Jämställdhet Av Reformer I Föräldrapenningen.* ISF Inspektionen för socialförsäkringen. Rapport 2013:7. Stockholm

Kitterød, R. H. and Rønsen, M. (2013) *Yrkes- og familiearbeid i barnefasen. Endring og variasjon i foreldres tidsbruk 1970–2010.* Rapporter 44/2013, Statistisk sentralbyrå

Lappegård, T. (2012) 'Couples' Parental Leave Practices: The Role of the Workplace Situation,' *Journal of Family and Economic Issues,* 33(3) pp. 298–305

Lyng, S. T. (2010) ' "Mothered" and Othered. (In)visibility of care responsibility and gender in processes of excluding women from Norwegian law firms', in: Lewis, P.and Simpson, R. (eds.) *Revealing and Concealing Gender: issues of visibility in organization research.* Basingstoke: Palgrave, pp. 76–99

Rege, M. and Solli, I. F. (2013) 'The Impact of Paternity Leave on Fathers' Future Earnings.' *Demography,* 50(6) pp. 2255–77

Skrede, K. and Aarskaug Wiik, K. (2012) 'Forsørgerstruktur og inntektsfordeling: Mer likestilling og større ulikhet?', in: Ellingsæter, A. L. and Widerberg, K. (eds.): *Velferdsstatens familier.* Oslo: Gyldendal

Smeby, K. W. (2013)' Fedrekvoten – Stykkevis Og Delt Eller Fullt Og Helt?', in: Brandth, B. and Kvande, E. (eds.) *Fedrekvoten Og Den Farsvennlige Velferdsstaten.* Oslo: Universitetsforlaget, pp. 150–164

Sørensen, B. Aa., Seierstad, G. and Grimsmo, A. (2005) Tatt av ordet. Medienes forspill til framtidens arbeidsliv. Oslo: Arbeidsforskningsinstituttet

Wærness, K. and Knudsen, K. (2006) 'Likestilling og husarbeid: Norden i komparativt perspektiv' *Tidsskrift for samfunnsforskning,* 2, pp. 163–190

Appendix

Binary logistic regressions: Fathers' probability of having a gender-traditional work-family division, dependent on uptake of paid leave after introduction of the fathers' quota. The sample includes only fathers with gender equal ideals and a highly educated spouse.

Fathers' probability of having a gender-traditional work-family division	Model 1 Division of unpaid work B (SE)	Model 2 Division of paid work B (SE)	Model 3 Division of status B (SE)	Model 4 Division of income B (SE)
Total leave	-.18*** (.04)	0.11** (0.04)	0.16*** (0.02)	0.17***(0.04)
Age	0.02 (0.02)	0.02 (0.02)	0.01 (0.02)	0.02 (0.02)
Number of children	0.18 (0.20)	0.35(0.19)	0.24 (0.21)	0.34 (0.24)
Preference for career	0.16 (0.11)	0.17 (0.11)	0.21 (0.11)	0.12 (0.13)
Constant	-1.12 (0.61)	- 0.58 (0.62)	- 0.52 (0.62)	- 0.82 (0.71)
N	716	716	716	716
- 2 Log likelihood	675,2	643.6	629,5	531.8

** = significance level 0.01 *** = significance level 0.001

Changing Fatherhood? The Significance of Parental Leave for Work Organizations and Couples

Benjamin Neumann and Michael Meuser

1. Introduction

The public and scientific discussion about changing fatherhood in Germany reaches back to the 1980s. In particular in the last decade the number of studies about 'new' fathers has increased significantly. Also German family policy has started – as in the EU as a whole – to address not only mothers, but also fathers (Ehnis and Beckmann 2010; Hofäcker 2007). The new direction of family policy is expressed in the amendment of the German parental leave legislation in 2007, which included several important changes: parents' allowance money is paid for up to fourteen months. In order to get the money for the full fourteen months both partners are required to take parental leave for at least two months. If only one partner takes parental leave, parental allowance will only be paid for twelve months. The two additional months cannot be split between the partners. Both parents can apply for parental leave at the same time as well as separately. Parents' money is roughly two-third of the mother's or father's previous income: 67% of the last wage, but at least €300 up to a maximum of €1800. One aim of the amendment is to encourage women to return to work earlier after parental leave and to prevent a devaluation of their human capital. Another goal is to motivate fathers to participate more in family life. Such changes in family policy do not only demonstrate new perspectives for (and on) both mothers and fathers, but support the idea that fathers in particular should be more involved in child rearing activities. An intensified involvement of fathers is not only accepted, but explicitly encouraged (cf. Meil 2013: 568).[1]

---

1   In 2005 the former German family minister Ursula von der Leyen postulated: "This country needs new fathers"(Heute, Nov. 18t[h], 2005; www.heute.de/ZDFheute/inhalt/22/0,3672,2397814,00.html, <5.10.2007>). In an interview she confirmed her position: "This society will not be able to go on existing without developing the paternal role" (Der Stern 7/2007; www.stern.de/politik/deutschland/582597.html?nv=cb, <05.03.2007>).

Latest data from the Federal Statistical Office in Germany (Statistisches Bundesamt) show a significant increase in the use of paternal leave in Germany. Whereas in 2006 – before the amendment – only 3.5% of fathers took parental leave, the number grew to 20.8% in 2008 and culminated in 32% in 2015 (Statistisches Bundesamt 2015: 27). To put these numbers into perspective: two-thirds of German fathers still do not take parental leave at all. Among the 32% of fathers taking paternal leave, the majority (78.9%) only take the two months, whereas 92.4% of women take ten to twelve months of parental leave (ibid.: 7). Since the majority of fathers only take the two 'partner months' these months are often referred to as 'daddy months' in German public discourse. Furthermore, statistical data show that there are regional differences within Germany. The federal states Saxony and Bavaria located in the east and south of Germany have the highest number of paternal leave with 41% and 39.9% respectively, whereas North Rhine-Westphalia or the Saarland, located in the west of Germany register 25.1% and 20.1% respectively of paternal leave. However, since 2007 the development remains positive across all federal states.

Over the last ten years, there is a remarkable increase in research on fatherhood in Germany. In 2005 a special issue of the German "Journal for Family Research" (Zeitschrift für Familienforschung) was published with the title: *Men – the "neglected" gender in family research* (Tölke and Hank 2005). Since then, fatherhood became a prominent subject in family as well as in gender research. Research focuses on different aspects of fathers' intra-familial engagement. One part of the research deals with the socio-demographic determinants (such as income, education, region, ethnicity, etc.) of fathers taking parental leave. The factors that influence fathers' decision to take parental leave are analyzed (Pfahl and Reuyß 2010; Trappe 2013). Other studies develop typologies of fathering to explain differences in the usage of parental leave and in fathers' involvement in unpaid household and childcare (e.g. Vogt 2010; Richter 2012; Pfahl, Reuyß and Hundt 2015; Possinger 2013). Different kinds of studies focus on negotiations between the couple about the father's involvement in domestic work and childcare (Behnke 2012; Behnke and Meuser 2013; König, 2012; Peukert 2015). Furthermore, there are studies that examine conducive and obstructive factors in work organizations which influence fathers' intra-familial engagement (Possinger 2013; Pfahl, Reuyß and Hundt 2015).

Whether fathers take parental leave and to what extent they do, is not only negotiated within the couple. One has also to take into account how work organizations deal with fathers' claims to take parental leave. The negotia-

---

She went as far as prophesying that men will no longer find a wife if they are not willing to contribute equally to domestic work and childcare.

tions within the couple and the negotiations between the father and the work organization are closely connected. In this chapter we focus in particular on work organizations and show how they try to handle the temporal absence of male employees in a way that organizational routines are not endangered. We identify conducive factors that allow a higher rate of fathers taking parental leave as well as obstructive factors that inhibit fathers from taking leave, or that they take more than the usual two months. Further we will briefly explore how organizational rationales and couples' motives are related in a way that the usual duration of two months meets the interests of both. We rely on a current research project about fathers in parental leave.[2] After a brief overview about recent research on changing fatherhood and some remarks on method and data we present the first findings of our study. The findings are discussed with regard to international research on changing patterns of fatherhood.

2. Involved fatherhood, employment and masculinity

In order to understand the rationale underlying the attitudes of work organizations toward fathers who claim to take parental leave one has to take into account the relation of fatherhood and masculinity. Fathers' involvement in domestic work and childcare and their willingness to take parental leave are determined not only by negotiations among the couple, but also by cultural patterns of masculinity and expectations of employers. Numerous studies reveal that masculinity is still related to gainful employment and occupational career (Meuser and Scholz 2012; Scholz 2008; Baur and Luedtke 2008). The hegemonic construction of masculinity ties masculinity tightly, if not indissolubly, to the work sphere (Meuser 2010). This becomes impressively evident when men change their attitudes towards professional obligations. These men are still confronted with a resistant organizational culture in enterprises and other work organizations. Fathers who try to reduce their working hours to increase family time challenge the norms of the work sphere (cf. Ranson 2001). They question the prevalent expectation that men do not have any duties besides gainful employment. Therefore, fathers requesting or taking parental leave may still be considered as "poor workers" by their employers or companies (Rudman and Mescher 2013: 335). Still, reducing the working

---

2   The Project "Fathers in Parental Leave.: negotiations and decision making among the couple and the work-sphere" is funded by Mercator Research Center Ruhr. The project is located at TU Dortmund University, Ruhr-University Bochum and University Duisburg-Essen. Members of the research team are: Stefanie Aunkofer, Ilse Lenz, Michael Meuser, Benjamin Neumann, Katja Sabisch and Christine Wimbauer.

hours is often interpreted as a lack of professional committment. According to Gesterkamp (2006: 149), these anticipated operational difficulties in terms of a reduced attendance at the workplace only seem to be a secondary reason. The main reason seems to be the demonstration of distance to the gainful employment itself and the insinuated erosion of strict morals of work. Furthermore, signalizing the wish to reduce ones amount of work can provoke conflicts among colleagues, since it may raise questions about commitment, solidarity and loyalty to the team, and how the additional work will be shared. Also the man's masculinity is often questioned by his colleagues (Doucet 2006: 209; Merla 2008).

Although, according to German legislation, both parents are entitled to take paternal leave there is a widespread expectation in business companies that women will make use of this right. Men are not expected to take parental leave, at least not for a longer time. Following common gender stereotypes of seeing the mother as the primary caregiver, a mother's claim to take parental leave is perceived as an expression of her legitimate and 'natural' maternal commitment to the child, whereas an assumption of a comparable 'natural' commitment of the father does not exist. According to Gesterkamp (2006: 149), "especially men often fail to give plausible reasons why they want to reduce their working hours. Compared to women in the same situation they lack societal approved gendered roles beyond the work-sphere". Many companies in Germany commit themselves to 'family-friendliness', which is declared as an important value. Those companies are eager to get the certificate 'audit work and family' *(audit beruf und familie)*. As discovered in our recent study, many of the measures designed to reconcile work and family only address female employees. The indispensability of the male workforce (fathers included) still seems to be an undisputable norm to many employers. The desire of fathers to participate more in family life is affected by the institutional limits of the labour market. The new culture of fatherhood has to be implemented against an existing structure that accepts a changing fatherhood only so far as it does not reduce the father's indispensability for the labour market (Born and Krüger 2002; Oberndorfer and Rost 2004). Some studies show that companies express their sympathy if fathers seek to increase their family involvement. However, most companies will not support these attempts because they assume operational difficulties that may arise (Possinger 2009: 62). Even within the relatively open-minded companies we spoke to, a lot of fathers face some difficulties while taking parental leave. Against this backdrop it is not surprising that 68% of German fathers do not make use of paternal leave.

Those who take paternal leave, in particular those who take it for a longer time than two months, as well as those who reduce their working time in favor of family time, are challenged to bring their familial engagement into accordance with the cultural image of masculinity. Various studies show that it is important for fathers to make sure that child care is compatible with masculinity. This shows that the figure of the involved father has no legitimate place in the pattern of hegemonic masculinity (Doucet, 2006; Magaraggia, 2013). In a study on Belgian fathers who stay at home for at least six months, Merla discovered that these fathers "reported diffuse feelings that others sometimes considered them as effeminate or weak, or put into question their sexual orientation" (Merla 2008: 123). No less than explicit allegations of being unmanly,[3] such diffuse feelings indicate that for men it is not uncomplicated to reconcile child care and masculinity. They feel the challenge to demonstrate that reducing working hours and doing family work does not result in a loss of masculinity. There is only little research on strategies fathers use to face this challenge.

In the following some preliminarily findings of the ongoing study on fathers taking parental leave are presented. The study focuses on fathers taking parental leave and how this is negotiated between the couple as well as in the workplace. Here, we concentrate on the latter sphere and refer mainly to interviews with human resource managers in private enterprises and other work organizations. In addition, we rely also on a former study on involved fatherhood.[4]

3. Data and Method

The study aims to reconstruct the decision processes taking place before the father takes parental leave. The focus lies on two different dimensions: the first one deals with the couple and their negotiations on how parental leave is timed and shared among the couple. The second dimension is about the work organization where the father has to claim his right to take parental leave. In both dimensions the study focuses on the significance of gender stereotypes. Related to the two dimensions, the study consists of two parts: interviews with couples and expert interviews with human resource managers.

In order to reconstruct the negotiations that preceded the fathers' decision to take the leave, the partners are interviewed together. The couple's interview generates two sorts of data: the couple's history reported by both

---

3   In an experimental study, Rudman and Mescher (2013: 336) found "that male leave requesters suffered femininity stigma, such that perceivers judged them as weaker and more communal, but also as less agentic and dominant".
4   In this study, funded by the German Research Foundation, 36 couples were interviewed (cf. Behnke 2012; Behnke/Meuser 2012, 2013; Lengersdorf/Meuser 2016).

partners (dimension of content) and the couple's interaction during the interview (formal dimension of discourse organization). The way *how* the couple tells the joint history *in situ* give hints to the partner's relationship. Also, the efforts of the partners to negotiate certain aspects of their family life become visible. Therefore, the couple's interview is particularly suited to reconstruct the joint construction of the partnership, the family and private gender arrangements (Behnke and Meuser 2013).[5] Additional expert interviews with human resource managers aim to comprehend how work organizations deal with claims for parental leave made by male employees. Human resource managers are addressed as experts due to their status in the organization's hierarchy. They have privileged access to information about the organization's personnel development and decisions, and the careers of the employees working in the organization[6].

To date, sixteen couples and eight human resource managers have been interviewed. The couples belong to different social milieus; a few migrant couples are also included. With one exception heterosexual couples were interviewed. The expert interviews took place predominantly in private enterprises, but also in public corporations. Both, couples' and expert interviews were conducted in two regions: in North Rhine-Westphalia (with a low rate of fathers in parental leave) and in Bavaria (with a high rate of fathers in parental leave).

4. Parental leave, fathers and work organizations: preliminary findings

Regarding the length of the paternal leave, our findings correspond with the statistical data mentioned above. According to the interviewed human resource managers, most mothers take at least twelve months of parental leave. The duration of maternity leave ranges from about seven or eight months (on the executive level, where parental leave is apparently shorter) to fourteen months and above (on the lower hierarchical levels).[7] Before the amendment of the parental leave legislation in 2007 many women had taken two to three

---

5 The method of the couple's interview is a mixture of the biographical-narrative interview and the group discussion (cf. Behnke/Meuser 2013; Kruse 2015: 159–165; Przyborski/ Wohlrab-Sahr 2008: 122–131).

6 Concerning the term 'expert' and the methodology of the expert interview cf. Meuser/ Nagel 2009.

7 The length of parental leave can exceed the maximum of twelve, plus two months of parents' money.

years of maternal leave. Since then their parental leave has shortened. The shortening of maternal leave is outlined by the following quotation of a representative and seems to be typical for the other interviewees we spoke to,:

> Well, if someone returns quickly [back to the job], after some months, so that one perhaps did not even take parental leave, that is, I believe, still considered differently by many, as if a woman at least takes off a year or a similar period of time. But if you take longer than two years off, the colleagues and all the others are wondering, [...]. Well, it is unusual that someone stays longer than two years. Two years seem to be a limit. (Company F)

4.1 Fathers' leave: a 'longer vacation'

The majority of fathers take two months of parental leave, which seems rather unproblematic to the companies and institutions we talked to. All institutional representatives told us that the two partner months, introduced in 2007, have been well established until now. One representative describes these two months as the fathers' 'classical' choice in parental leave arrangements:

> It is typical of men working in administration to take the eight weeks during the first 14 months of life [...] there have been several longer sections of parental leave lasting for a duration of three, four months. Also without part-time. But always still the eight weeks. (Company C)

Many representatives argued that the two months of paternal leave, especially when split into one month at the birth of the child and one month at the end of the partners leave, were unproblematic to compensate because the company would handle these four to eight weeks like an extended vacation.

> Yes, it differs [resettlement for men and women after the parental leave] already because, normally men do not leave too long, but rather work part-time and stay for a few hours during parental leave. Thus it is actually not a real issue, because it is just a natural consequence, that it is that short. If we talk about two months, it is, so to speak, a long holiday, if one exaggerates a bit. (Company D)

Framing the two months in terms of an elongated vacation expresses how a lot of companies perceive paternal leave – especially in contrast to the maternity leave of women. Framing men's parental leave this way the representatives make several things clear: first, that up to two months of paternal leave can be coped with as a vacation, and that this is even more unproblematic when the two months are split up. Secondly it implies that this kind of leave is seen (and handled) as an extended kind of holiday for recreation and time with the family. None of the interviewed representatives who portrayed paternal leave like this mentioned that parental leave can be exhausting and stressful, especially if the father does not take the leave parallel to his partner.[8] Finally, the two months can be seen as a limit that states to which extent the absence of fathers can be coped with, and when the difficulties begin. Although the two months seem to be well established, they also seem to be a limit, since an extension of these two months in terms of a longer paternal leave (e.g. six months and more) can provoke resistance and cause irritation.

This does not necessarily mean that there will be problems if fathers take longer leaves, e.g. for three, six or twelve months, but a longer leave cannot be seen as a 'vacation leave' and would have to be treated differently. To some extent this implies that the "manpower" of men seems to be still indispensable (especially in contrast to women – cf. e.g. Björnberg 2002), but it also illustrates that the assumption of indispensability can become fragile if a growing number of fathers take parental leave, especially for more than two months. Still, a lot of companies reckon that female employees will become pregnant and that their (wo)manpower must be compensated for, but ignore that the availability of male employees can become uncertain. This highlights the persistence of the common traditional perspective of a gendered division of the work sphere and the domestic sphere. It still exists even though changes become apparent.

4.2 Importance of role models

Studies focusing on possible challenges men face within the German work sphere show that taking parental leave or expressing an extended interest in family life or recreational time can provoke conflicts between colleagues and/or managers (Gesterkamp 2006; Possinger 2013; Neumann 2015). In our study we discovered that managers in particular have a huge influence on how the parental leave arrangement can be used. Although the managers cannot refuse the parental leave they can influence the process of decision-making on a subtle level, e.g. holding in prospect certain career problems. Such problems were anticipated by some of the couples we interviewed as well.[9] The relation between decision-making within the work sphere and the family or couple is a very close one. Even if such problems do not occur often, this fact will not encourage most of the fathers to take longer periods of parental leave. Some

---

8   Some of the fathers we interviewed underestimated this too.
9   Coletrane et al. (2013) observe a significant drop in the earnings of men, if they are unemployed for family reasons. "[M]en who opt for a 'daddy track,' by choosing flexible work trajectories suffer lower long-term earnings, just as women who opt for a 'mommy track' suffer an eventual earnings penalty. Thus, our findings suggest that the flexibility stigma is relatively gender neutral. Regardless of gender, if a parent quits work or stays unemployed for family reasons, that person is likely to experience lower earnings in the long run." (ibid.: 297).

of the experts we interviewed stated that employees (especially fathers) get more confident if there are visible role models. The fear of losing the job or of returning to a different (and felt as inappropriate) position within the company, or of reducing one's career prospects, remains and is often taken into account during the process of negotiation and decision-making.

Positive effects of role models were highlighted in many interviews, particularly if these role models are located at the management level.[10] One of the representatives we spoke to illustrates this by referring to a manager who took paternal leave and was filmed for company publicity:

> Well, that is one of the colleagues who, for example, we portrayed in such a video. It is of course really helpful for the company's corporate culture, if we have executives who talk openly about the topic [...] well, he really turned his gaze into the camera and said, if you really want to do it, just do it. And of course that is a very, very important message. (Company D)

Another expert illustrates the importance and the effect such a role model can have:

> Mr. Eggert[11], an executive, went on parental leave, the first one in the company, and in doing that he drew attention to the topic, which then did, yes, let me put it this way, led to discussion, but afterwards the whole topic met with great acceptance because it was simply new. And since then it is normal for all kind of employees, yes, regularly, that employees are leaving for parental time. (Company E)

For some companies it seems to be a rather radical decision for an employee on the management level to take parental leave. This indicates that taking leave seems to be relatively accepted on lower hierarchical levels, but rather uncommon and (rather) not welcome on middle or higher management levels. The effect is bigger if a male employee in a leading position takes parental leave:

> I mean, it is of course a strong sign if the personnel manager, as an executive employee, is the first one who announces that he is going to take parental leave. Of course that has an effect on all the other employees, right? He got the ball rolling, yes. (Company E)

Furthermore, it is important to highlight that the visibility of role models is not the only relevant aspect in motivating fathers to take parental leave. Quantity is also significant. The general increase of the number of men taking parental leave furthers not only the normalization of men taking leave, but also

---

10 Magnus Bygren and Ann-Zofie Duvander (2006) also found that the possibility of fathers' taking parental leave is influenced by other fathers.
11 All names are anonymized.

of men doing childcare, and it destabilizes the expectation of male employees' unlimited availability for the organization.

So far we showed that the visibility of role models in particular can have an important impact on promoting paternal leave – both in terms of making use of paternal leave in the first place and taking a longer leave, but also for women in reducing their length of leave, especially for those women in higher hierarchical levels. The significance of visibility is further illustrated by the fact that it is perceived as a danger by those employers who are resistant to paternal leave, especially if an employee in management positions claims it, as the following example from one of the couples interviews shows. The interviewee, working within a 'family-friendly' certified company, describes a lot of resistance from the executive board. His boss told him to keep his paternal leave a 'secret', and not to talk about it to his colleagues, since it could encourage other employees to make use of this possibility, too. This is a negative point to the significance of visibility.

4.3 Supporting effects of 'family-friendliness'

Not only role models can support fathers who claim parental leave. A family-friendly mission statement by the organization can also have positive effects, as this father explained:

> If it would have been a company that is not certified in combining work and family life, expectations would not have been there in the first place. I would simply say that the company does not offer it. If I became a father it would concern me. I'd have to take care of a child. I'd have to see if I could keep my job if I decided to take parental leave and so on. The certificate sends another signal. Now I would assume that it's even less complicated. (Couple Buchholz)

On the one hand this example shows that even if a company is certified for compatibility of family and career, one cannot assume that there will not be any problems in taking parental leave. On the other hand, it illustrates that certification itself holds some significance for fathers who want to engage in childcare.[12] A growing number of corporations are interested in being certified as family friendly. This is part of the *publicity* of organizations. Fathers can rely on this in making claims for a longer period of paternal leave. They feel more encouraged to claim their rights because they reasonably assume that the company cannot simply deny its family-friendly commitment. The compa-

---

12 A company's commitment to family friendliness is often critically seen as mere symbolic policy. But even a symbolic policy opens up new chances for employees to make their claims, because they can refer to the company's statements.

ny would risk its positive image, which is important because it is a competitive advantage in relation to non-certified companies.[13] One interviewee confirms this, but also makes clear that the culture a company proclaims to have has to be realized as well, especially on the management and board levels:

> There are many problems where it is lacking and where a mission statement would facilitate, but that isn't the case, and as long as the current executive chairman is in office. Certainly till next year, February, I don't believe it will change. After February a younger chairman will move up [replacing the former], and he has two kids, which are as old as mine, nine and ten, but the mother in the family isn't working. It's a classical role allocation. He makes his career and is never at home, she's always at home with her children, and yes, we have to see. It will take a long time, I believe, until it is stored in our brains. (Company G)

A mission statement or a certification of a company as family-friendly could help to encourage claims for parental leave, but it cannot be taken for granted. It must be implemented by the executive staff, but, according to this interviewee, this takes time, and further, one cannot simply expect that a generational change in top management automatically promotes the implementation. Another interviewee points to a specific aspect of organizational resistance. Even if top management is supportive, middle management is often resistant:

> It is always a question of the direct superior. Very often. How progressive he supports this subject or works against it. (Company A)

Implementing an organizational culture that is supportive to fathers taking parental leave is not only a matter for top management. The above-mentioned implicit norm of men's indispensability is very effective at middle management level. On this organizational level the missing manpower of the father in leave must be compensated for.

4.4 Generational shift and changing attitudes: changing practices?

The generational aspect expressed in the penultimate quotation above, was mentioned by some of the representatives in a broader sense as well. They perceive a generational shift in terms of changing attitudes about gender or the gendered division of labor. They assume that a lot of the problems the present generation of employees is facing will resolve itself in the course of

---

13 In a former study on dual career couples, human resource managers argued that family friendliness is an advantage in competing with other companies for highly qualified applicants (Behnke/Meuser 2003). Some respondents in the current study locate family friendly policies in the context of diversity.

generational change, instead of being an effect of an active change in politics and corporate policies:

> *We intensively dealt with Generation Y and spoke to trainees about roles and how they feel about having family. It goes in the direction of living together with a partner, not only in terms of childcare but domestic duties etc. There is nearly no one among our current trainees – and we have performed a workshop [...] with very different professional groups, from hospitals, from the chemical sector, from the hotel sector, etc. – and there were a few, very few, who stated that the woman has to be home to educate the children and that [the men] have to bring the money home. And the other way round. Few women said yes, I only want to take care of the child and I do not want a proper profession or to earn money. (Company B)*

The impression that there are generational changes going on may seem plausible against the backdrop of the increase of fathers taking parental leave, but one has to take into account that the expressed attitudes toward gender, sexuality,[14] an egalitarian share of family work and child care etc. is not necessarily congruent with the actual practices within couples. In the couples interviews it becomes evident that most couples practice a rather 'modernized' traditional arrangement regarding family work and child rearing tasks. On the one hand, a lot of them express their agreement and appreciation of sharing those tasks in an egalitarian way, but on the other hand, they practice a rather traditional division of labor. This is consistent with findings from other studies, which found thar a re-traditionalization takes place after the birth of the first child (cf. Oberndorfer and Rost 2004; Schulz and Blossfeld 2012; Wippermann, Calmbach and Wippermann 2009: 64–65). As a result of a longitudinal study on the division of housework, Schulz and Blossfeld (2012: 204) report that the "transition to parenthood and parenthood itself slow down egalitarian progress and enforce a latent adaption to traditional gendered housework patterns". Indeed, not all of our respondents seem to be satisfied with the effects of re-traditionalization, but seem to lack strategies and role models for alternative arrangements. Re-traditionalization is also related to structural conditions like the higher wage of the husband in many families, or absence of an infrastructure of institutionalized child care.

The power of gendered norms of parenthood and possible moderate shifts of generational attitudes, as well as the lack of alternatives seem to condense in the slight changes we mentioned above (e.g. a reduced length of maternal leave, an increase in paternal leave). But still, at least in Germany, taking parental leave seems obligatory only for women but not for fathers:

---

14 One respondent emphasized that his company pursues a policy of diversity, including appreciating diverse sexual orientations and gender identities (e.g. trans-persons etc.).

It is clear for women anyway. For them it is somehow normal that in any case they are away for a while. (Company B)

In the eyes of the representatives parental leave taken by mothers is a matter of course, whereas taking leave by fathers is seen as a deliberate decision.[15] Some respondents explain this by referring to biological differences. A (female) human resource manager argued quite explicitly:

But I think it is above all a biological issue. [...] This is just a women's matter. I think here we cannot get away from our evolution. Since the Stone Age women have taken care of children, and I think this is a basic need somehow. (Company B)

A mother's claim to take parental leave is seen as an expression of her natural and therefore legitimate maternal commitment to the child, whereas a comparable commitment from the father is not assumed. Corresponding to findings from our couples' interviews, maternal leave still seems to be a natural constant, whereas paternal leave remains optional (cf. Björnberg 2002). This gender bias has consequences in terms of companies' approaches to deal with fathers' and mothers' claims. They are handled and interpreted differently. The typical two partner months taken by fathers are framed as a luxurious addition to support mothers, who remain in the gender-specific position of the primary parent responsible for childcare. In this regard the assumed generational change with its alleged change in gender roles and gendered stereotypes has to be interpreted with caution.

4.5 Organizational policies and couple's gender beliefs

In this regard we find that the common stereotypical gendering within work organizations corresponds with the rather 'traditional' gender perspective of a lot of couples we interviewed.[16] Mr. Albert, for example, describes that there are just plain differences between men and women, and explains this by stating that women can give birth and men cannot, and that the bonding between a mother and her child is more intense. He also makes clear that in his perspective there are limits of equity and equality which cannot be transgressed. In this regard it is obvious for him that it cannot be the purpose for a mother to work fulltime after giving birth, besides having a negative effect on the child's development.

---

15 To what degree mothers' leave is seen as a matter of course is expressed in the following quotation: "If a woman comes back soon it is puzzling why she does not stay at home for a longer time."(Company F)
16 Not all couples referred to such gendered stereotypes. One couple e.g. described themselves only as 'parents' and rejected the gendered distinction between 'mother' and 'father'.

In our sample, some mothers rejected a longer parental leave of fathers. This can be discussed by referring to the notion of *maternal gatekeeping* (Allen and Hawkins 1999; Gaunt 2008). These mothers are not willing to share care responsibilities equally with the father, or even to leave them to him. Retrospectively, a father regrets that he has not taken a longer leave and explains that "his wife would have lost it" if he had taken a longer leave:

> *Mr. Gabler: Well, thinking back two months it does almost seem to be too short. Afterwards I regret not taking three, four or five months, but I think you [his partner] would have lost it.*

> *Ms. Graf: (laughing) At some point it's enough. I was looking forward to spending daytimes together. Me with the baby alone. That's something completely different. One has the entire responsibility. (Couple Graf-Gabler)*

This corresponds with widespread beliefs about mothering, fathering and the needs of a child. The topic of breastfeeding was present in most of our interviews. Breastfeeding seems to be a 'natural constant'; compared with this all other interests and considerations are secondary, even economic reasons as the following excerpt shows.

Besides valuing 'natural' breastfeeding more than feeding by bottle a couple explains that they would rather take a loss of family income then give up their traditional gender roles:

> *Mrs. Niem: Well, it's an infant and it belongs to its mother. And for me it was more important to breastfeed as long as I could – and I mean authentic breastfeeding instead of giving the bottle, in order to give the child a good start. This seems more important to me than to return to work as fast as I can. He [Mr. Niem] could have handled the care for sure, but there's a physical fact that only women can breastfeed. And that seemed more important to me. And that's why he has to take care of the money. [..].*

> *Mr. Niem: But our family income would be higher [if Mrs. Niem would work fulltime, while Mr. Niem handles the care work].*

> *Mrs. Niem: From an economic point of view that would be more efficient.*

> *Mr. Niem: From an economic point of view that is true, but as we already said, that would be against our understanding of roles that only you can breastfeed.17 (Couple Niem)*

Even though it would be financially profitable for the family's income if the father feeds the baby by bottle, the gendered beliefs about fathers' and moth-

---

17 The understanding of roles he mentioned is that the mother has to breastfeed the baby instead of giving him the bottle. Therefore even expressing breast milk into a bottle would be no alternative. This role concept is shared by both partners.

ers' roles within the family – especially in regard to the child's wellbeing – and referring to 'physical facts' let it seem to be without any alternative for some couples to practice the traditional gendered division of labor, at least during infancy.[18] Just as organizations see the mother as the primary caregiver, the majority of the couples do, too. The institutional attribution of childcare to the mother – as it is expressed in the interviews with the representatives of work organizations – corresponds to beliefs about mothers being the primary caregiver held by the majority of couples.

This finding is compatible with findings of the former study on involved fatherhood mentioned above. This study reveals that in the majority of couples who were interviewed both partners (implicitly) agree that the mother is the primary caregiver. It further shows that traditional gender beliefs are not absent among couples who share parenthood and that these beliefs are a serious obstacle against a father's involvement that goes beyond supporting the mother (cf. Lengersdorf and Meuser 2016). Even mothers who intend to share care work equally with the father fell back into traditional patterns of claiming primary responsibility for child care, as the following example taken from the former study, an excerpt from an interview with Mrs. Hoffmann (Hf) and Mr. Hoffmann (Hm), illustrates.

> Hf: There were, there are, I think, there were situations or things where I thought he doesn't make it right or he cannot do it so well, yes [...] And then letting go and saying, no, he is doing this, and he should do it how he does it [...] It happens again and again, doesn't it?
>
> Hm: Uhm.
>
> Hf: But anyway, putting children to bed or if the children hurt themselves or something, then I cannot free myself from thinking inwardly, no, now they must be with mum (Lengersdorf and Meuser 2016: 155).

Compared to Mrs. Niem, Mrs. Hoffmann does not offensively claim to be the primary caregiver, but she reproduces the cultural pattern unintentionally: it "happens". The cultural "feminization of care is so deeply inscribed into their maternal habitus that reflecting on this cannot change the habitualized practice. The pre-reflexive, incorporated routine of doing care is more effective than rational considerations and intentions to change the routines" (Lengersdorf and Meuser 2016: 156). A gendered division of labor is often reproduced against the intentions of both mother and father.

---

18 This example corresponds to findings of Schulz and Blossfeld (2012) that economic theories referring to cost-benefit calculations cannot sufficiently explain the gendered division of labor in the household.

5. Discussion and outlook

On the whole, the expert interviews with representatives of companies and organizations reveal that a change of organizational culture is necessary to motivate more fathers to take parental leave and /or to take more than the two 'daddy months'. A certain change is already going on, but still quite hesitantly in most organizations, although the majority of organizations have implemented programs for reconciling work and family life, subscribe to the value of family friendliness and put diversity on their agenda. Referring to international findings about fatherhood, parental leave and the compatibility of family and care, von Bresinski (2012) and Nelles (2012) point out that companies frame (or begin to frame) family-friendliness as an important company value which helps to recruit and keep well-educated and qualified professionals. They also show that such a focus in a company's culture can raise the company's productivity (cf. OECD 2007: 79–84), as well as the efficiency of staff members, and has a positive influence on well-being and the sickness absence rate.

But, in accordance with the established gendered division of labor as well as common gender beliefs and stereotypes, measures developed in this context are predominantly addressed to female employees. Against this backdrop, male employees who claim more than two months of parental leave still evoke astonishment and disturb the organizational routine. Two months are widely accepted because of the legislation of paying parents' money for twelve plus two months if both partners take parental leave.[19] In the nine years in which the present legislation has existed, organizations have established routines of compensating two months of fathers' absence. It seems that two months of paternal leave does not seriously breach the implicit norm of men's unlimited indispensability.

Of course, compensating for a longer absence is challenging regardless of the sex of the absent employee. However, gender beliefs and stereotypes seem to be the reason why the absence of a female employee is more accepted (and taken for granted) than the absence of a male employee. Nevertheless, in higher hierarchical levels female employees are also increasingly confronted with the demands of being unlimitedly available. Consequently, female managers are requested to keep their parental leave as short as possible and to return to full-time employment early on. Generally, the higher the position within the

---

19 It seems that the legislation generated a stance in organizations that the two months cannot be refused to fathers because they are fixed by law. This implies that the law is interpreted in such a way that the two additional months are explicitly assigned to fathers. According to this, one can ask whether a longer leave for fathers would be accepted if – as in Iceland – the parental leave allocation is 5-2-5: five months for the mother, five months for the father and two months of free availability.

organization, the more frequently an employee is seen as indispensable. But gender intersects with hierarchy. Therefore it is easier for female managers to justify a longer paternal leave than for male managers.

Organizational culture has much impact on fathers' involvement in parental leave. This illustrates that research on (changing) fatherhood cannot be limited to the familial sphere; it also has to be taken into consideration that the occupational sphere mediates to what extent new, more family-centered concepts of fatherhood can be realized. But organizational culture is by no means the only important factor. On the one hand it is embedded in a cultural gender discourse where gender beliefs and images are the blueprints of the organizations' gendered attributions mentioned above. On the other hand the present state of dealing with paternal leave in organizations is in accordance with negotiations between the majority of the couples on how to divide the parents' money months.

The increase of fathers taking parental leave from 3.5 to 32% between 2006 and 2015 indicates that policies can influence couples' decisions relating to the question of who will take parental leave and to which extent. This remarkable increase would not have happened without the amendment of 2007. However, one should not overdraw expectations concerning the possibilities of political steering. 78.9% of fathers take only two months. As we have shown, the way organizations deal with fathers' claims to take parental leave is one reason for not being too optimistic concerning the impact of policy programs. Notwithstanding, private gender arrangements are perhaps even much less accessible to political steering than the labor market and the occupational sphere. It proves extremely difficult to break up incorporated routines and habitualizations of parenting. Family policy can help to increase the options for couples; expecting more would underestimate the inertia of incorporated and habitualized practices in private gender arrangements. Nevertheless, experiences from the Nordic countries show that family policy has effects. Here, over a period of several decades, fathers became increasingly involved in family work. But this also indicates that changing private gender arrangements takes time.

References

Baur, N. and Luedtke, J. (2008) Männlichkeit und Erwerbsarbeit bei westdeutschen Männern, in: Baur, N. and Luedtke J. (eds.) (2008) *Die soziale Konstruktion von Männlichkeit. Hegemoniale und marginalisierte Männlichkeiten in Deutschland.* Opladen/Farmington Hills: Verlag Barbara Budrich, pp. 81–103

Behnke, C. (2012) *Partnerschaftliche Arrangements und väterliche Praxis in Ost- und Westdeutschland.* Opladen/Berlin/Toronto: Verlag Barbara Budrich

Behnke, C. and Meuser, M. (2003) *Doppelkarrieren in Wirtschaft und Wissenschaft, in: Zeitschrift für Frauenforschung und Geschlechterstudien,* 21(4) pp. 62–74

Behnke, C. and Meuser, M. (2012) "Look here mate! I'm taking parental leave for a year" – involved fatherhood and images of masculinity, in: Oechsle, M., Müller, U. and Hess, S. (eds.) (2012) *Fatherhood in Late Modernity: Cultural Images, Social Practices, Structural Frames.* Opladen/Farmington Hills: Verlag Barbara Budrich, pp. 129–145

Behnke, C. and Meuser, M. (2013) „Aktive Vaterschaft". Geschlechterkonflikte und Männlichkeitsbilder in biographischen Paarinterviews, in: Loos, P., Nohl, A-M., Przyborski, A. and Schäffer, B. (eds.) (2013) *Dokumentarische Methode. Grundlagen, Entwicklungen, Anwendungen.* Opladen/Berlin/Toronto: Verlag Barbara Budrich 2013, pp. 75–91

Björnberg, U. (2002) 'Ideology and choice between work and care: Swedish family policy for working parents'. *Critical Social Policy,* 22(1) pp. 33–52

BMAS (2013) *Lebenslagen in Deutschland. Vierter Armuts- und Reichtumsbericht der Bundesregierung.* Bonn: Bundesministerium für Arbeit und Soziales

Born, C. and Krüger H. (2002) Vaterschaft und Väter im Kontext sozialen Wandels. Über die Notwendigkeit der Differenzierung zwischen strukturellen Gegebenheiten und kulturellen Wünschen, in: Walter, H. (ed.) (2002) *Männer als Väter. Sozialwissenschaftliche Theorie und Empirie.* Gießen: Psychosozial-Verlag, pp. 107–143

Brandth, B. and Kvande, E. (1998) 'Masculinity and child care: the reconstruction of fathering', *The Sociological Review,* 46(2) pp. 293–313

Bresinski, B. von (2012) Aktive Vaterschaft und Beruf vereinbaren. Elternzeit für Väter im europäischen Vergleich, in: Walter, H. and Eickhorst, A. (eds.) (2012) *Das Väter Handbuch. Theorie, Forschung, Praxis.* Gießen: Psychosozial-Verlag, pp. 635–655

Bygren, M. and Duvander, A-Z. (2006) 'Parents' Workplace Situation and Fathers' Parental Leave Use', *Journal of Marriage and Family,* 68(2) pp. 363–372

Coletrane, S., Miller, E. C., DeHaan, T. and Stewart, L. (2013) 'Fathers and the Flexibility Stigma', *Journal of Social Issues,* 69(2) pp. 279–302

Doucet, A. (2006) *Do Men Mother? Fathering, Care and Domestic Responsibility.* Toronto: University of Toronto Press

Ehnis, P. (2009) *Väter in Erziehungszeiten. Politische, kulturelle und subjektive Bedingungen für mehr Engagement in der Familie.* Sulzbach: Ulrike Helmer Verlag

Ehnis, P. and Beckmann, S. (2010) ,"Krabbeln lerne ich bei Mama, laufen dann bei Papa". Zur Einbeziehung von Vätern bei Elterngeld und Elternzeit – eine kritische Betrachtung,' *Feministische Studien* 28, pp. 313–324

Gesterkamp, T. (2006) Das Väterdilemma: Die Balance zwischen Anforderungen im Beruf und Engagement in der Familie, in: Mühling, T. and Rost, H. (ed.) (2006) *ifb-Familienreport Bayern 2006. Zur Lage der Familie in Bayern. Schwerpunkt: Väter in der Familie.* München: Bayrisches Staatsministerium für Arbeit und Sozialordnung, Familie und Frauen, pp. 141–153

Hofäcker, D. (2007) Väter im internationalen Vergleich, in: Mühling, T. and Rost, H. (eds.) (2007) *Väter im Blickpunkt. Perspektiven der Familienforschung.* Opladen: Verlag Barbara Budrich, pp. 161–204

Kassner, K. and Rüling, A. (2005) „Nicht nur am Samstag gehört Papi mir!" Väter in egalitären Arrangements von Arbeit und Leben, in: Tölke, A. and Hank, Ka. (eds.) (2005) *Männer – Das „vernachlässigte" Geschlecht in der Familienforschung.* Wiesbaden: VS-Verlag, pp. 235–264

König, T. (2012) *Familie heißt Arbeit teilen. Transformationen der symbolischen Geschlechterordnung.* Konstanz: UVK

Koppetsch, C. and Speck, S. (2015) *Wenn der Mann kein Ernährer mehr ist. Geschlechterkonflikte in Krisenzeiten.* Berlin: Suhrkamp

Kruse, J. (2015) *Qualitative Interviewforschung. Ein integrativer Ansatz.* Weinheim/Basel: Beltz Juventa

Lengersdorf, D. and Meuser, M. (2016) Involved Fatherhood: Source of New Gender Conflicts?, in: Crespi, I. and Ruspini, E. (eds.) (2016) *Balancing Work and Family in a Changing Society: the fathers' perspective.* Basingstoke: Palgrave Macmillan, pp. 149–161

Magaraggia, S. (2013) Tensions between Fatherhood and the Social Construction of Fatherhood in Italy, *Current Sociology,* 61, pp. 76–92

Matzner, M. (2004) *Vaterschaft aus der Sicht von Vätern.* Wiesbaden: VS Verlag

Meil, G. (2013) 'European Men's Use of Parental Leave and their Involvement in Child Care and Housework', *Journal of Comparative Family Studies,* 44(5), pp. 557–570

Merla, L. (2008) 'Determinants, Costs, and Meanings of Belgian Stay-at-Home Fathers: An International Comparison', *Fathering,* 6, pp. 113–132

Meuser, M. (2012) ‚Geschlecht, Macht, Männlichkeit – Strukturwandel von Erwerbsarbeit und hegemoniale Männlichkeit,' *Erwägen, Wissen, Ethik* (EWE), 21(3) pp. 325–336

Meuser, M. and Nagel, U. (2009) The Expert Interview and Changes in Knowledge Production, in: Bogner, A., Littig, B. and Menz, W. (eds.) (2009) *Interviewing Experts.* Houndmills/Basingstoke: Palgrave Macmillan, pp. 17–42

Meuser, M. and Scholz, S. (2012) Herausgeforderte Männlichkeit. Männlichkeitskonstruktionen im Wandel von Erwerbsarbeit und Familie, in: Baader, M. S., Bilstein, J. and Tholen, T. (eds.) (2012) *Erziehung, Bildung und Geschlecht. Männlichkeiten im Fokus der Gender-Studies.* Wiesbaden: Springer VS, pp. 23–40

Nelles, H-G. (2012) Väter – ein Gewinn für Unternehmen?!, in: Walter, H. and Eickhorst, A. (eds.) (2012) *Das Väter Handbuch. Theorie, Forschung, Praxis.* Gießen: Psychosozial-Verlag, pp. 657–667

Neumann, B. (2015) Elternzeitnahme durch Väter. Chancen und Konfliktfelder innerhalb des Paarkontextes, in: Scholz, S. and Dütsch, J. (eds.) (2015) *Krisen, Prozesse, Potenziale. Beiträge zum 4. Studentischen Soziologiekongress. 04.–06.10.2013 in Bamberg.* Bamberg: University of Bamberg Press, pp. 123–152

Oberndorfer, R. and Rost, H. (2004) ‚Auf der Suche nach den neuen Vätern', *Gewerkschaftliche Monatshefte,* 55, pp. 490–499

OECD (2007) *Employment Outlook 2007.* OECD Publishing. Available at: http://www.oecd-ilibrary.org/employment/oecd-employment-outlook-2007_empl_outlook-2007-en [download: 24.02.2016]

Peukert, A. (2015) *Aushandlungen von Paaren zur Elternzeit. Arbeitsteilung unter neuen Vorzeichen?* Wiesbaden: Springer VS

Pfahl, S. and Reuyß, S. (2010) Das neue Elterngeld: Erfahrungen und betriebliche Nutzungsbedingungen von Vätern, in: Badura, B., Schröder, H., Klose, J. and Macco, K.(eds.) (2010) *Fehlzeiten Report 2010. Vielfalt Managen: Gesundheit fördern, Potenziale nutzen. Zahlen, Daten, Analysen aus allen Bereichen der Wirtschaft.* Berlin/Heidelberg: Springer Verlag, pp. 225–233

Pfahl, S., Reuyß, S. and Hundt, A. (2015) *Väter in Elternzeit. Ein Handlungsfeld für Betriebs- und Personalräte.* Berlin: DGB Bundesvorstand Projekt ‚Vereinbarkeit von Familie und Beruf gestalten'/ver.di Bundesverwaltung Bereich Genderpolitik

Possinger, J. (2013) *Vaterschaft im Spannungsfeld von Erwerbs- und Familienleben. „Neuen" Vätern auf der Spur.* Wiesbaden: Springer VS

Przyborski, A. and Wohrab-Sahr, M. (2008) *Qualitative Sozialforschung. Ein Arbeitsbuch.* München: Oldenbourg

Ranson, G. (2001) 'Men at Work. Change – or No Change? – in the Era of the "New Father"'. *Men and Masculinities* 4, pp. 3–26

Richter, R. (2012) *Väter in Elternzeit – Umsetzungen und Strategien zwischen Familie und Beruf. Dissertation.* Paderborn: Institut für Erziehungswissenschaft. Fakultät für Kulturwissenschaften der Universität Paderborn

Rudman, L. A. and Mescher, K. (2013) 'Penalizing Men Who Request a Family Leave: Is Flexibility Stigma a Femininity Stigma?', *Journal of Social Issues,* 69(2) pp. 322–340

Scholz, S. (2008) Männlichkeit und Erwerbsarbeit bei ostdeutschen Männern. Paradoxe Identitätskonstruktionen, in: Baur, N. and Luedtke J. (eds.) (2008) *Die soziale Konstruktion von Männlichkeit. Hegemoniale und marginalisierte Männlichkeiten in Deutschland.* Opladen: Verlag Barbara Budrich, pp. 105–122

Schulz, F. and Blossfeld, H-P. (2012) The Division of Housework in the Family. Results from a Longitudinal Analysis, in: Oechsle, M., Müller, U. and Hess, S. (eds.) (2012) *Fatherhood in Late Modernity: Cultural Images, Social Practices, Structural Frames.* Opladen/Farmington Hills: Verlag Barbara Budrich, pp. 193–209

Statistisches Bundesamt (2015) Öffentliche Sozialleistungen. Statistik zum Elterngeld. Beendete Leistungsbezüge für im Jahr 2013 geborene Kinder. Januar 2013 bis März 2015. Wiesbaden: Statistisches Bundesamt

Tölke, A. and Hank, K. (eds.) (2005) *Männer – Das „vernachlässigte" Geschlecht in der Familienforschung.* Wiesbaden: VS-Verlag

Trappe, H. (2013) Väter mit Elterngeldbezug: Nichts als ökonomisches Kalkül?, *Zeitschrift für Soziologie* (ZfS), 42(1) pp. 28–51

Vogt, A-C. (2010) *Warum Väter ihre Erwerbstätigkeit (nicht) unterbrechen. Ökonomische versus sozialpsychologische Determinanten der Inanspruchnahme von Elternzeit durch Väter.* München: Rainer Hampp Verlag

Wippermann, C., Calmbach, M. and Wippermann, K. (2009) *Männer: Rolle vorwärts, Rolle rückwärts.* Opladen/Farmington Hills: Verlag Barbara Budrich.

3. Cultures, Rationalities and Management

Ambivalent Benevolence: The Instrumental Rationality of Father-friendly Policies in Swiss Organizations

Brigitte Liebig and Christian Kron

1. Introduction

In recent years new images of 'caring masculinities' and 'active fatherhood' have caused growing attention for questions concerning the reconciliation of family and work with respect to men (Werneck, Berham and Palz 2006). New generations of well-educated young men self-confidently assert claims to reduce work time and demand improved support for their parental obligations and needs in work organizations (Volz and Zulehner 2009; Parment 2009). Due to these transformations and the shortage of skilled workers many work organizations in Europe already provide a large range of family friendly policies (BMFSFJ 2010). And while for many years organizations primarily addressed women when issues of care and work were concerned, increasingly men have also become stakeholders today (European Commission 2013). Part-time work, job sharing and top sharing have been invented to involve men who care for children more strongly in family-friendly programs. However, corporate strategies and family-friendly measures addressing fathers as employees still show considerable limitations with respect to their effects (Prognos 2005). As data illustrate, for many European countries only small changes characterize employment patterns for men: overtime and weekend work turns out to still be widespread among fathers and – compared to men without children – fathers even seem to increase their workload (Kalicki, Peitz and Fthenakis 2006; Klenner and Pfahl 2008). The rate of part-time working fathers remains low – and fathers working part-time are not sharing equal time in housework and child-rearing (Puchert et al.2005).

A trend towards active fatherhood – especially amongst well educated young men – can also be identified in Switzerland (Pro Familia 2011). However, Switzerland shows the highest number of men's actual weekly hours of work, and a very high gap in female and male part-time work, compared to other European nations (European Commission 2013). As a recent report on the political support of equal parenting illustrates, Switzerland ranks at the very last place of 21 high income OECD countries (Fatherhood Institute 2010).[1] Consequently, Switzerland is characterized by a very low percentage of men in the part-time workforce (15.9%) (BFS 2015). More than that: statistics show that more men without children work part-time than fathers, and that the number of men who are involved in care and household labor is considerably low (BFS 2013). Large pay gaps and different developments in the real wages of men and women persist and perpetuate traditional patterns in the division of labor in partnerships (Liebig, Gottschall and Sauer 2016). Drawing on Esping-Andersen's (1990) typology of welfare states, Switzerland may be assigned a "strong breadwinner model" up until today: within the liberal conception of the Swiss welfare state, family and fatherhood still rank as a private matter. Public financing and assistance for families are low, including support for family childcare services, which are – in an international comparison – extremely costly (Häusermann and Zollinger 2014). Even young couples seem to follow traditional family models, in spite of modern notions of partnership (Levy and Widmer 2013). Quite uniquely in the European context, it also seems that up until today paternal leave only receives small support in parliament, and that a sound legal foundation for paternal leave does not exist in Switzerland (Liebig and Peitz 2014; Valarino and Gauthier 2016).[2] Within the last two decades more than twenty political initiatives for implementing paternity leave (respectively, 'parental leave' including men) have failed (Belser 2014). In recent years private companies and administrations have voluntarily developed activities and measures in order to ease father's work-life dilemmas, many of them by offering flexible work models, part-time work or nurseries located close to the office. But policy goals concerning fathers seem to barely gain a foothold in Swiss work organizations.

This chapter starts from the questions of why men do not make use of family-friendly offers in great numbers, and what is the contribution of work organizations. The moderate success of family-friendly measures that include men generates a need for more knowledge and understanding of men's situation in work organizations. Little is known about organizational factors and mechanisms which prevent male employees from realizing involved fatherhood, as well as the premises of a successful implementation of father-oriented family-friendly activities. The chapter aims to approach these issues by focusing on Swiss work organizations. After a short review of previous re-

---

1   The index draws on OECD data and on a set of 10 'family fairness' indicators, including elements such as parental leave, the ratio of time that men and women spend in childcare, and the ratio of men and women doing unpaid domestic work.
2   Maternity leave only became legal in 2005 in Switzerland, after long term bottom-up political activities.

search and theoretical considerations, it presents results from a recent study on family-friendly organizations in Switzerland. The results highlight informal rules and normative expectations as invisible barriers for the reconciliation of work and family for men. The conclusion will pose these findings in the context of current rationalities of gender equality policies.

2. Theoretical perspective

As international research on fatherhood illustrates, changes for men and masculinities seem more advanced in terms of 'caring masculinities' than in everyday practices in work organizations (Holter, Riesenfeld and Scambor 2005; European Commission 2013). Numerous studies have shown that traditional notions of masculinity and associated work roles dominate organizational life, and also influence social perceptions of fatherhood (Tölke 2007; Zerle and Krok 2008). These contribute to representations of working fathers as "good providers" (Bernard 1981) and ignore the care responsibilities of men (Burnett et al. 2013). Organizational careers are tailored according to traditional gender arrangements in the family, and seem to allow no deviations from the normal work/time ratio for men (f.i. Collinson 2010). Beyond that, gendered norms and perceptions of competence, efficiency and productivity remain unquestioned in the world of work organizations and do not only impede women's professional careers but allow only very few men to test alternative career paths and orientations (Heilmann et al. 2015).

The paradoxes between organizational activities in the field of 'family-friendliness' and the persistent practices of fathers also illustrate the challenges of institutional equality policies in their implementation and management by the organizations. Based on neo-institutionalist approaches (DiMaggio and Powell 1991) theoretical perspectives in the field of gender studies have highlighted that organizations can be considered as institutional actors, which develop various strategies in order to adapt to changes and expectations within their environment (e.g. Müller 2010; Funder and May 2014). When external and internal interests collide, a decoupling of officially proposed 'rational' ways of action and unwritten, informal rules allows organizations to combine different, contradicting aims. That means, organizations can introduce various formal regulations, but at the same time everyday practices in organizations can follow opposite rules on an informal level.

Drawing on these thoughts it can be assumed that family-friendly measures for fathers in work organizations seek for both: legitimacy with respect to a growing public awareness and changing needs of fathers, and organizational aims of economic growth, which in many organizations still seem strongly related to traditional work biographies of men (full-time, one hundred percent, life-long). Involved fatherhood seems diametrically opposed to organizational interests, since it challenges the full labor market availability of men (see also Behnke and Meuser 2012). Powerful elements of the decoupling between "talk, decision and action" (Brunsson 1989) are constituted by normative rules and expectations concerning achievement, career and success (e.g. Murgia and Poggio 2009; Possinger 2013; Oechsle and Beaufaÿs 2016). Also these normative expectations are linked to specific ideas, which refer to traditional masculinities inside and outside of the organization. They contradict changing attitudes of men and fatherhood and steer subtly but extremely effectively the claiming of father-friendly measures by fathers. And they mediate between official goals of fostering active fatherhood in organizations and a rather unchanged practice. These assumptions are supported by findings, which illustrate the primarily female connotation of family-friendly measures in organizations today (Prognos 2005). Historically related to the achievements of women's rights, the reconciliation of work and life as well as family-friendly activities has broadly been defined as a woman's issue (see Lewis and Humbert 2010; Oechsle, Müller and Hess 2012).

The motivations and strategies of men and fathers contribute to the perpetuation of traditional cultural representations of masculinity and fatherhood in organizations. As Kvande (2012) shows, organizational norms and rationales constitute part of fathers' identities as employees. Fathers hardly challenge gendered norms in the workplace or engage themselves for an improvement of their situation between work and life (Possinger 2013), and they rarely develop a 'sense of entitlement' for making claims (Hobson and Fahlen 2009). Employment still constitutes the core of male identities (Scholz 2009), even if it seems to no longer demonstrate exclusive status (see Gärtner and Riesenfeld 2004). For men, the choice of an 'alternative way of life' is often associated not only with a conscious decision against a professional career, but also with a "rebalancing of male identity" (Meuser 2007).

Starting from these findings and perspectives this chapter works from the assumption that the implementation of family-friendly measures for men in work organizations can only be understood as a result of complex interdependences between formal and informal rules. The focus of our analysis is set on the informal factors and mechanisms within which family-friendly programs get translated into organizational realities for men. In approaching these dimensions we intend to uncover some of the conditions which affect the implementation of measures and the realization of active fatherhood in organizations.

3. Methods

The analysis is based on case studies in nine large and medium-sized work organizations in the public and private sectors in Switzerland, of which eight have been officially certified as "family friendly" in 2014 and/or in the years before.[3] The organizations under study include four federal administrations, three large companies in the field of finance, insurance, and army technology, as well as two medium-sized companies in the design and software industry. Within the organizations, organizational policies and mission statements on father-friendliness have been analyzed. Further, fifteen expert interviews with human resource officers, diversity managers and equal opportunity officers were conducted, to gain more information about the motives and cultural framing of these policies. In a second step, thirty-two fathers, who were employed within the selected organizations participated in half-standardized qualitative interviews: these included questions about their personal perception of family-friendly measures, their experienced support by superiors and colleagues, the meaning of part-time work for careers, and the reconciliation of family and work. Respondents were on average about thirty-eight years old, the majority (about 70%) had an academic background. About two thirds of the fathers were working full-time and about 58% held management functions.

The analysis of qualitative data aimed at a reconstruction of the informal aspects of the implementation of father-friendly policies in the everyday work culture of the organizations. Interviews were digitally-recorded and transcribed – partly completely, partly in more or less detail, based on their relevance to the analysis. Qualitative analysis has been conducted according to the procedures of qualitative content-analysis (see Mayring 2010) and followed a mixed strategy of deductive and inductive interpretation. That means the guideline for interviews was based on theoretical assumptions, which allowed a deductive procedure. On the other hand, new thematic aspects were derived from the narratives of the interviews, for which categories have been inductively generated. In particular, the interpretation of interviews with fathers aimed at a detailed reconstruction of subjectively experienced barriers for involved fatherhood.

In addition to the qualitative analyses, an online-survey of 8901 employees within seven organizations has been conducted, which resulted in 1777 valuable data sets on men and women (total return rate 21.1%). 71.9% of

---

3   Findings are based on the results of the study "Family-friendly organizations and fatherhood. Conditions, barriers, and effectiveness of family-friendly measures in work organizations". It has been carried out with the friendly support of the Swiss National Science Foundation (Project ID 100017_146106 / 1) in 2013-2015.

respondents were male, with an average age of 44.9 years; 59% of the male respondents indicated having care responsibilities for children (this group is called 'fathers' here). 34.2% of all male employees had tertiary education, 37.9% specified holding management functions and 57.6% had a gross income over 100 000 Swiss francs per year, which is above the average income in Switzerland in administration and private industry. The data can be estimated as approximately representative, but only for the family-friendly companies included; they cannot be generalized without reservations for other Swiss companies.

4. Results

Men in care-giving roles have increasingly become an issue in Swiss work organizations. As the analysis of documents on family-friendly policies shows, a large range of activities and measures characterizes the organizations, of which the most widespread have been selected for this study: paternity leave, flexible working time, part-time work, home office, telework, child-care and other special social services which are provided by employers in order to facilitate the compatibility of family and work. Three organizations offer special awareness campaigns to remove existing cultural barriers against part-time work by men. More than that, organization representatives state that executive positions can also be held on a part-time basis (at least at 80%).

At the same time, our interviews and statistical data illustrate a strong egalitarian orientation of fathers within the organizations studied. This is true especially for younger generations of men (see chart 1): almost two out of three fathers up to thirty-four years of age consider the role of the house-husband as important to fathers today, while merely half of fathers older than fifty-four years share this point of view.

Chart 1: Percentage of the respondents who rated the specific roles of men as "important" or "very important" for fathers today.

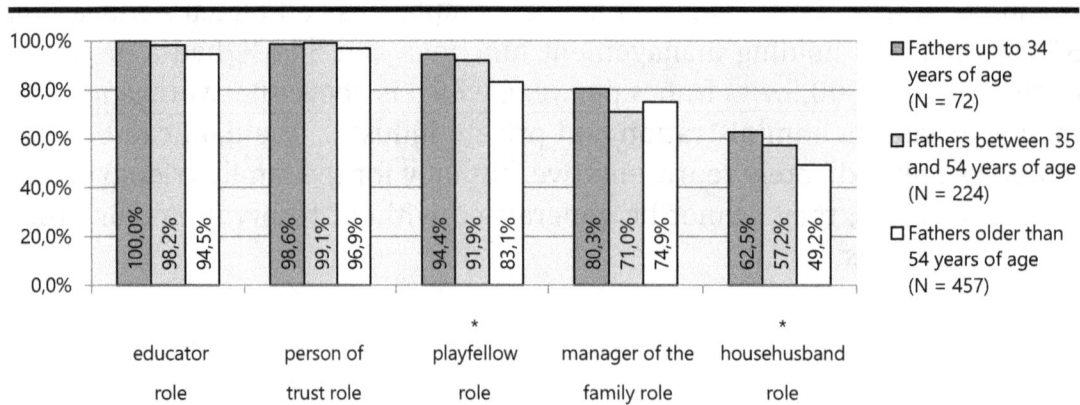

Note. *Fathers up to 34 years of age differ significantly from fathers older than 54 years of age according to their rating of the importance of these specific roles of men (p < .05).

Most of the fathers who were interviewed in this study distance themselves from images of fatherhood as the sole nurturer of the family: instead, they believe that children profit from care and education by both parents, intend to actively support their female partners, and to build a close relationship to their children. Many fathers report problems of reconciling work and family duties and wish to spend more time with their children. Also the vast majority of men rated the organizational activities in the area of family-friendliness as important (see Kron 2016). However, these men hardly seem to participate in these measures: the part-time levels of men within the seven organizations included in the survey is considerably lower (14.2%), than that of female employees (74.5%), which adequately reflects the participation of men in part-time work in Switzerland in 2014 (BFS 2015). Unpaid time-off because of fatherhood has been chosen by only 6.6% of these men, compared to 19.7% of the responding mothers.

But why do efforts to support fathers show only limited effects – even in organizations which have been labelled as 'outstanding' with respect to family-friendliness? Why do part-time arrangements remain the exception? As the analysis shows, various factors contribute to this situation.

4.1 The instrumental rationality of family-friendliness for men

As it turns out, on the basis of interviews with experts and fathers within the organizations studied, family-friendly policies for fathers are primarily estimated as an economic necessity. Equality or justice, that constitute the frame of reference for gender-equality policies for women, hardly play a role in organizational discourses, where father-oriented forms of family-support are concerned. Rather they are perceived as an efficient means to increase visibility as a family-friendly employer in times of skills shortage. The dominance of this instrumental rationality is in a more general way highlighted by an expert, who is reasoning about the meaning of trust-based working hours and the opportunity of home office work in his firm:

> *Trust-based working hours – initially we thought "hmm, does that work?" But it is now very much appreciated because of its flexibility – by all the staff and the executives. I think in fact it also serves the intentions of the company. It's not that people work less necessarily, but the self-determination also creates a loyalty to the employer. People are more motivated if they are not controlled and managed closely and thus ultimately more productive. With the home office we have also had good experiences. Actually, people continue to work, even if they have worked here during the day, they still continue to work in the evening* (expert, design industry, 2014).

The flexibility of working hours, as a core element of family-friendliness in organizations, is described here with implicit reference to the concept of "diversity management'" (Cox and Blake 1993). It can boost the attractiveness of the organization as an employer and promises a cost-effective means to achieve increased job satisfaction, and the retention and motivation of employees (see also Prognos 2005). This way of thinking can be especially found in industries based strongly on engineering and technical knowledge. These organizations have not only failed to recruit and promote women, but also have attracted fewer and fewer men for qualified jobs in recent years. Firms strongly promote family-friendliness in order to gain more attention from younger generations of highly qualified men.

4.2 Management practices related to fatherhood

The instrumental rationality of family-friendliness for men as fathers also constitutes a frame of reference when management practices related to involved fatherhood are concerned. On the one hand these practices still refer to traditional concepts of masculinity, which are strongly employment-centered and still conceive fathers' mainly as the breadwinner of the family. At the same time rather unchanged expectations concerning the role of women as full-time carers for the family can be identified in almost all organizations.

> *But I feel that men are more under pressure to continue to work a hundred percent, and for women it is actually normal that they say "yes, then I will not work for some time, and then I'll come back part-time". And you discuss less than if a man comes and says "I want to reduce 20 percent"; then quite a*

discussion happens with the respective team leaders (father, design industry, 2014).

Fathers, who explicitly reduce their workload in order to participate more in caring for children, challenge the informal requirements of work-related male biographies. As the interviewees report, active fathers are still perceived as deviators from the organizational norm, and are mostly experienced as 'exotic' or 'weak' in the organizational environment (see also Gärtner 2012). Further, the rather distant and estranged way of dealing with parental obligations of fathers in organizations is demonstrated in the following quote from an interview with a human relations manager:

> *There is a need for more creative freedom to design the relation between work and leisure time. But actually there is no difference, if one goes hang-gliding, goes golfing or takes care of children* (expert, male, software industry, 2014).

While the respondent generally seems to support the creation of more "freedom" for the reconciliation of work and life, his words demonstrate rather limited experience in caring duties, since he puts fatherly obligations on the same level as leisure activities such as hang-gliding or golfing. But more than that, in his eyes, a reduction of work hours because of a stronger commitment to family work also seems to have no more legitimacy than an exemption because of voluntary involvement in sport or leisure, and therefore appears to be offensively devalued here.

Apart from distanced connotations of fatherhood, the seeming evidence of an incompatibility between active fatherhood and professional career characterizes the organizations studied here. While a reduction in workload is expected in cases of becoming a mother, a reduction of work hours in cases of fatherhood can still cause the loss of prestige and of career opportunities.

> *Yes, everything has advantages and disadvantages (...) I think one can do certain things, when you also achieve at the same time. It is always a give and take. If you always take, then it can turn out negatively, if you don't achieve* (father, insurance company, 2014).

4.3 The role of superiors and colleagues

The informal character of measures fostering involved fatherhood in the organizations, and traditional representations of fatherhood practices, are accompanied by informal and precarious agreements, when decisions about a reduction of work hours or absences because of children are concerned. The capability of fathers to withdraw from work strongly depends on negotiation, firstly between superiors and the father as an employee. As our interviewed fathers state, a close personal relation to superiors that is characterized by mutual trust seems essential, when "extraordinary" requests concerning home office or part-time work are made. But still – an approval of time-outs for fathers because of family concerns is by no means guaranteed:

> *And my boss, I do not know if he would understand (...). Perhaps if I only once or rarely came up with such things, I think that would work, but if it would be regular, then he would probably say something like "hey, can you not organize yourself better?" or" does your wife not do that?* (father, financial industry, 2014)

Further, the instrumental perspective on family-friendliness coincides with the commonly shared assumption that an exchange of benefits between employer and employee has to be assured *("if somebody is good in his job, then he has chances to reduce")*. Accordingly, the capability of fathers to withdraw from the workplace strongly depends on the trust of superiors that a balance between the benefits of the employer and those of the working fathers is assured. As the following quote illustrates the informal rule of reciprocity counts for both the employer and the employee:

> *Well, I do understand my boss, because I also believe that it needs reciprocity. Well, I have made use of the trust of my boss, it is really the case, trust is a very important issue; you have to trust in the situation, the employee has to trust his boss, and vice versa. And when the relationship is built on trust, and you have the feeling it functions this way, then it will function* (father, design industry, 2014).

As this father explains, an exemption from full-time work can only be successful if the informal law of reciprocity can be guaranteed. Trust influences the credibility of the employee that he will 'pay back' the losses because of his release, and therefore his legitimate application for time off. Men who explicitly call for more time to raise their children tend to compensate for the apparent profit losses by demonstrating even greater work performance, flexibility and commitment to employers.

Empathy and understanding for employees' needs seems to grow when a close relation between employer and employee can be established. This relation is fostered when superiors have had experiences with fatherly duties themselves. Otherwise, fathers can expect only a limited understanding of their specific situation. This is also the case when a team's colleagues are concerned. Although young fathers report that the birth of their child has been an occasion for congratulations in the firm, they also describe that colleagues soon signal limits for compensating long term absences due to involved fatherhood.

The strain which active fathers and their needs put on their teammates seems to get reinforced in modern organizational environments. In the context of lower hierarchies and teamwork, autonomous work units are responsible for output and success. The social dynamics of teams, including the definition of common goals, a sense of togetherness and joint responsibility for target achievement, constitute an unspoken contradiction to solidarity with fathers since they jeopardize unwritten rules; consequently, family concerns remain largely a matter of individual responsibility. The silent reluctance to accept regular absences of fathers due to part-time work gets expressed in various ways – sometimes also in form of a 'forgetfulness' by colleagues:

> *Yes, insofar that basically, actively, and again and again, important meetings and dates are set on that day, which I have off. And this can get problematic, when people somehow almost systematically (smiles) forget again and again, and let you know: "oh yes, you are not here, this is funny!"* (father, software industry, 2014)

The 'forgetting' of fatherly duties or time-off by colleagues, which was reported more than once by interviewees, signifies not only a collective mindset and a claim that men should 'normally' be present at the workplace one hundred percent, but also a collective resistance to changing perspectives on work and the lives of men due to the obligations of the work context. The decision to reduce work hours means refraining from participation in exciting projects, and to be no longer recognized as a full member of the team. Part-time workers who "miss what is going on" will not be able to fulfill common objectives and will have negative impact on the team. More generally, experiences with parenthood in the immediate work environment of fathers turn out to be most important for active fatherhood, as our survey data show; teammates without children often seem not to apprehend the challenges due to the reconciliation of work and family:

> *In the team, we also have employees who have children and those who still have none. And those who have no children cannot imagine how it is when a child is sick, feels unwell, and why somehow I cannot give the child up. This understanding comes, I think, only by one's own experience* (father, insurance company, 2014)

These qualitative findings are validated by survey data, which illustrate that a common social experience can support the reconciliation of work and family (see table 1). Fathers with a high number of colleagues and superiors who work part-time in favor of having more time for their children report significantly more often that their coworkers show understanding in case of conflicts arising from trying to reconcile work and family life ($\beta = .232$, $R2 = .05$).

Table 1. The importance of common social experience: linear regression to predict the amount of understanding shown by coworkers in case of conflicts arising from trying to reconcile work and family life.

Predictor	B	SE	β	R2
Amount of agreement to have a lot of colleagues and superiors, who work part time in favor of having more time for their children.	.235	.042	.232*	.05*

Notes. *p < .001, β = standardized coefficients, R2 = coefficient of determination

4.4 Active fatherhood as social divide

Men who try to reconcile work and family report facing more reservations than women when they make use of family-friendly offers (see Kron 2016). As shown in chart 2 about half of male (51.4%) and female (45%) online survey respondents who care for children, agreed with this particular statement. But men who care for children also feel significantly less often supported by their superiors than women (52.3% vs 73.9%), and they report significantly less often than women (60.9% vs 76.1%) that their female colleagues show understanding in cases of conflict between work and family. Apparently men neither get the same amount of understanding from their male (56.%) nor from their female colleagues (60.4%). In other words: mothers can still count on more support from superiors and male and female coworkers in cases of work-family conflicts.

Chart 2: Acceptance of fathers in work organizations: amount of people who slightly or fully agree with the following statements:

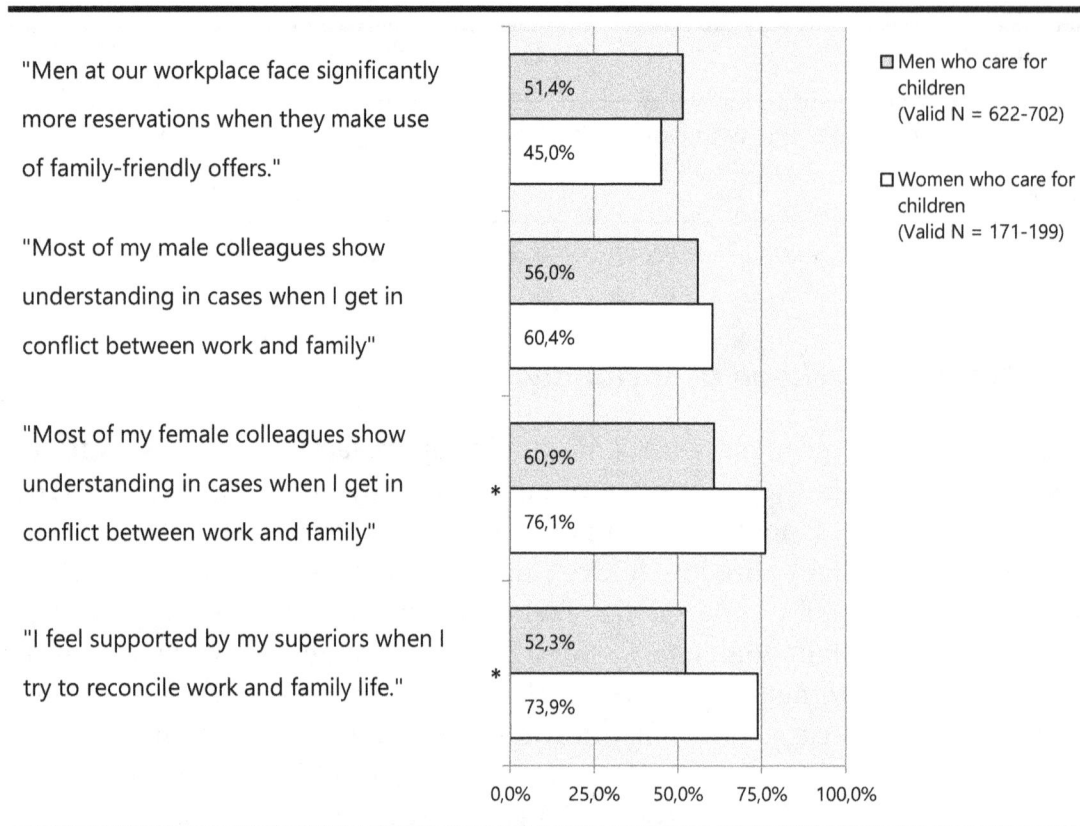

Statement	Men who care for children (Valid N = 622-702)	Women who care for children (Valid N = 171-199)
"Men at our workplace face significantly more reservations when they make use of family-friendly offers."	51,4%	45,0%
"Most of my male colleagues show understanding in cases when I get in conflict between work and family"	56,0%	60,4%
"Most of my female colleagues show understanding in cases when I get in conflict between work and family" *	60,9%	76,1%
"I feel supported by my superiors when I try to reconcile work and family life." *	52,3%	73,9%

Note. Men who care for children agree significantly more often with the particular statement than women who care for children (p < .01).

The instrumental rationale also contributes to the fact that family-friendly policies for men obviously focus on achievers, i.e. on young men in white collar professions as well as high performing employees. In expert interviews these groups of men are more or less openly referred to as a privileged target group – "rare employees, who have to be cared for". Blue collar workers – and older men – do have less bargaining power *("yes, we have different populations of course; I think in production, in the blue collar sphere, it gets less communicated and discussed")*.[4] Less qualified fathers do not turn up as beneficiaries of measures such as part-time work or unpaid paternity leave – if only because of their location in the wage system. The social divides generated between different categories of employees are illustrated by the fact that fathers with a gross income of about CHF 100'000 receive significantly more family-friendly

---

4   The limited focus of family-friendly policies on young female employees and the exclusion of women's care obligations, which occur in the second half of professional biographies, has been shown by Le Feuvre et al. (2014)

offers than those without supervisory functions, or with a lower gross income. Table 2 also shows that better-educated and higher-income workers on average use more family-friendly offers:

Table 2. Knowledge and use of family friendly offers by men who care for children

Men who care for children		Age		Professional status		Education		Income	
		Up to 39 years	Older than 39 years	Superior	Employee	With tertiary education	Without tertiary education	Over CHF 100'000.-	Up to CHF 100'000.-
Valid N		175	578	330	406	250	488	424	211
Number of known family friendly offers	Ø	4.21	4.09	4.46**	3.84**	4.34	3.99	4.49**	3.50**
Number of used family friendly offers	Ø	1.62**	1.18**	1.25	1.33	1.63**	1.09**	1.40*	1.17*

*Note. * Men of these particular groups differ significantly according to the amount of known and/or used family friendly offers with *p < .05 and **p < .01.*

4.5 Complicit masculinities

As it has already been suggested above, the business rationale also contributes to contradictions between "male breadwinner" and "caring dad" as part of male identities (see Aumann, Galisky and Matos 2011). Those fathers who belong to target groups of family-friendly measures today certainly cannot be assigned to "protest masculinities" (Connell and Messerschmidt 1995). Differently to women, they do not perceive themselves entitled to make a claim (Hobson 2012). Fathers rarely challenge hegemonic constructions or embody alternative ideals of masculinity and – quite contrary to women – do not query the limitations of active fatherhood in work organizations. This is also documented by the following excerpt of an interview with a father, who was obliged to look after his children because his wife was severely ill:

> *This (work absence) has been in consultation with the employer, and the employer has supported me. He said: "Look Arno, you have this situation: your wife is now in the hospital, and we see that you have your child, let's see what is possible. And this was a very generous gesture from the employer that he (...), and vice versa, I have seen that the work processes for which I have been responsible can continue to run. Of course, my employer got a super loyal employee, because I knew what I owe him. And then I have invested even*

more, when I had spare capacity again, and within two years I have subsequently even made good the 150 hours again (...). So, now, I think, it's a give and take (father, public administration, 2014).

As this quote illustrates, the use of measures which actually should aim at supporting fathers are interpreted as a reward for a high level of commitment. The respondent shares the organizational norms and rationales, and considers the reduction of workload as a concession by his superior and employer. Men fear twice as much as women that negative consequences might arise for their colleagues, if they reduce their work hours (Liebig, Peitz and Kron 2016). More than that, fathers accept precarious solutions and informal arrangements; they anticipate the limited resilience of their colleagues, and try to avoid failures as much as possible:

When the child is ill and nobody can stay at home, then somebody has to make themselves not so popular with the boss or the team, and cancel the meeting. Well, but the next time it is the partners turn (father, design industry, 2014).

As a consequence, fatherhood strongly exists as a "private matter" in organizations. While many interviewees think about a reduction of work hours, they are not willing to sacrifice their career. In case of conflict the majority of men still decide for keeping their professional options. Even fathers living in dual-earner partnerships develop strategies which intend to relieve the organization from their responsibility, while at the same time they are looking for solutions for the incompatibility of work-family issues with their private sphere.

5. Conclusion

This chapter started from the question, why family-friendly policies in work organizations fail to attain significant attention by fathers, and how work organizations contribute to this fact. Drawing on theories of gender and organization the perspective focused on the informal rules and mechanisms which influence the reconciliation of work and family for men. The study was based on the analysis of nine work organizations, of which eight ranked at the top of 'family-friendliness' in Switzerland in 2014.

Extrapolating from the organizations studied here the scope and practical applicability of family-friendly policies for fathers turns out to be quite limited. As it has already been noted for other countries (Lewis and Humbert 2010), the connotation of family-friendliness still seems basically geared towards females, and the challenges of the reconciliation of family and work are often defined as a problem for women only. But beyond that we found that when family-friendly activities include men, they seem primarily driven by an instrumental rationality. The idea of family-friendliness as a 'business case' dominates, while the morally and ethically based argument of social justice, which has been (and partly still is) constitutive for family-friendliness for women, is not available and has no point of reference, when fathers are concerned (see Liebig, Peitz and Kron 2016). Work organizations consider family-friendliness for fathers as a reward for high commitment and achievement, not as a social right.

The economic rationale refers to traditional conceptions of masculinity and fatherhood in society, and is equally inscribed into the organizational objectives of family-friendliness for men as it is enacted in work relations and practices. It shapes the identities of working fathers, and is reflected in attitudes dominating their work environment. As we can see, current policies do not challenge traditional representations of fathers – rather, they support culturally dominant conceptions of masculinity, which still basically relate men to the role of the breadwinner (see also Burnett et al. 2013). The implicit/explicit rules of the game generate and perpetuate "complicit masculinities" (Connell 1995) that do not challenge institutionalized contradictions of responsibility. As a consequence, the issue of work time reduction hardly arises for many fathers, but rather the question of how full-time work can be organized so that it still allows the fulfillment of basic paternal obligations.

These results reflect the fact that current gender equality discourses in Switzerland strongly point to *economic benefits* in order to motivate companies to introduce equality measures (Lanfranconi 2014). But not only with respect to women we can see that these discourses strongly influence the success of measures, by providing arguments and guiding practices for their implementation. On the basis of our results it can be stated that the 'business discourse' which frames father-friendly policies in work organizations does not necessarily foster active fatherhood. Rather, it both enables and constrains the use of equality policies by men at the same time, and turns out to be an important element of the contradictions inherent in postmodern work organizations. It can be assumed that the contradictory effects of this discourse can unfold especially strongly in Switzerland, where it is framed by a lack of a legal foundation for parental leave (Liebig and Peitz 2014). Up until today the voluntary character of parental leave negatively affects the legitimacy of active fatherhood within the corporation, as well as related concerns of fathers and supervisors.

In reference to neo-institutionalist thought (see DiMaggio and Powell 1991), we can assume family-friendly policies for fathers as an "empty shell"

(Hoque and Noon 2004), which basically serves to adapt to expectations of modern society, while at the same time limiting fathers' options for involved fatherhood. A closer look at the informal dimensions of work organizations quickly reveals various signs of "organizational hypocrisy" (Brunsson 1989), i.e. considerable contradictions between official claims for family-friendliness on the one hand and unwritten rules of work on the other. For example, policies claim that part-time work is available for fathers, yet – as we have shown here – full time engagement is the implicit norm of jobs and careers. Or organizations officially direct family-friendliness measures to all, but informally only to those men who promise return on investment. This is confirmed by the fact that family-friendly policies for fathers easily seem to be thwarted by 'greedy' working cultures (Kvande 2012).

Economically driven discourses on family-friendliness also produce and maintain social inequalities between men as fathers on one side, and men (and women) without children on the other, and contribute to 'family responsibility discrimination' (von Bergen 2008). And they hide the issue of equal opportunity between men of different classes or professions. This is indicated by the fact that fatherhood shows up as a new category of social inequality between men. As it can be stated for women (Le Feuvre et al. 2014), men are subject to multiple forms of discrimination based on a combination of parenthood, age and qualification. As we can see from our data, family-friendliness for men is limited to well-educated young men as powerful stakeholders, and it rather counts as a promotion program for 'top talents'. Other groups of men seem beyond the horizon of family-friendly measures (see also Liebig, Peitz and Kron: forthcoming)

From our study we can conclude, that work organizations in Switzerland are still not in a "mode of agency" (Dass and Parker 1999) when involved fatherhood is concerned. They react with strong ambivalence – if not to say 'hypocritically' – based on a limited understanding of gender roles as well as of the management of diversity in organizations. In order to integrate the diverse social realities of men into family-friendly programmes, work organizations still have to make considerable moves, and to conceive of themselves as part of societal changes characterized by a new self-understanding of men as fathers.

References

Aumann, K., Galinsky, E. and Matos, K. (2011) *The New Male Mystique: National Study of the Changing Workforce.* New York: Families and Work Institute.

Behnke, C. and Meuser, M. (2012) "Look here mate! I'm taking paternal leave for a year" – involved fatherhood and images of masculinity, in: Oechsle, M., Müller, U. and Hess, S. (eds.) *Fatherhood in Late Modernity: Cultural Images, Social Practices, Structural Frames.* Opladen: Budrich, pp. 129-145

Belser, K. (2014) ,Ist ein Elternurlaub heute in der Schweiz mehrheitsfähig? Ergebnisse einer Umfrage bei den Parteien', *Frauenfragen,* 2, pp. 8–18

Bernard, J. (1981) ,The Good-Provider Role: Its rise and fall', *American Psychologist,* 36(1) pp. 1–12

BFS (Bundesamt für Statistik) (2015) *Schweizer Arbeitskräfteerhebung 2014.* Neuchâtel. Eidgenössisches Departement des Innern EDI. Available at: http://www.bfs.admin.ch/bfs/portal/de/index/news/medienmitteilungen.html?pressID=10114 [retrieved 29.10.15]

BFS (Bundesamt für Statistik) (2013) *Das Engagement der Väter in Haushalt und Familie.* BFS Aktuell. Neuchâtel: Eidgenössisches Departement des Innern EDI

Bundesministerium für Familie, Senioren, Frauen und Jugend (BMFSFJ) (2010) (ed) Europäischer Unternehmensmonitor Familienfreundlichkeit. Berlin: BMFSFJ

Brunsson, N. (1989) *The Organization of Hypocrisy: Talk, Decisions, and Actions in Organizations.* Chichester: John Wiley & Sons

Burnett, S. B., Gatrell, C. J., Cooper, C. L. and Sparrow, P. (2013) 'Fathers at Work: A Ghost in the Organizational Machine', *Gender, Work & Organization,* 20, pp. 632–646.

Connell, R. (2010) ,Im Innern des gläsernen Turms: Die Konstruktion von Männlichkeiten im Finanzkapital', *Feministische Studien,* 1(10), pp. 8–24

Connell, R.W. and Messerschmidt, J. W. (2005) Hegemonic Masculinity: Rethinking the Concept, *Gender & Society* 19(6) pp. 829–859

Cox, T. H. and Blake, S. (1991) 'Managing Cultural Diversity: Implications for Organizational Competitiveness', *Academy of Management Executive,* 5(3) pp. 45–56

Dass, P. and Parker, B. (1999) 'Strategies for managing human resource diversity: From resistance to learning', *Academy of Management Executive,* 13(2) pp. 68–80

Di Maggio, P. and Powell, W. (1991) (eds.) *The New Institutionalism in Organizational Analysis.* Chicago: University of Chicago Press

Esping-Andersen, G. (1999) *The Social Foundations of Post-Industrial Economies.* Oxford: University Press

European Commission (2013) *The Role of Men in Gender Equality: European Strategies & Insights.* Study on the Role of Men in Gender Equality. Luxembourg: Publications Office of the European Union. Available at: http://ec.europa.eu/justice/gender-quality/files/gender_pay_gap/130424_final_report_role_of_men_en.pdf [retrieved 2.3.16].

Fatherhood Institute (2010) *The Fairness in Families Index 2010–2011,* Abergaven-
ny. Available at: http://www.fatherhoodinstitute.org/wp-content/uploads/
2010/12/FI-FiFI-Report-2010_FINAL.pdf [retrieved 2.3.16].

Funder, M. and May, F. (2014) Neo-Institutionalismus: Geschlechtergleichheit als
Egalitätsmythos?, in: Funder, M. (ed) *Gender Cage – Revisited. Handbuch zur
Organisations- und Geschlechterforschung.* Baden-Baden: Nomos, pp. 195–225

Gärtner, M. (2012) *Männer und Familienvereinbarkeit. Betriebliche Personalpolitik,
Akteurskonstellationen und Organisationskulturen.* Opladen: Budrich University Press

Gärtner, M. and Riesenfeld,V. (2004) Geld oder Leben? Männliche Erwerbsorien-
tierung und neue Lebensmodelle unter veränderten Arbeitsmarktbedingun-
gen, in: Boeckle, B. and Ruf, M. (eds.) *Gender-Reader – Eine Frage des
Geschlechts. VS Verlag für Sozialwissenschaften. Wiesbaden,* pp. 87–104

Häusermann, S. and Zollinger, C. (2014) Familienpolitik, in: Knöpfel, P. (eds.) *Handbuch der Schweizer Politik* Zürich. NZZ Libro, pp. 911–934

Heilmann, A., Jähnert, G. Schnicke, F., Schönwetter, C. and Vollhardt, M. (eds.)
(2015) *Männlichkeit und Reproduktion. Zum gesellschaftlichen Ort historischer
und aktueller Männlichkeitsproduktionen.* Wiesbaden: Springer VS

Hergatt Huffman, A. H., Olson, K. J., O'Gara, T. C., and King, E. B. (2014) 'Gender Role
Beliefs and Fathers' Work-Family Conflict', *Journal of Managerial Psychology,*
29(7) pp. 774–793

Hobson, B. (ed) (2013) *Worklife Balance: The Agency and Capabilities Gap.* Oxford:
Oxford University Press

Hobson, B. and Fahlén, S. (2009) 'Competing Scenarios for European Fathers: Applying Sen's Capabilities and Agency Framework to Work Family Balance', *The
Annals of the American Academy of Political and Social Science,* 642(1) pp. 214–
233

Holter Ø. G, Riesenfeld, V., Scambor, E. (2005) 'We don't have anything like that
here!' – Organisations, Men and Gender Equality, in: Puchert ,R., Gärtner, M.
and Höyng, S. (eds.) *Work Changes Gender: Men and Equality in the Transition
of Labour Forms.* Opladen: Verlag Barbara Budrich, pp. 73–104

Hoque, K. and Noon, M. (2004) 'Equal Opportunities Policy and Practice in Britain:
Evaluating the "empty shell" hypothesis', *Work, Employment & Society,* 18(3)
pp. 481–506

Kalicki,B., Peitz,G. and Fthenakis,W. E. (2006) Die Bewältigung des Übergangs zur
Vaterschaft, in: Werneck, H., Beham, M. and Palz, D. (eds) *Aktive Vaterschaft.
Männer zwischen Familie und Beruf,* Gießen: Psychosozial-Verlag, pp. 80–93

Klenner, C. and Pfahl, S. (2008) *Jenseits von Zeitnot und Karriereverzicht – Wege aus
dem Arbeitszeitdilemma. Analyse der Arbeitszeiten von Müttern, Vätern und
Pflegenden und Umrisse eines Konzeptes,* WSI Diskussionspapier Nr. 158, Düsseldorf, Hans-Böckler-Stiftung

Kron, C. (2016) Was Väter wollen, in: Liebig, B., Peitz, M. and Kron, C. (eds.) *Väterorientierte Massnahmen für Unternehmen und Verwaltungen in der Schweiz.
Ein Handbuch.* Mering: Rainer Hampp, pp. 29–50

Kvande, E. (2012) Control in Post-Bureaucratic Organizations – Consequences for
Fathering Practices, in: Oechsle, M., Müller, U. and Hess, S. (eds.) *Fatherhood in*

Late Modernity: Cultural Images, Social Practices, Structural Frames. Opladen: Verlag Barbara Budrich, pp. 233–248

Lewis, S. and Humbert, A. L. (2010) 'Discourse or reality: "Worklife Balance" Flexibility and Gendered Organizations', *Equality, Diversity and Inclusion,* 29(3) pp. 239–254

Lanfranconi, L. (2014) ,Chancen und Risiken des Wirtschafsnutzendiskurses in der aktuellen betrieblichen Geschlechtergleichstellungspolitik der Schweiz', Swiss Journal of Sociology, 40(2) pp. 325–348

Le Feuvre, N., Kuehni, M., Rosende, M. and Schoeni, C. (2014) 'Le genre du 'vieillissement actif': du principe de traitement équitable à la multiplication des injonctions contradictoires', *Swiss Journal of Sociology,* 40(2), pp. 307–324.

Levy, R. and Widmer, E. (eds.) (2013) *Gendered life courses between standardization and individualization: A European approach applied to Switzerland.* Zürich/Berlin: LIT

Liebig, and Peitz, M. (2014) ,Vaterschafts- und Elternurlaub in der Schweiz: Der lange Weg zu einer elternfreundlichen Familienpolitik', *Frauenfragen,* 2, pp. 34–40

Liebig, B., Gottschall, K. and Sauer, B. (2016) Introduction. Gender Equality: Policies and Practices in Switzerland, in: Liebig, B., Gottschall, K. and Sauer, B. (eds.) *Gender equality in context: policies and practices in Switzerland.* Opladen/Berlin/Toronto: Barbara Budrich Publishers, pp. 9–18

Liebig, B., Peitz, M. and Kron, C. (eds.) (2016) *Väterorientierte Massnahmen für Unternehmen und Verwaltungen in der Schweiz. Ein Handbuch.* Mering: Rainer Hampp Verlag

Liebig, B., Peitz, M. and Kron, C. (forthcoming) *Familienfreundliche Organisation und Vaterschaft. Herausforderungen einer väterorientierten Personalpolitik* (submitted)

Mayring, P. (2010) *Qualitative Inhaltsanalyse. Grundlagen und Techniken.* Weinheim: Deutscher Studienverlag

Meuser, M. (2007) Vom Ernährer der Familie zum involvierten Vater? Männlichkeitskonstruktionen und Vaterschaftskonzepte, in: Meuser, M. (ed.) *Herausforderungen, Männlichkeit im Wandel der Geschlechterverhältnisse.* Köln: Rüdiger Köppe Verlag, pp. 49–62

Müller, U. (2010) Organisation und Geschlecht aus neo-institutionalistischer Sicht. Betrachtungen am Beispiel von Entwicklungen in der Polizei, *Feministische Studien* (10) pp. 40–55

Murgia, A., Poggio, B. (2009) Challenging Hegemonic Masculinities. Men's Stories on Gender Culture in Organizations, *Organization,* 16(3) pp. 407–423

Oechsle, M., Müller, U. and Hess, S. (2012) Fatherhood in Late Modernity, in: Oechsle, M., Müller, U. and Hess, S. (eds.) *Fatherhood in Late Modernity: Cultural Images, Social Practices, Structural Frames.* Opladen: Verlag Barbara Budrich, pp. 9–36

Oechsle, M. and Beaufaÿs, S. (2016) Hidden rules and competing logics in Germany, in: Brandth, B., Kvande, E. and Halrynjo, S. (eds.) *Work-Family Dynamics: Competing Logics of Regulation, Economy and Morals.* Abingdon: Routledge (forthcoming)

Parment, A. (2009) *Die Generation Y – Mitarbeiter der Zukunft.* Wiesbaden: Gabler

Possinger, J. (2013) *Fürsorgliche Vaterschaft im Spannungsfeld von Erwerbs- und Familienleben.,Neuen Vätern' auf der Spur.* Wiesbaden: Springer

Prognos AG (2005) *Väterfreundliche Maßnahmen im Unternehmen. Ansatzpunkte – Erfolgsfaktoren – Praxisbeispiele.* Available at: http://www.Prognos AG .com/fileadmin/pdf/Vaeterbroschuere2005.pdf [retrieved: 3.1.2016]

Pro Familia Schweiz (2011) *Was Männer wollen! Studie zur Vereinbarkeit von Beruf und Privatleben.* Bern Available at: http://www.profamilia.ch/tl_files/Dokumente/jobundfamilie/Studie%20Was%20Maenner%20wollen%20-%20 Publikation.pdf [retrieved 20.4.16]

Puchert, R., Gärtner, M. and Höyng, S. (eds.) (2005) *Work Changes Gender: Men and Equality in the Transition of Labour Forms.*Opladen: Budrich.

Scholz, S. (2009) Männer und Männlichkeitenim Spannungsfeld zwischen Erwerbs-und Familienarbeit, in Aulenbacher, B. and Wetterer, A. (eds) *Arbeit. Perspektiven und Diagnosen der Geschlechterforschung.* Münster: Westfälisches Dampfboot, pp. 82–99

Tölke, A. (2007) ,Familie und Beruf im Leben von Männern', *Berliner Journal für Soziologie,* 17(3) pp. 323–342

Valarino, I. and Gauthier, J-A. (2016) 'Paternity Leave Implementation in Switzerland: A Challenge to Gendered Representations and Practices of Fatherhood?', *Community, Work & Family,* 19(1) pp. 1–20

Volz, R. and Zulehner, P. M. (2009) Männer in Bewegung. Zehn Jahre Männerentwicklung in Deutschlan*d. Forschungsprojekt der Gemeinschaft Katholischer Männer Deutschlands und der Männerarbeit der Evangelischen Kirche in Deutschland.* Baden-Baden: Nomos

von Bergen, C.W. (2008) '"The times they Are a-Changin": Family Responsibilities Discrimination and the EEOC', *Employee Responsibilities and Rights Journal,* 20(3), pp. 177–194

Werneck, H., Beham, M. and Palz, D. (eds.) (2006) *Aktive Vaterschaft.Männer zwischen Familie und Beruf,* Gießen: Psychosozial-Verlag

Zerle, C. and Krok, I. (2008) *Null Bock auf Familie? Der schwierige Weg junger Männer in die Vaterschaft.* Gütersloh: Verlag Bertelsmann Stiftung

Fatherhood in Transition: From Standard to Precarious Archetypes in Italian Contemporary Work Organizations

Annalisa Murgia and Barbara Poggio[1]

1. Introduction

A few years ago we published an article in which we analyzed the stories recounted by fathers who had taken parental leave about their experiences in coping with gender cultures in their organizations (Murgia and Poggio 2013). We were interested in how cultural resistance and hegemony practices in organizations may affect the implementation of changes promoted at a normative level. We focused in particular on how specific forms of masculinity and fatherhood are mobilized and institutionalized in organizations and how normative changes can challenge this cultural order. In the analysis of the fathers' narratives we identified three main archetypes of the relationship between father and organization, using as metaphors three male figures of Greek mythology, Atlas, Epimetheus and Prometheus, the Titan brothers who rebelled against the hegemony of Zeus, albeit with different attitudes and receiving different punishments.

This work allowed us to reflect upon the fact that the symbolic orders of gender in organizations cannot be challenged at a normative level if the change does not affect the organizational culture as well, becoming embedded in everyday organizational practices.

The article was based on narrative interviews conducted in Italy in the public and private sectors. We did not stress the point at that time, but here we would underline that the contexts analyzed were represented by organizations characterized by 'standard' employment relations, based on dependent, full-time and permanent work.

---

1   The present article is an entirely collaborative effort by the two authors, whose names appear in alphabetical order. If, however, for academic reasons individual responsibility is to be assigned, Annalisa Murgia wrote sections 4 and 5; Barbara Poggio wrote sections 1, 2, 3 and 6.

Some years later, and amid an employment scenario rather different from the one in which the above-mentioned research was conducted, both because of the growing precarization of the labor market and because of the onset of the economic crisis, we intended to introduce a new perspective on this issue by considering the experience of fathers working in contexts in which employment has become more flexible and unstable. To this end, we conducted a new series of interviews with fathers with fixed-term employment contracts, and we analyzed emerging issues and the main differences between their experiences and those of the men involved in our previous research. It was soon evident from the analysis of the new materials collected that the archetypes identified in the first research failed to give proper account of those experiences. Consequently, we tried to find a different interpretative lens, and to identify a new image better able to represent the emerging situations.

In the first part of this chapter we outline the theoretical background about the relationship between fatherhood, work and organizations. Then we will focus on the Italian context, considering the normative framework of parental and fatherhood leaves with specific attention to ongoing changes in the labor market and working conditions, and stressing the shift of emphasis from the organizational dimension to the more individualized one typical of workers with non-standard work arrangements. We shall then describe the methodology used and thereafter discuss the main outcomes of the analysis in light of the new metaphorical figure identified, in order to take the new work scenarios into account as well. In our search for this further archetype we again drew on the mythological repertoire, identifying in the fourth Titan brother, Menoetius, a feature that seemed more closely to match the experiences emerging from the analysis of the new, more recent interviews. We shall conclude the presentation by discussing the emerging prospects in terms of policies and strategies for action.

2. Models of fatherhood at work

In recent decades, the theme of fatherhood has assumed increasing importance in the sociological debate (Marsiglio 1995) and the body of research on fathers, fatherhood and men in households has grown significantly (Lupton and Lesley 1997; Dienhart 1998; Dermott 2009). Numerous studies have highlighted the changes that have characterized the experience of fatherhood. They use labels such as 'new' and 'active' (Gill 2003) and terms such as 'involved' and 'sharing' to suggest that the traditional view of the father, centered on the image of the male breadwinner, should be gradually replaced by a more modern paternal figure able to develop closer and more active relationships with his children (Cohen 1993; Dermott 2005), to express stronger emotions and affection towards them, and to devote more time and attention to them (Gershuny 2000; Sandbergh and Hofferth 2001; Dermott 2005). There has thus emerged over time a growing cultural prescription that fathers should be much more involved than in the past in the growth of their offspring (Griswold 1993; La Rossa 1997).

However, despite the ongoing changes in the notion of fatherhood, some aspects of the paternal role seem to have changed very little. In recent decades, a debate has arisen on the reasons why the cultural images of fatherhood have changed much more than the actual behavior of fathers with their children. This has generated a disparity between the notion of fatherhood and the concrete practices of fathers (La Rossa 1988). The involvement of the father with his children, in fact, often appears to be limited to activities such as play and relaxation, excluding everyday activities such as the preparation of meals or housework (Sanchez and Thomson 1997; Di Giulio and Carrozza 2003). Various studies on fatherhood have therefore focused on the reasons why fatherhood practices still seem remote from their collectively constructed representation. Among the reasons most often identified are the persistence of patriarchal gender relations; the welfare state systems that continue to be based on the role of the mother as the main parent, considering fathers to be relatively marginal; the resistance of employers to providing the means to reconcile work and private life, and their sanctioning of men who do not match the expectations of the labor market; the reluctance of mothers to relinquish their predominant role in the household in a context where they struggle to gain recognition in other life-areas (Dermott 2003; Pfau-Effinger 2005). Also, research conducted in Italy has highlighted the cultural resistance encountered by fathers who reject the traditional model to adopt alternative practices (Magaraggia 2013).

In what follows, the focus will be on the interweaving between parenthood and work, and in particular on the use of parental leave. Enactment of the law on parental leave in Italy in the early 2000s gave equal entitlement to its use by mothers and fathers. The law's explicit purpose was to alter the division of labor within the couple and within organizations, thereby challenging the dominant gender patterns (Poggio 2006). The request to take time off from work following the birth of a child can be understood in this sense as a form of 'active' fatherhood that supersedes the traditional notion of a father figure distant from the practices of nurture and care. It challenges the hegemonic model of masculinity that still today permeates and sustains the dominant organizational culture.

In fact, within every organization there are rules, implicit and explicit, which discipline the behavior and interaction of members: they define who should do what, and how they should do it. These rules also define gender positioning and gender relations, thus expressing the normative order immanent in the organizational culture (Davies and Harré 1990). Therefore, just as motherhood has always struggled to find citizenship within work organizations (Poggio 2002), so fatherhood – when it no longer pertains to the private and personal dimension and is claimed as a right to take time off from work to be with the children – runs the risk of penalizing the career prospects of men, as it happens to women. Also men, when they ask themselves whether they should take parental leave on the birth of their children, are faced by a series of established practices that define explicit and implicit gender contents transmitted by the dominant organizational culture. They must therefore negotiate with the regulations laid down by the state (in this case those on parental leave), with organizations and their management of working time (Murgia and Poggio 2009, 2012), and with the mothers and the organizations for which they work (Brandth and Kvande 2002). The outcome of the negotiation of these various processes, labelled "fathers' practices" (Morgan 1996), is often the relinquishment of leave, or at least its limited use when it has no compulsory duration.[2]

3. Fatherhood in Italy: regulation and changing labor market

The Italian welfare system is rather familistic in nature, so that the activities of care and treatment are often on the shoulders of families. This hampers achievement of a more balanced gender division of care-work, because the emphasis placed on gender asymmetry by familistic development models reduces the willingness to invest financial and emotional resources in the creation of new familial arrangements (Mills et al. 2008). This is reflected in the limited availability of, and access to, parenting support services,[3] which are

---

2   In Italy, according to INPS data, in 2011 the users of parental leave were 89% women and only 11% men. Among parents with children aged under 8, parental leave was taken by 45.3% of mothers compared with 6.9% of fathers (ISTAT 2011, Moss 2014).

3   On considering, for example, the coverage for child care, comparison between the available places and the potential users of child-care services for children aged between 3 months and 3 years of age shows that the Italian average service coverage is 6.5% with a maximum of 15.2% in Emilia Romagna and a minimum of 1% in Calabria and Campania.

generally rather expensive. A direct consequence is the significant involvement of grandparents in child care (Cittadinanzattiva 2012).

Concerning parental leave in particular, it was only in 2000 that a law was enacted to regulate the matter by recognizing childcare as a parental responsibility and not just a maternal one (Naldini and Saraceno 2008). According this law (no. 53), both mothers and fathers with a salaried job – whether open-ended or temporary – can apply for parental leave for a maximum of six months each, to also be used by the partners simultaneously, until the child is eight and for up to a maximum of ten months. But if the father takes leave for a continuous period amounting to more than three months, the six-months limit is extended to seven, and the total amount of leave entitlement for the two parents becomes eleven months. During the period of parental leave, for six months and until the child's third birthday, the law grants an allowance amounting to 30% of the parent's pay, regardless of his/her income. Parental leave is instead unpaid if the child is aged 3–8 years old, but the period is covered by social security contributions.

For non-dependent workers the situation is different: male professional freelancers (VAT-registered workers)[4] are entirely excluded from parental leave, while male project workers[5] are entitled to take leave of absence (for up to three months) only if the mother is dead or severely ill, if she has abandoned the child, or if the father has custody.

Instead, specific legislation on paternity leave is almost non-existent in Italy. Only in 2012 was legal recognition introduced, but it was entirely symbolic, as it consists of only one day.[6] The recent labor-market reform (the "Jobs Act") has made certain changes to the use of parental leave.[7] But once again it has failed to address the significant gender asymmetry in care work that persists in Italy. Indeed, the reform law has reiterated the central importance of protecting motherhood because no reference is made to fatherhood or parenthood. Also rather modest are the changes with respect to paternity leave, which in Italy is usable only in the event of the mother's death or abandonment of the children: the leave is extended to self-employed fathers, who were

---

4 In Italy self-employed workers are entrepreneurs, professional freelancers, contract workers and 'project workers'.

5 These are workers who pay contributions into a special fund of the National Social Insurance Agency (INPS) dedicated to self-employed workers.

6 On the birth of a child, the father – once again only if he is a salaried employee – has the right (and duty) to take one day off from work within five months after the birth of the child, to which may be added two extra days deducted from the mother's period of compulsory maternity leave.

7 Parental leave has been extended to the first twelve years of the child's life, and the allowance of 30% of the salary has been prolonged to six years. The law also makes it possible to apply for a part-time work schedule as an alternative to leave, or to opt for a split schedule (taking hours rather than days).

previously entirely excluded; and fathers married to self-employed women are allowed to use part of their maternity leave (which has a total duration of five months).

In light of this legal framework, one may certainly argue that the Italian regulatory context still gives scant support to fathers, especially those working on non-standard contracts. This is a problem that cannot be overlooked when considering the changes taking place in fatherhood with respect to working conditions, given the large growth of temporary contracts in the Italian labor market, and also in relation to the more general processes of globalization and work flexibility. In Italy, in fact, the increase of precarious jobs has radically recast the labor market hierarchy by widening the gap between insider and outsider workers. The use of these employment contracts has several advantages for organizations in terms of flexibility and reduced labor costs. But from the workers' point of view, employment on a fixed-term contract very often means experiencing precariousness due first to irregular income and then to the lack of welfare benefits, such as training, paid holidays, sickness leave, maternity leave, unemployment benefits, social security contributions and, of course, parental leave (Gherardi and Murgia 2013). The economic crisis has exacerbated this situation by increasing the risk of precariousness especially for the younger generation, hampering their projects for the future (Murgia and Poggio 2014).

Research carried out in Italy has shown that labor market flexibility and employment instability influence the decision to have children, especially among men. Low wages and sporadic employment, especially in the case of men – and if the family of origin cannot give support – induce young couples to postpone parenthood until they have more stable employment (Bertolini and Musumeci 2014; Pandolfini 2010). Men seem to feel a greater sense of inadequacy if they do not earn a regular income; a condition which distances them from the traditional male-breadwinner model. Re-processing the data issued by ISTAT (2009)[8] shows that the percentage of men aged between 26 and 45 years with children is significantly lower for those with atypical jobs (41.1%) than for those with a standard employment (54.7%) or entrepreneurs (65.4%), professionals (52%) or self-employed workers (56.7%). Only among the unemployed is there a smaller percentage of men with children (23.2%).

Although these are significant issues, few studies on fatherhood have addressed them. Most research continues to focus on fathers employed with standard contracts. Among those studies which have been conducted on the matter, of particular interest is Halrynjo (2009). This examined the role of

---

8   We thank Rossella Bozzon, a colleague from the University of Trento, for re-processing the ISTAT data.

men in the division of care work and constructed a typology of four different positions: the 'career' position, the 'care 'position, the 'care and career' position, and the 'patchwork career' position. Analysis of this last position explored non-standard work patterns (characterized by reduced hours, fragmented trajectories, etc.) and showed that men in this situation do not necessarily devote more time to childcare, although they appreciate being able to reconcile work and private life notwithstanding the dictates of the hegemonic male model. Also, Carreri (2014), in a qualitative study conducted in Italy on couples in which both partners were highly-educated workers, employed on short-term contracts but in high-skilled jobs, highlights that fathers tend discursively to emphasize the positive rather than negative aspects of working with short-term contracts in relation to fatherhood, since work flexibility enables greater investment in the family in terms of identity, time and energy.

However, both Halrynjo and Carreri show that, despite the recognition that such careers have some positive aspects, the difficulties related to insecurity, lack of continuity and career prospects, as well as low wages, are critical factors for fathers with fixed-term employment contracts. This aspect emerges more forcefully in other studies. Considering the use of parental leave in particular, Bertolini and Musumeci (2014) found that a reason frequently cited by fathers to justify their decision not to take parental leave was the impossibility of interrupting their work, especially if they were employed on short-term contracts. This was due not only to concern about a reduction of the salary, but also to the fear of not obtaining a renewal of the contract. This fear seems to be exacerbated by the economic crisis (Musumeci et al. 2015), which is seen as a factor behind the re-traditionalization of gender roles.

One therefore observes a conflict between, on the one hand, the growing desire of fathers to be more closely involved with their children and more responsive to the new cultural model of the "responsible father" (Doherty et al. 1998), and on the other, the perception that they cannot evade, first, the demand of the labor market that they should be constantly available lest they pay the cost of severe career penalizations (Musumeci and Solera 2013), and second, fulfillment of the role of main breadwinner that the still dominant cultural model continues to assign them.

To complete the scenario, mention should also be made of the changes that characterize the relationships of flexible workers with organizations. It has been pointed out that, in the case of permanent workers, organizations are obstacles to the use of parental leave because of the prevalence of symbolic gender orders that assign different tasks and responsibilities to women and men. What happens, however, when the relationship between workers and organizations becomes looser because of the flexibility of the labor market? How do the processes of individualization and precarization affect the attitude of fathers to using parental leave and taking time off from work to look after their children? The greater freedom from conditioning by organizations would suggest the greater freedom of fathers in the management of family life. However, in addition to the above-mentioned critical issues for fathers (including the fear of losing their jobs, as well as failing to fulfill the dominant cultural expectations), there is also the concern about the emergence, in the neoliberal organizational scenario, of personnel management methods based on the substitutability of workers and the reduction of labor costs (Gherardi and Murgia 2013). The symbolic space for recognition of the worker's needs and personal life-dimensions therefore becomes more circumscribed; and the requirements of space and time for parenting obtain even less recognition than before from organizations.

4. Research Design

This study is based on materials from two different research projects, each of which involved fathers employed on short-term contracts, both employees and freelancers. The first was an international research project entitled *"Trapped or Flexible? Transitions and Risk Missing Policies for Young High-Skilled Workers in Europe"* (Samek Lodovici and Semenza 2012), funded by the European Commission, in which we were involved in 2011 and 2012. As part of the project, 30 in-depth interviews were conducted in Italy, in the areas of Milan, Trento and Bologna (three cities in the north of the country), with men and women aged between 27 and 34 with at least five years of work experience. The second source of this study is a smaller-scale qualitative research project, carried out in 2015 in the Province of Trento, through interviews with 10 fathers aged between 25 and 45 employed on fixed-term contracts, in order to reconstruct their work trajectories and how they were interwoven with familial and parental choices and experiences.

Both research projects employed the narrative interview technique, the main purpose of which is to elicit stories concerning the experiences of the interviewees (Vodak and Wagner 2006; Riessman 2008). All the interviews were audio-recorded and transcribed in their entirety. They were then subjected to narrative analysis (Poggio 2004; Riessman 2008). This kind of analysis makes it possible to determine how dominant social orders are constructed and the ways in which social actors contribute to, or oppose, hegemonic practices (Bamberg 2004). Moreover, a narrative approach is particularly useful for the analysis of changes, both individual and organizational: stories, in fact, are discursive tools to make sense of change, and they are always based on the occurrence of a change – on the upsetting of a balance between a 'before' and an 'after' (Todorov 1971). Finally, narratives provide particularly effective materials for the analysis of changes in gender orders (Gherardi and Poggio 2007) because they are able to bring hegemonic practices to light and deconstruct them (Martin 2001).

The analysis built on previous research work – cited at the beginning of the chapter – which had concentrated on a series of interviews with Italian fathers, employed in organizations both public and private, who had made use of parental leave. They focused on the difficulty of changing the gender models present in organizations, identifying three main plots in the fathers' experiences. Drawing on Greek mythology, we referred to the Titan brothers Atlas, Epimetheus and Prometheus, three divinities who rebelled against the command of Zeus.

The first archetype identified, that of Atlas (the Titan condemned to support the sky on his shoulders), referred to situations in which the research had highlighted cases of explicit opposition to the dominant gender model by fathers who, having decided to take parental leave and devote themselves to childcare, had suffered serious consequences from their employers, such as being downgraded. The image of Atlas emphasized the magnitude of the challenge made to the hegemonic gender order by refusing to follow the practices of hegemonic masculinity and engaging in practices of resistance.

The image of Epimetheus (a Titan who, although belonging to the rebel Titans, took the side of Zeus – together with his brother Prometheus – in the war between the Titans and the Olympians) was used to refer to situations with a closer intertwining between practices of resistance and of hegemony. Here parental leave was experienced as a contingent necessity, without questioning the dominant model of gender in the organization and in the couple. Often these men complied with the hegemonic model of the male breadwinner, a man with a full-time job involved in care-work as a helper rather than being in a symmetrical position with his partner. And the organization accepted the arrangement without raising too much resistance, considering the situation as an emergency.

Finally, the third archetype – Prometheus (who had entered the war, siding with Zeus, only towards its end, obtaining as a reward to have the Olympus gate opened for him) – was adopted for a case where parental leave for fathers was described as a privilege tolerated by the organization, which – if it remained an exception, an extraordinary event rather than a routine practice – could become a reason for pride in the organizational identity. Taking leave from work to care for children was regarded as an unusual practice, but unproblematic because it did not entail redefinition of a model of work based on constant availability and physical presence.

The analysis of these stories evidenced that they were accounts of challenges against dominant symbolic gender orders as forms of resistance to, or acceptance within, the organizations to which the interviewees belonged, and the extent to which they positioned themselves internally or externally to the hegemonic models of masculinity of organizations.

With hindsight, however, it seems that the stories and archetypes identified are no longer sufficient to account for the contemporary experience of working fathers, because the profound changes taking place in the labor market – in particular the increasing flexibilization and precarization, on the one hand, and the economic crisis on the other – have also had consequences on fatherhood and practices to balance parenting and work. When focusing on the use of parental leave, for example, one finds a striking polarization between protected workers (with salaried and open-ended jobs) and unprotected ones (especially freelancers and employees with a fixed-term contract). Precarious fathers, in fact, are not eligible for the rights granted to standard employees, neither *de jure* – in the case of those who are self-employed – nor *de facto,* as when leave is possible on paper (e.g. in the case of employees with fixed-term contracts) but in practice cannot be taken for fear that the contract will not be renewed.

The questions addressed by our research were therefore the following: what happens when the right to parental leave is not available or is effectively unusable? How is fatherhood changing in the current scenario of work characterized by a large increase in precarious workers, both employed and self-employed?

5. Menoetius: the multiple experiences of precarious fatherhood

On the basis of the analysis of the collected stories, which we interpreted by setting them in relation to those considered in the above-mentioned previous research, we identified a further archetype of the working father apparently better able to represent the experiences of precarious fathers. This archetype is Menoetius, the fourth brother of Atlas, Epimetheus and Prometheus, who – unlike his brothers – did not survive the war between the Titans and the Olympians. In the updated story that we present below, Menoetius symbolizes the father deprived of his rights at work, who also tries to resist the hegemonic model of masculinity – as his brothers did – but who is not able to challenge the organizational culture, even if he would like to, mainly because he cannot access rights (this is the case of freelancers) or because he is afraid of losing his job (this is the case of those who are instead employees, but with a fixed-term contract).

Analysis of the texts of the interviews with non-standard workers yielded a representation of them difficult to summarize in a single image and a single story. However, we decided to refer to a single archetype, that of Menoetius, the etymological roots of whose name are the terms *menos* (might, power) and *oitos* (doom, torment), because in the various stories collected there was a constant ambivalence between, on the one hand, the endeavor of these fathers to establish non-traditional relational styles centered on closeness with their children, and on the other, the constraints and obstacles imposed on them by work precarization, but also by the persistence of traditional gender symbolic orders with which they are intertwined.

As heterogeneous as they are, the stories of the fathers interviewed were characterized by a representation of gender roles that was different, at least in part, from the model of the male breadwinner. In the interviews with fathers in precarious jobs, in fact, although varying degrees of involvement in child-care were found, the claim that child-care is not a male task was significantly less frequent than in the interviews with fathers employed on standard contracts.

For me it is normal that my wife and I are absolutely on the same level. Instead, in my dad's home the man worked and the woman stayed at home (...). My mother worked and looked after the children, while my father did very little. But that was entirely normal. I don't know if it was a deliberate choice, if it was for cultural reasons or a mix of cultural reasons and laziness. It was partly that, of course, but management of the children was certainly very unbalanced between the parents. Dad was the one who helped you with homework and took you swimming at the weekends, and during supper asked you how things had gone at school. Mamma did everything else, but I think it was a normal situation at that time, although both my parents came from educated families. He played with me, but much much less than I play with my daughter, and the amount of attention devoted to me was different from what I devote to my daughter. [IT technician, 38 years, two children, one aged 4 and one coming]

I'm at home with the children in the evening when I finish all my other activities and hobbies. Not that I'm someone who stays shut up at home all day, so it's something that affects me to a relative extent. I act the father when I have to act like a father not like a mother-hen. I'm less involved in management of the children because I never know whether or not I'll be teaching all year. I have to hustle to find things so that I can scrape together a salary to pay my bills at the end of the month. So I'm almost always out, and I'm not constantly attached to the family. I'm not a mother-hen. For me the children must grow and be independent. They're still small, however. [Gym teacher, 40 years, two children, aged 8 and 6]

Hence, whilst on the one hand there are fathers who stress the importance of closeness to and care of the children, giving them a central role in their lives, on the other, there are men who adopt relational models characterized by a more traditional division of roles, and who instead stress the importance of distance. It is interesting to note, however, that the figure of the absentee father is no longer perceived as something that can be taken for granted and that is socially legitimized. In the second interview excerpt, for example, after describing his limited presence with the children, the interviewee feels it necessary to deploy a justificatory rhetoric which interprets his absence, on the one hand, in educational terms linked to the children's achievement of independence, and on the other, as the result of precariousness and having to "scrape together a salary".

Precariousness may also be described as a factor which instead strengthens the desire for involvement in the father's role as a space for self-realization. Also in these cases, however, there are evident ambivalences between investment in parenthood and job dissatisfaction.

If you ask me what I am, I answer '*** [child's name]'s father'. It's a wonderful thing. You can fulfill yourself in many ways, but ... so far the only thing that I've achieved and done well has been my daughter (...). Before I didn't feel fulfilled; now I do, even though I haven't been successful in work ... It's probably a bit like the fox and the grapes, I say that work is sour because I haven't achieved anything, but it's also a choice at some point. If you can be a better worker, that's fine. Otherwise never mind! *** [child's name] has everything she needs, so I think that this means being fulfilled. She hasn't got her own home, but so what? Who said she should be a home-owner? She's got a roof over her head, so ... I tell you that my experience of fatherhood is the only thing makes me really proud, the most important thing. [Commercial promoter, 36 years, one child aged 7]

The above story reflects – reversing the traditional model – the trade-off between investment in professional life and in the family, suggesting some sort of incompatibility between the two life-spheres. Whilst detachment from work seems to be the result of an unsatisfactory professional career marked by precariousness, on the other hand the desire to fully experience fatherhood is not described as a fallback solution, but rather as an important and almost unexpected discovery, a source of identity and satisfaction.

The ability to establish a close relationship with the children, which takes priority over work, therefore cannot be reduced to mere justificatory rhetoric. This is demonstrated by the stories of some fathers, currently employed on fixed-term contracts, who left more stable careers precisely because of an organizational model – still dominant in Italy – which refuses to recognize the experience of fatherhood.

> *Fatherhood has been great. Obviously the company didn't like it at all. In fact, when I went back [after a period of parental leave], my boss told me. "Okay, now you'll go abroad for five months". That was one of the reasons why I said: "Okay guys, you haven't understood anything. I quit". At the family level, it's absolutely necessary for the father and mother to share the management of the children.* [IT technician, 38 years, two children, one aged 4 and one coming]

We collected the experiences of fathers who left their jobs after taking parental leave, preferring fixed-term term contracts to permanent employment and a regular income. Besides, it seems important to stress the absence, in the stories of the precarious fathers interviewed, of any reconciliation measures. Indeed, in answering a question about policies that could facilitate a better balance between family life and work, the majority of respondents did not even consider the possibility of benefitting from organizational policies. Instead, they referred to the timing of child-care services.

> *In the end, I believe that the best reconciliation service would be to ensure that the timings for my daughter are compatible with the work schedules of her parents. This unfortunately we still ... I mean, the school was created when the woman stayed at home and it was already difficult when the children got out of school at 12 o'clock. Now they leave at 4pm, but it's too early. Leaving at 4pm instead of 5pm means 400 euros more a month for babysitters, or grandparents.* [Commercial promoter, 36 years, one child aged 7]

The dimension of reconciliation of work and family life, and in particular the (non) use of parental leave, makes it possible to highlight significant differences among the fathers interviewed who worked on fixed-term contracts. These differences are linked to the different structural conditions that characterized the fathers' experiences in terms of their own employment, the employment status of the partner, and the immediate family.

The first aspect concerns the type of job. In fact, there are jobs in which flexibility can be an advantage and others in which it is a disadvantage. Moreover, in a context of scant normative protection, the characteristics of organizations or the sensitivity of employers also become important.

> *I didn't ask [for parental leave] because my contract expired in June ... and in fact I didn't know how it worked, and then my wife was at home until the end of September. Then my contract expired in June and they renewed it until the end of September, so I didn't ask.* [Warehouse officer, 34 years, one child aged 7 months]

I have a fixed-term contract at a foundation and I'm a freelance tennis coach. [....] At the foundation I have a flexible schedule of 38 hours a week on a 4-month average. So I don't have obligatory working hours, and from this point of view my family/work balance is exceptional. [Programmer and Tennis coach, 37 years, one child aged 5 months]

I believe that a person's absence affects small and medium-sized enterprises, so it's more a fear for your job. Then it depends a bit on the maturity of the employer, because in the end if he doesn't understand the context ... everything depends on the sensitivity of the employer. [...] The family is seen as something external to work. [Industrial Automation Technician, 32 years, one child aged 2]

The chance of experiencing fatherhood with a certain serenity is therefore linked to the presence of different forms of support and employment, in which flexibility gives a certain freedom and does not destabilize the organization of family timings.

Another significant discriminant is the employment status of the partner. In fact, if the partner has a permanent job – as she did in most of the cases considered – precariousness is less problematic; all the more so if the man's work is a source of professional satisfaction, regardless of the contractual form of his employment. The permanent character of the mother's job – which is sometimes also the result of renunciation, as in the case described in the excerpt below – to some extent provides security by enabling the father to do the work that he enjoys. It may also allow him to take time off to spend with his child.

She was a lawyer in another city and then got a job at the chamber of commerce. She has always preferred the family to work and her ambitions, and in fact we live here and lead a tranquil life. As regards work, she has a permanent contract, and also this gives me peace of mind. We've concentrated on the family. [...]. Knowing that she has a steady income makes me feel more at ease. Okay, doing what I like is fine. Then, if I'm at home for two months, it's not a problem. [...] If it was the only income in the family, yes, I wouldn't have even had the first [child]. The precondition is a regular income. We can keep ourselves and start a family. So if there's a job, there will certainly be other children. [Web designer, 34 years, one child aged 2 years]

I'm lucky to have my partner who works hard, she's the one who brings the money home [laughs] and for me that's great, and fortunate, because without her, everything that I enjoy in life I'd probably enjoy less, like before she started working. [Sales rapresentative, 33 years, one child aged 4]

The above-reported stories – which were recurrent among the interviews, depict an organization of the couple whereby the division of care work is less asymmetrical than in the cases analyzed in the previous research, and on the basis of which we constructed the ideal-typical figures of Atlas, Prometheus and Epimetheus. In fact, in the case of Menoetius – who represents the ambivalence of the experiences of precarious fathers – there is a greater balance in child-care, although it does not alter the gender differences due to professional investment. Whilst on the one hand there are women who pursue stable professional careers and have greater economic security than their partners, on the other, they pay the price for it by working in unsatisfying jobs, or at any rate ones with less investment in terms of time. This allows men to assume the risk of precarious work, so that they can take stimulating jobs and at the same time have the flexibility to devote time to relationships with their children. These, therefore, are cases in which there is a better balance of unpaid care work within the couple; but the same cannot be said of investment in, and identification with, paid work, even if it is precarious and uncertain.

A third important condition – this too present in several of the stories considered – is the support offered by the family of origin.

> *The worry of having a family and being a father is legitimate, but a vital role is played by the family, our parents, my brothers, who are in fact always ready to lend a hand. So this worry is somewhat mitigated by their constant presence.* [Accountant in a cooperative, 36 years, one child aged 8 months]

> *We're lucky because my wife's mother lives nearby, let's say, one hour by coach from here, and whenever we're in difficulties, she has to come. What else can you do? Either you take a day off, especially with the older girl, or my mother-in-law has to come.* [Gym teacher, 40 years, two children, aged 8 and 6]

As shown by several studies on the Italian context, for non-standard workers the family of origin is the main safety net with respect to discontinuity of income and employment, independent housing, and also support for child-care (Addabbo and Borghi 2001; Fullin 2004). The extended family, in fact, seems still to be an indispensable source of protection which intervenes when difficulties arise, especially in terms of income. From this point of view, the balance that seems to have been created in the Italian labor market among precarious jobs, the welfare system, and the family only strengthens the role of the family in the reproduction of social inequality (Saraceno 2000; Ranci 2014). Low levels of job security, high unemployment, and a lack of social rights make workers with fixed-term contracts even more dependent on their families than in the past. This fuels strong generational imbalances based on asymmetries in treatment and types of protection (Murgia 2010).

It is generally evident that this labor market and the organizational models currently present within many organizations do not give full citizenship to parenthood when there are no other supporting factors. In this scenario, fatherhood seems to be fully experienced only when effective support is available; support that may be provided by a high-skilled job in an organization with favorable working hours, by the high level of security of the partner's job, or the assistance, in both economic and care terms, of the immediate family. In the absence of these conditions, the possibility to live the experience of fatherhood (both as a choice and as a practice) is very limited.

6. Managing fatherhood and flexible organizational models: New policies wanted

In this study, which draws on previous research focused on the stories of fathers who had taken parental leave – thus challenging the gender cultures of the organizations to which they belonged – we have tried to take a step forward, starting from the awareness that in recent years the Italian labor market has undergone significant changes, with inevitable consequences for the lifestyles and reconciliation choices of individuals. In particular, we have found that the condition of young fathers – and beforehand the decision to experience fatherhood – can be increasingly less understood in light of a model of standard employment with only one organization. It is increasingly subject to the process of precarization and to the constraints and opportunities that characterize the new forms of non-standard employment. This does not mean that the cultural models present in contemporary organizations lose importance because of the individualization of experiences and choices; rather, the current scenario has more complex features with a plurality of dimensions that give rise to diverse experiential combinations. It is therefore difficult to identify a single archetype of fatherhood amid precariousness, although it is possible to delineate a series of dimensions that unite the experiences of these 'new fathers'. The image of the fourth brother, Menoetius, is therefore composite and ambivalent: on the one hand, it strains towards change, towards the ideal type of the present and nurturing father; on the other, it is pushed back by the changes taking place in the labor market and the lack of measures to support fatherhood for new workers, within the framework of the traditional symbolic order.

In this scenario, both the regulatory and organizational contexts have failed to respond proactively to the ongoing changes by identifying solutions and strategies that enable families to cope with the new structure and to meet the challenges arising in the labor market. Precariousness seems to have had different consequences for the fathers interviewed: on the one hand, if the answer is the intensification of work, precariousness is an evident obstacle to more active and present parenting; on the other, in the case of fathers with high-skilled jobs and with substantial family resources and professional networks, these may provide opportunities to consolidate involvement in the paternal role, described as a source of self-fulfillment.

Both situations, however, are connoted by an ambivalence betrayed by dissatisfaction with one of the two domains (the profession versus fatherhood). The discussion on practices of resistance to hegemonic models of gender within organizations therefore appears to be significantly different for fathers working with non-standard contracts, with respect to those of fathers with a standard job, since the legislation itself denies – or makes not exercisable – their right to use parental leave. What possible solutions could therefore ensure a better balance between the desire to experience fatherhood to the full and the constraints and pressures deriving from the new work arrangements? We shall now try to identify some of the strategies that might prove useful in promoting real change in this regard.

At the organizational level, it would be opportune to extend organizational policies (like company kindergartens or time-saving services) to staff on non-standard contracts, who instead are often excluded from them. More generally, work should be done on the organizational culture, so that parenthood is considered one of the possible biographical events that occur in the workers' careers, thus avoiding the penalization (or even non-renewal of the contract) of those who have used work/life balance measures.

More generally, it would be appropriate to shift to local interventions, and in particular to integrated policies, which can also arise from synergies between public and private actors. Among these interventions should be policies on the hours of services, which should take account of the fact that the new forms of work often have schedules that differ from those of the Fordist system. They are characterized by greater discontinuity and therefore make planning more difficult. Moreover, it is important to discard the assumption that fixed-term work is more flexible. There is no reason to believe, in fact, that atypical workers can better manage their working time. It is instead more likely that the fear of not having their contracts renewed induces such workers to avoid using policies of work/life balance.

Finally – and most importantly – it seems urgent to take action on the regulatory side through interventions that grant greater citizenship to non-standard work in terms of rights and welfare. More generally, it is necessary to press for the introduction of different forms of social protection, such as a basic income, which could offset the flexibilisation of the labor market, reducing the current asymmetry among the different contractual forms and favoring greater employment security and sustainability (Murgia and Poggio 2014). This would ensure greater income continuity for temporary workers, also enabling them to plan parenting choices with greater tranquility. More specifically, one can envisage the adoption of initiatives aimed at supporting, in particular, parents with precarious jobs by providing subsidies and leave entitlements. As just seen, recent changes to the regulations on leave have in fact only been minor adjustments, not implying a redefinition of the normative framework. The latter still appears to be patterned on the characteristics of standard workers, whose need of a reconciliation with respect to parenthood will paradoxically continue to decrease.

What appears clear is the urgent need to remedy the imbalance between the different opportunities available to those who enjoy standard working conditions and those who increasingly experience precariousness in work and life. Continuing in this direction, however, means, on the one hand, that parenthood decisions will increasingly depend on structural factors external to the will of the young men and women entering the labor market; on the other hand, it will be difficult for a more complete model of fatherhood to find fully active and concrete realization.

References

Addabbo, T., Borghi, V. (2001) *Riconoscere il lavoro. Una ricerca sulle lavoratrici con contratti di collaborazione nella provincia di Modena.* Milano: Angeli

Bamberg, M. (2004) Considering Counter Narratives, in: M. Bamberg, and M. Andrews, (eds) *Considering Counter Narratives: Narrating, Resisting, Making Sense,* Amsterdam: John Benjamins, pp. 351–71

Bertolini, S., Musumeci, R. (2014) 'Diventare genitori in tempi di crisi: verso una ritradizionalizzazione dei ruoli di genere', *Sociologia Italiana – AIS Journal of Sociology,* 4, pp. 31–54

Brandth, B., Kvande, E. (2002) 'Reflexive fathers: negotiating parental leave and working life', *Gender, Work & Organization,* 9(2) pp. 186–203

Carreri, A. (2014) 'Fatherhood and Precarious Work: A Supporting relation Between Systems of Meanings', *About Gender,* 3(6) pp. 87–115

Cittadinanzattiva (2012) *Report: Indagine 2012 sugli asili nido comunali,* available at: http://www.cittadinanzattiva.it

Cohen, T.F. (1993) What do fathers provide? Reconsidering the economic and nurturant dimensions of men as parents, in J.C. Hood (ed) *Men, Work and Family,* Newbury Park: Sage, pp. 1–22

Davies, B., Harré, R. (1990) 'Positioning: The Discursive Production of Selves', *Journal for the Theory of Social Behavior,* 20(1) pp. 43–163

Dermott, E. (2009) *Intimate Fatherhood. A sociological analysis.* London: Routledge

Dermott, E. (2005) 'Time and Labour: Fathers' perceptions of employment and childcare', *Sociology Review,* 53(2) pp. 91–103

Dermott, E. (2003) 'The Intimate Father: defining paternal involvement', *Sociological Research Online,* 8(3), Available at: http://www.socresonline.org.uk/8/4/dermott.html

Di Giulio, P., Carrozza, S. (2003) Il nuovo ruolo del padre, in: A. Pinnelli, F. Racioppi, R. Rettaroli (eds) *Genere e demografia.* Bologna: il Mulino, pp. 311–338

Dienhart, A. (1998) *Reshaping Fatherhood: The Social Construction of Shared Parenting.* Thousand Oaks: Sage

Doherty, W.J., Kouneski, E.F., Erickson, M.F. (1998) 'Responsible Fathering: An overview and conceptual framework', *Journal of Marriage and the Family,* 60, pp. 277–292

Fullin, G. (2004) *Vivere l'instabilità del lavoro.* Bologna: Il Mulino

Gershuny, J. (2000) *Changing Times: Work and Leisure in Postindustrial Society.* Oxford and New York: Oxford University Press

Gherardi, S., Murgia, A. (2013) 'By hook or by crook: temporary workers between exploration and exploitation', *Research in the Sociology of Organizations,* 37, pp. 75–103

Gherardi, S., Poggio, B. (2007) *Gendertelling in Organizations: Narratives from Male-dominated Environments.* Stockholm: Liber AB

Gill, R. (2003) Power and the Production of Subjects: A Genealogy of the New Man and the New Lad in: B. Benwell (ed) *Masculinity and Men's Lifestyle Magazines.* Oxford: Blackwell, pp. 34–56

Griswold, R.L. (1993) *Fatherhood in America.* New York: Basic Books

Halrynjo, S. (2009) 'Men's work–life conflict: career, care and self-realization: patterns of privileges and dilemmas', *Gender, Work & Organization,* 16(1) pp. 98–125

Istat (2009) *Famiglie e soggetti sociali,* Available at: http://www.istat.it/it/archivio/81546

Istat (2011) *La conciliazione fra lavoro e famiglia* (Statistiche Report, 28-12-11). Available at: http://www.istat.it/it/archivio/48912

La Rossa, R. (1997) *The Modernization of Fatherhood: a Social and Political History.* Chicago: University of Chicago Press

La Rossa, R. (1988) "Fatherhood and Social Change". *Family Relations,* 37, pp. 451–457

Lupton, D., Barclay, L. (1997) *Constructing Fatherhood: Discourses and experiences,* London: Sage

Magaraggia, S. (2013) 'Di certo mio figlio non lo educo allo stesso modo dei miei'. Relazioni intergenerazionali e trasformazioni dei desideri paterni', *Studi culturali,* 10(2) pp. 189–210

Marsiglio, W. (1995) Fatherhood scholarship: an agenda and overview for the future, in: W. Marsiglio (ed) *Fatherhood: Contemporary Theory, Research and Social Policy.* Thousand Oaks: Sage, pp. 1–20

Martin, P. (2001) "Mobilizing Masculinities": Women's Experiences of Men at Work,' *Organization,* 8(4) pp. 587–618

Mills, M., Mencarini, L., Tanturri, M.L, Begall, K. (2008) 'Gender equity and fertility intentions in Italy and Netherlands', *Demographic Research,* 18(1) pp. 1–26.

Morgan, D. (1996) *Family Connections: An Introduction to Family Studies.* Cambridge: Polity Press

Moss, P. (2014) (ed) *International Review of Leave Policies and Related Research 2014,* Institute of Education, University of London. Available at: http://www.leavenetwork.org/lp_and_r_reports/

Murgia (2010) *Dalla precarietà lavorativa alla precarietà sociale. Biografie in transito tra lavoro e non lavoro.* Bologna: Odoya

Murgia, A., Poggio, B. (2014) Experiences of precariousness by highly-skilled young people in Italy, Spain and the UK in: L. Antonucci, M. Hamilton, S. Roberts (eds) *Young People and Social Policy in Europe: Dealing with risk, inequality and precariousness in times of crisis.* London: Palgrave, pp. 62–86

Murgia, A., Poggio, B. (2013) 'Fathers' Stories of Resistance and Hegemony in Organizational Cultures', *Gender, Work & Organization,* 20(4) pp. 413–424.

Murgia, A., Poggio, B. (2012) (eds.) *Padri che cambiano. Sguardi interdisciplinari sulla paternità contemporanea tra rappresentazioni e pratiche quotidiane.* Pisa: ETS

Murgia, A., Poggio, B. (2009) 'Challenging Hegemonic Masculinities. Men's Stories on Gender Culture in Organizations', *Organization,* 16(3) pp. 407–423

Musumeci, R., Naldini, M., Santero (2015) *First time Italian fathers' discourses on childcare and paid work reconciliation between anticipation and experience,* paper presented at the 5th ESPAnet Conference Inequality and democracy: public policies and social innovation, 5–6 February, Autonomous University of Barcelona

Musumeci, R., Solera, C. (2013) Women's and men's career interruptions in Europe: the role of social policies, in: S. Finding, A. Kober-Smith (eds) *Politiques familiales et politiques d'emploi "genrées" au Royaume-Uni et en Europe, "Observatoire de la société britannique",* 14, pp. 37–72

Naldini, M., Saraceno, C. (2011) *Conciliare famiglia e lavoro. Vecchi e nuovi patti tra i sessi e tra le generazioni.* Bologna: Il Mulino

Pandolfini, V. (2010) *'Work-life balance in a capability perspective: an Italian case study of "flexible couples"',* Transfer: European Review of Labor and Research, 18(1) pp. 45–54

Pfau-Effinger, B. (2005) 'Welfare State Policies and care arrangements', *European Societies,* 7(2) pp. 321–347

Poggio, B. (2002) Who's Afraid of Mothers?, in: M. Kostera, H. Höpfl (eds.) *Interpreting Maternal Organisations,* London: Routledge, pp. 13–26

Poggio, B. (2004) *Mi racconti una storia? Il metodo narrativo nelle scienze sociali.* Roma: Carocci

Poggio, B. (2006) Flessibilità, conciliazione e trappole di genere, in: C. Barbarulli, L. Borghi (eds) *Forme della diversità. Genere, precarietà e intercultura.* Cagliari: CUEC, pp. 207–215

Ranci, C., Brandsen, T., Sabatinelli, S. (2014) (eds.) *Social Vulnerability in European Cities The Role of Local Welfare in Times of Crisis,* Basingstoke; Palgrave

Riessman, C.K. (2008) Narrative Methods for the Human Sciences. Thousand Oaks: Sage

Samek Lodovici, M., Semenza, R. (2012) (eds.) *Precarious work and high-skilled youth in Europe.* Milano: Angeli

Sanchez, L., Thomson, E. (1997) 'Becoming Mothers and Fathers: Parenthood, Gender, and the Division of Labor', *Gender & Society,* 11(6) pp. 747–772

Sandberg, J.F., Hofferth, S.L. (2001) 'Changes in children's time with parents: US 1981–1997', *Demography,* 38(3) pp. 423–436

Saraceno, C. (2000) Gendered Policies: Family Obligations and Social Policies in Europe, in: T. P. Boje, A. Leira (eds) *Gender, Welfare State and the Market.* London: Routledge, pp. 135–156

Todorov, T. (1971) *Poétique de la prose.* Paris: Seuil

Wagner, I., Vodak, R. (2006) 'Performing success: identifying strategies of self-presentation in women's biographical narratives', *Discourse & Society,* 17(3) pp. 385–411

Of *ikumen* and *ikuboss:* An Inquiry into Japan's New Fathers as Consumers, Employees and Managers

Christoph Schimkowsky and Florian Kohlbacher

1. Introduction

It has become common to speak of Japanese society as undergoing social transformations (Kingston 2012). Among the main venues of these processes are demographic change – population ageing, declining birthrates, later births and marriages – as well as the labor market, which is more and more shaped by an increase of non-traditional modes of employment, especially among younger workers (*furītā,* NEET, etc.). The institution of the family is not excluded from these changes but a transformation of its culture and structure are accelerated by the changing social environment (Rebick and Takenaka 2006). One example of changes within Japanese family culture is the emergence of *ikumen:* fathers who are actively involved in childcare (see e.g. Kohlbacher and Schimkowsky 2014). The term *ikumen* is composed of the Chinese character for upbringing and rearing (as in child-rearing, *ikuji*) and the English word men. At the same time, the neologism is a play on words with the term *ikemen:* another relatively recent word which describes good-looking men and where *ike* comes from *iketeru* (colloquial: cool), thus implying that child-rearing fathers are "cool". The term was coined in 2006 by Maruta Masaya, an employee of the advertising and market research company Haku-hōdō. *Ikumen* reached its current level of popularity in 2010, when it came out among the Top Ten Words of the Year *(ryūkōgo)* and Nagatsuma Akira, MHLW Minister at the time, stated that he wants to spread the term *ikumen* as one countermeasure against the declining birth rate (Ishii-Kuntz 2013: 37). Starting from this point, the term also became much more frequently used in newspapers (Mizukoshi, Kohlbacher, Schimkowsky 2016).

Today, the *ikumen* boom has spawned several accompanying terms, such as *papa tomo* (father friends), which draws inspiration from the phrase *mama tomo; ikujī* (child caring granddads) and most recently *ikubosu,* work superiors who support mothers and fathers and understand their needs (Schimkowsky and Kohlbacher 2016). The emergence of these terms, along with the aforementioned popularity of *ikumen* in the media, highlights Japan's increasing engagement with male childcare (Ishii-Kuntz 2013: 38).

Overall, however, "traditional" conceptions of men as breadwinners still remain dominant in Japan (North 2009; Yasuike 2011). With the persisting culture of long working hours as one major reason, there is a significant gap between the time fathers and mothers spend with their offspring (Makino et al. 2010). Regarding time invested in the family, Japanese fathers also perform poorly in comparison to fathers from Western nations (Ishii-Kuntz 1992, 1994, 2013). In spite of this, Japanese children are more likely to view their fathers as the center point of the family than Western children (Ishii-Kuntz 1992, 2013) and show respect for the breadwinner role that keeps the father from spending more time with the family (Yasuike 2011). However, Japanese fatherhood is not a homogenous practice (Yeung 2013). Not only can a change of the Japanese father ideal be traced historically (Holloway and Nagase 2014; Ishii-Kuntz 2013; Nakazawa and Shwalb 2013), but the discourse on fatherhood in contemporary Japan is diverse as well (Nakatani 2006). Social problems such as bullying and teenage suicides have been discussed in relation to the absence of fathers from families and have led to doubts about the breadwinner ideal (Nakatani 2006). Furthermore, the influence of men's and fathers' movements, the spread of IT technology and social networks, and family policy including a promotion of involved fathering as a response to declining birth rates have stimulated public discussion (Ishii-Kuntz 2013). Today, progressive trends among Japanese fathers are so visible that Nakazawa and Shwalb (2013) speak of an "era of involvement with children". Japan thus seems to follow a global trend of "new fathers", which are defined by their more active participation in the physical-affective care of their offspring and by more egalitarian relationships with their wives (Hook and Wolfe 2012; Yoshida 2012).

The aim of this chapter is twofold. Offering an introduction to Japan's "new fathers", we will discuss the often difficult position working fathers have in work organizations in Japan and introduce public and private campaigns that strive to make company policies and executive behavior more amiable to fathers. Afterwards, we will investigate companies' engagement with fathers as customers through a discussion of products, marketing- and advertising campaigns directed at fathers. Discussing companies' engagement with involved fathers as part of their workforce and customers, we find that, due to the *ikumen* phenomenon, work organizations in contemporary Japan encounter several stimuli causing them to rethink their approach to fathers inside and outside of the company.

2. The phenomenon of *ikumen*

While fathers have traditionally held a distant position in the Japanese family, the last few years have seen changes in the image of fathers. The Japanese public increasingly recognizes the importance of paternal involvement in everyday family life, and more and more men are making efforts to actively engage in childcare. This is illustrated through *ikumen*, a popular term used in Japan to describe fathers who are actively involved in child-rearing (Ishii-Kuntz 2013). *Ikumen* has received widespread media attention, such as in television programs, newspapers, magazines and manga. Guidebooks for *ikumen* are published and even contests picking the *"Ikumen of the Year"* can be found. With the creation of the Ikumen Project by the MHLW (Ministry of Health, Labor and Welfare) in 2010, the trend has received backing from the Japanese government, which hopes to use these "nurturing fathers" to counter the demographic double threat of declining birth rates and demographic ageing in Japan (Coulmas 2007; Kingston 2012; Kohlbacher and Schimkowsky 2014). Such government patronage presents much needed support for the *ikumen* phenomenon. Even though recent decades have seen changes in the attitudes Japanese men hold towards childcare and household chores, there is still a significant gap between the *ikumen* boom portrayed in the media and the everyday life of Japanese men (Mizukoshi, Kohlbacher, Schimkowsky 2016). On the one side Japanese celebrities are honored through *Ikumen of the Year* Awards and even illustrious foreigners such as Prince William are enthusiastically described as *ikumen.* On the other side, however the actualization of the *ikumen* ideal propagated by the media remains difficult for the majority of Japanese men due to the work culture and the continuous perception of child-rearing ultimately belonging to a female sphere of duties.

Next to these social and political dimensions, the *ikumen* phenomenon is also relevant to businesses and work organizations. Public and private campaigns encourage companies to be considerate of fathers in their workforce. Further, attention has also been called towards the business potential companies see in the *ikumen* phenomenon (Holloway and Nagase 2014: 60) and an increase of *ikumen* goods, defined by Ishii-Kuntz as childcare products that are especially accessible for men (Ishii-Kuntz 2013: 57). With the exception of only a few studies (Coskuner-Balli and Thompson 2013; Bettany, Kerrane, Hogg 2014; Kohlbacher and Mizukoshi 2013; Mizukoshi, Kohlbacher, Schimkowsky 2016) however, relatively little work has been done on the relationship of consumption and fatherhood. This is striking considering that the relationship of consumption and motherhood has received considerable attention in consumer research (for example: Minahan and Huddleston 2013).

3. Fathers as employees: obstacles and initiatives[1]

In spite of its popularity, the *ikumen* phenomenon remains difficult to grasp. Depending on the definition, the size of the *ikumen* population varies dramatically: 32.6% of all fathers state that they change diapers almost daily (BERI 2012: 7) but only 2.03% of all new fathers took a paternity leave in 2013 (MHLW 2014). It is possible that the *ikumen* phenomenon is not primarily defined by the fathering habits of ordinary Japanese men but by a media-hype. Our research shows that a significant part of the *ikumen* population seems to stem from celebrity circles. For example, the *Ikumen of the Year* Award, hosted by Frontier International Inc. and the MHLW, only honors celebrities. Primary sources for the attention awarded to the *ikumen* phenomenon might lie in the novelty factor male childcare has for Japanese society (Ishii-Kuntz 2013: 62). Accordingly, Japanese men exhibit a cautious relationship with the term *ikumen.* In a 2012 survey by the advertising company ADK, only 16.6% of all fathers said they would identify as *ikumen* (ADK Kids Marketing Research Institute 2013: 15). Though the percentage of fathers identifying with the term increases with the younger age of the respondents, men's parental leave quota of 2.03% of all new and expecting fathers among permanent employees (fixed-term contract workers: 0.78%) stands in a stark contrast to a quota of 83.3% for women and demonstrates how rare a commitment to fathering still is (MHLW 2014: 13). This is even more obvious looking at the duration of these leaves: 41.3% of the 1.89% young fathers who took a "paternity leave" in 2012[2], did this for a duration of under 5 days (MHLW 2013: 16–17). The key reasons keeping Japanese men from a paternity leave seem to lie in anticipated problems in the workplace (Taga 2011: 53–54). Asked for their reasons for not taking a paternity leave, a 2011 survey among 2086 male full-time employees by the MHLW finds that 30.3% of all respondents felt that the workplace's atmosphere makes it difficult to take a paternity leave, 29.7% said that the company was too busy, and 25.1% mentioned that they think it would cause "trouble" (*meiwaku*) for the company and their colleagues. Other major factors included the availability of another person who takes care of the child (i.e. mostly spouses, 29.4%) or financial reasons, as the leave would mean a loss of income (22%)(MHLW 2012: 223). As in the case of Germany, the sustained influence of gender norms becomes most visible when men try

---

1 In addition to statistics published by the Japanese Ministry of Health, Labor and Welfare and several marketing research institutes/ advertising agencies, the findings in this and the next section are based on expert interviews, a content analysis of the Japanese "fathering magazine" FQ Japan and documents released by the government-backed "Ikumen Project", especially those related to the "Ikumen Company Award" and "Ikuboss Award" initiatives.

2 No updated numbers were reported for 2013.

to implement their changed attitudes (Meuser 2011: 74). The popularity of the *ikumen* phenomenon thus points at a gap between mindset and behavior. Fewer and fewer Japanese uncritically accept a "traditional" distribution of gender roles – husband as breadwinner, wife as housekeeper. The number of Japanese who "agree" or "somewhat agree" with such a division of roles fell from 60.1% in 1992 to 51.6% in 2012[3] (CAO 2012). The majority of Japanese men also agree that domestic work should be shared by husband and wife (tadaima! 2013: 8). Further, the number of men who state that they want to engage more actively with childcare and household work also rose from 47.7% in 2005 to 54.2% in 2009 (BERI 2011: 29). Men's actual participation in childcare and household tasks registers a rise as well, albeit a slow one. From 1999 to 2011 the number of fathers who bathe their children rose from 65.6% to 75.2%. Tasks that are less common among men, such as putting the child to bed (1999: 30.1%, 2011: 37.3%) or taking the child to kindergarten and picking it up again (*sōgei*, 1999: 22%, 2011: 26.7%) also show increasing levels of male involvement (Ishii-Kuntz 2013: 47). Comparing data from 2006 and 2011, Benesse observes a similar trend (BERI 2012: 7). The overall picture however is still sobering. The participation rate of Japanese fathers is very low when compared to fathers in other countries or when measured against the time Japanese women spend on housework and childcare (Holloway and Nagase 2014: 69).

Government and private initiatives

In order to close this gap between mindset and behavior, the Japanese government founded the Ikumen Project in 2010. One of the initiatives of the Ikumen Project is the *ikumen kigyō awādo* (Ikumen Company Award) which has been bestowed on businesses with exemplary father-friendly policies since autumn 2013. The award aims to promote a change in consciousness on an institutional level, encouraging Japanese companies to support fathers in their workforce in order to enable active fatherhoods in the sense of *ikumen*. In its first year, awards were granted to seven of forty-nine applicant enterprises. Grand Prizes were awarded to Tokyo-based Kao Corporation and the Southern Tohoku Kasuga Rehabilitation Hospital. Kao, a major chemical and cosmetics company, was honored for measures such as distributing an awareness pamphlet to male employees who have just become fathers, as well as their direct superiors. The pamphlet explains the company's childcare leave system, necessary formalities, case examples and experience reports of men who have taken a leave, thus promoting the use of the company's childcare leave system and

---

3   However, this is already a lot more than 41.3% in 2009.

advancing managers' understanding of the system (Ikumen Project 2013). In 2014, the award was conferred to another seven companies, the Grand Prize being awarded to the Gifu-based construction company Earth Create. In this company, where a majority of employees are men, workers who have a child that is not a high school student yet have the option to "prepone"/postpone the start/end of their working hours. One of the company policies that were lauded by the award, this guideline makes it easier for fathers to participate in their child's school life, in events such as sports day or parent's day (Ikumen Project 2014). The size of the enterprises honored by the award vary dramatically. This becomes especially evident when comparing the three recipients of the Grand Prize: Kao has 6,100 employees, the Kasuga Rehabilitation Hospital around 200 and Earth Create just 22. Employee-wise the biggest company among the awardees is the Nippon Life Insurance Company, which has 70,806 employees (Ikumen Project 2013, 2014). Father- and childcare-friendly measures taken by enterprises are often also featured in companies' CSR reports. For example, so-called sustainability reports published by the Kao Corporation include a section that addresses work-life-balance issues and presents company policies aiding employees in combining family and work. Measures supporting fathers, such as the awareness pamphlets, are explicitly listed, as are numbers of male employees who have taken a parental leave (Kao Corporation 2014). Similarly, the Earth Create homepage advertises the attention the company's work-life-balance policies have received from the media and the Ikumen Company Award. Interestingly, the pride companies seem to take in their measures targeting fathers does not just include company policies, but also extends to customer-oriented activities. In its 2010 CSR report (Akachan Honpo 2010), the childcare chain Akachan Honpo dedicates a whole page to introducing its father-oriented projects, such as the Pre-Papa Night Tour and the development of father-friendly *ikumen* goods, both of which will be discussed shortly (4.). Next to public campaigns, the desire to be perceived as a modern enterprise can thus be identified as another factor influencing companies' engagement with fathers.

Making executives childcare-aware

Recognizing that executives play a crucial role in determining the work-life-balance possibilities of their employees, *ikuboss (ikubosu)* has become another key word (Schimkowsky and Kohlbacher 2016). The term describes superiors who understand the needs of young parents and are supportive of working mothers and *ikumen* in their workforce. Calls for more *ikuboss* managers have come from both public and private actors. In line with the Ikumen Company Award, in 2014 the Ikumen Project also bestowed an Ikuboss Award for the first time. The award was granted to five *"ikubosses"*, who were honored, as in the case of a department head of a Tokyo based digital marketing company, for activities such as proposing a childcare support project to the company's management and establishing a corresponding committee. The department head was also applauded for responding to subordinates who experienced problems in balancing work and family life on a case-by-case basis. Further, the head of the safety control department of the branch of a multinational pharmaceutical company was honored for encouraging male employees to take a paternity leave, describing it as a valuable experience. Another point the manager was commended for was not judging employees who go home early as people that "do not do overtime work" *(zangyō shinai hito)* – a criticism which can imply an insufficient level of devotion to one's company or lack of solidarity with the rest of the work force – but praising them as time-efficient workers. As overtime work is often expected, employees regularly do not feel able to go home as long as the majority of their collogues remain or the current work project is unfinished, even if they have already finished their own work (Fathering Japan 2014a). As this leads to longer working hours, it shortens the time parents spend with their children on working days.

The Ikumen Project is not the only actor that is supporting and promoting childcare-minded managers. In Gunma prefecture, public bodies already began in 2012 to host *ikuboss* training seminars that aim to change executives' way of thinking *(kigyō toppu no ishikikaikaku)*. Hiroshima prefecture supports an Ikumen Company Alliance *(ikumenkigyō dōmei)* that, similarly to the training seminars in Gunma, aims to change the views and attitudes of managers. The alliance further strives to encourage male employees to take a childcare leave and introduce *ikumen*-supporting company policies and initiatives to other enterprises in the prefecture (Hiroshima Prefecture 2014). Aichi prefecture created an *ikumen* support website. While so far contents on this website still have to be considered as sparse, it features a list of "five lessons for companies that support *ikumen* and *ikuboss*" that includes slogans such as "*ikubosses* vitalize the workplace!" or "work-life-balance is an important management strategy!" (Aichi Prefecture 2015).

The crucial role executives play for the development of a childcare friendly society is emphasized by private bodies as well. An example of this is the 2006-founded NPO *Fathering Japan.* Aiming to raise the numbers of "smiling" fathers, the NPO has become a significant actor in Japan's discussion of fatherhood in the recent years. In the announcement of its Ikuboss Project, Fathering Japan reports that, according to the questionnaires the NPO had fathers fill out after participating in seminars or workshops, an overwhelming number of responses said: "Parental leave? I can't even take a paid holiday when something is up with the children!" or "Please do something about my stubborn boss". While the NPO feels that the importance of work-life-balance has reached many fathers, it considers the way of thinking of managers in their 40s and 50s as a "bottleneck" hindering involved fathers and concludes: "if there were more *ikubosses,* society would change"(Fathering Japan 2014a). With the start of the project in March 2014, Fathering Japan added seminars for employers to its activities. In December 2014, the NPO founded the Ikuboss Company Alliance *(ikubosu kigyō dōmei)* together with eleven businesses, including All Nippon Airways and the Mizuho Financial Group. The primary object of the alliance is to create a network of companies that allows businesses to share knowledge and introduce childcare-related company policies to each other. Together with Fathering Japan, the alliance is also supposed to host events for training and educating new *ikubosses,* and, as an association of child-care-friendly companies, send a message to society (Fathering Japan 2014b, 2015). Companies clearly seem interested in the project: Since January 2015, it was joined by major Japanese companies such as Sony, Kao and Shiseido, and has, with the addition of Panasonic in March 2016, grown to fifty-nine members. At the end of July 2015, Fathering Japan added a whole branch to the alliance, namely the Ikuboss Company Alliance for Small and Medium Enterprises *(ikubosu chūshōkigyō dōmei)*, which as of writing includes thirty-seven companies from all over Japan (Fathering Japan 2015; Schimkowsky and Kohlbacher 2016). Being covered by established media such as the Yomiuri and Mainichi Shimbun, TV Tokyo, Bloomberg and the national broadcaster NHK, the NPO's Ikuboss project receives significant attention.

So far, we have focused on public and private campaigns that not only aim at increasing the numbers of *ikumen,* but, recognizing the work environment as a major factor obstructing fathers' involvement in childcare, pay special attention to the role of companies and executives. This focus on public campaigns is shared by other studies on Japanese fathers (Holloway and Nagase 2014; Rebick 2006; Rebick and Takenaka 2006). As a record of government initiatives, these studies help view the emergence of new fathers against the historical background of political measures trying to influence Japanese practices of family, work and gender. However, focusing only on such measures does not suffice, as the *ikumen* phenomenon and trend to more involved fathering is not singlehandedly created and maintained by government initiatives and public campaigns. Instead, it is supported by a wider "father culture" (*chichioya bunka,* Ishii-Kuntz 2013: 223). While examples of such a culture can be found in the trope of "child rearing men" in current Japanese television series (At Home Dad (2004), Stepfather Step (2012), Oh, My Dad!! (2013)) and mangas (Usagi Drop (2005-2011), Ikumen! (2011-)), we now want to shift our attention to the role of an *ikumen* market and the consumer side of the phenomenon. We will thus illustrate that companies not only interact with involved fathers through company policies but, through *ikumen* goods and marketing initiatives, also engage with fathers as customers and consumers.

4. Fathers as consumers: ikumen goods and company initiatives

Mentioning the business potential of *ikumen,* Ishii-Kuntz (2013: 57) brings up the case of *ikumen* goods. As our analysis of products presented as *ikumen goods* in the Japanese media has shown, these are mostly new versions of already established products that are modified to be more father-friendly. Two major modification strategies can be identified: facilitation of product use, and design adjustments to conform to gender norms. The first strategy is deployed to make the product usable by fathers on a basic, physiological level. Fathers who want to cut their children's fingernails might encounter the unexpected problem that children's nail scissors are designed with mothers as primary users in mind, which results in the scissors' holes being too small for men's fingers. The nail scissors made by Akachan Honpo's in-house brand *papa mo OK (Also for Daddy)* identified this problem and made the holes bigger. The second strategy is to increase the product's appeal for men. For example, bicycles made for transporting small children (to kindergarten, etc.) increasingly come in dark colors, and baby slings are produced in a gender neutral design – or even in a Japan-exclusive camouflage design, as in the case of the US-American Original Baby Carrier. In the majority of cases, both strategies are combined. Buggies are experiencing a breakaway from colorful, lightweight models to unisex models with gender-neutral colors and adjustable handle height. Adjusting the product design thus enables companies to extend their consumer group to include fathers. A more comprehensive definition of the *ikumen* market can be attempted through a content analysis of the self-titled *ikumen* journal *FQ Japan*. While articles advertised on the magazine's cover include reports on shared father-child activities such as father-child-trips *(fushitabi)*, articles about the lifestyle of modern dads and reviews of essential *ikumen* goods such as strollers or children seats, and thus promise diverse magazine contents, product-related articles prove to be the most dominant form of content inside the magazine. Articles with an explicit focus on consumer items, published in categories with titles such as *Top Gear Selection* or *What's New,* amount to an average of 48.94% (excluding advertisements: 37.75%) of the magazine's contents. Still, there is no even split of product-focused and content-focused (i.e. articles giving fathering advice or commenting on related topics) articles in the magazine. Embedded product information, such as info boxes with product suggestions, are found in about half of all content-focused articles. For example, an article recommending bug-catching as a father-child activity is complemented with an info box listing the product details of hats and outdoor shoes. Comprehensive content-focused feature articles advertised on the magazine cover are regularly accompanied by a related product special that spans multiple pages. A number of articles in the 2013 Summer issue of *FQ* which presented outdoor activities such as camping as a male domain of parenting, was supplemented by an extensive list of relevant outdoor products such as a trekking backpack with built-in baby carrier or a feeding bottle made of stainless steel (FQ JAPAN 06.2013: 30–33). Thus, *FQ Japan* is not only itself an example of a consumer item spawned by the *ikumen* phenomenon, but its editorial focus on consumer recommendations also offers a possible definition of the *ikumen* market. Emblematic *ikumen* goods such as the ones mentioned above feature prominently in this. The cover of the magazine regularly tries to lure readers in with reviews of essential childcare products, such as devises for the transport of babies (i.e. buggies or baby slings), which take up 22.76% of all product-focused articles. However, the scope of product types featured in *FQ* is much wider and more diverse. Next to children's goods such as toys (16.22%) and children's clothes (11.65%) there are also articles about household items such as air purifiers (3.73%) or outdoor products (3.78%). The *ikumen* phenomenon and the *ikumen* market are not limited to parenting practices and accessories. Instead, they connect to a greater ideal of masculinity – fathers are supposed to go on trips with their family (outdoor goods, travel reports), protect their families (air purifier, safe groceries) and have style (fashion, luxury articles). This wide scope of fathers' expected consumer behavior is mirrored in advertisements placed in *FQ*, only 24.78% of which were for children's and childcare goods. This is only slightly more than advertisements for cars (20.7%), and advertisements for men's clothing and shoes (16.56%), which occupy a significant percentage as well. Furthermore, a full-page advertisement promoting smoking cessation products was also regularly found in the 2013 volume. Accordingly, the *ikumen* market not only consists of childcare goods for men but of products from diverse industries that are supposed to facilitate an involved and responsible fatherhood, and the fulfillment of dominant ideals of masculinity. An *ikumen* market thus should not be seen as limited to a set of products for child-caring fathers, but as a market in which the identity as an involved father emerges as a crucial motivation for consumption. Accordingly, *FQ Japan* not only reports on stereotypical *ikumen* goods but notifies its readers about products from different industries and explains which products are relevant for fathers and why. Fatherhood is declared the basis for consumption decisions (FQ JAPAN 01.2013: 70, 06.2013: 83, own translation):

> *When children are born the man becomes a father – but this does not mean that he stops being a man. The value system with which we look at things stays fundamentally the same. Still, there is change: whatever one does and whatever one sees, the child comes to mind. If this is the case, why not follow this direction? Let's look at all items from the perspective of (the) child(-raising)! In doing so, we might discover interesting things we did not see before.*

But how active are fathers as customers? To discuss this, we shift our attention to fathers' participation in consumption decisions. This has to be considered as especially low when it comes to buying childcare goods. A Hakuhōdō survey showed in 2012 that in 95.6% of the questioned couples, it is mainly the mother who decides on the purchase of childcare goods, with only 2% of fathers participating in purchase decisions. Men showed much higher levels of involvement when buying television sets (82%), cars (81.2%) or cameras (72.1%). Thus, the majority of consumption decisions are still made in accordance with dominant conceptions of gender roles (Hakuhōdō 2013). A Benesse survey conducted among Japanese fathers in Tokyo in 2009 revealed a similar trend. In about 80% of the questioned families, the wives have the final word when buying children's clothes (81%), and household- and childcare articles (79.4%) (BERI 2011: 105–107). Mothers are also dominant when choosing teaching materials (62.4%), children's books (61.1%) and extracurricular education and training activities (48.2%). However, BERI's survey also points at consumption decisions that are more likely to receive fathers' attention. 63.9% of the questioned parents made joint decisions when it came to toys, and in 10.2% of all cases this decision was primarily made by the father. With a result of 29.6% (overall involvement: 68.7%), this number is even higher when purchasing video games. Japanese fathers can thus be seen as being more likely to be involved in purchases of technical products. This is also visible in a total participation rate of 57.2% when buying strollers. Interestingly, identifying oneself as *ikumen* seems to be correlated with the probability of being involved in purchasing child-related products. A survey by ADK revealed that mothers are more likely to discuss purchase decisions regarding children's clothing and toys when their partner identifies as *ikumen* (53%), compared to partners who reject identification with the term (39%) (ADK Kids Marketing Research Institute 2013: 34). A further factor that has to be considered is the Japanese custom of *kozukai* which is practiced in over 70% of all married couples (ADK Kids Marketing Research Institute 2013: 32). According to this custom, domestic revenue is administrated by the wife, who provides her husband with a certain allowance *(kozukai)* for expenses such as lunch and after-work drinking with colleagues. Statistics show that the monthly allowance is lower for fathers (34.963 JPY) than for the average of all *kozukai* recipients (39.572 JPY; Shinsei Bank 2014: 29). On the other hand, engaging in shared father-child activities – such as going to see a baseball game – authorizes fathers to solicit additional funds from their wives, leading to a bigger available budget for involved fathers (Interview with Hakuhōdō Research Staff, June 2013). Involved fatherhood practice can thus be expected to increase the motivation *and* the ability to engage in child-related consumption behavior.

Accordingly, involved fathers are increasingly seen as potential customers by companies. Next to special products for fathers, companies' avid interest in gaining fathers as customers is evident from customer-generating and customer-binding company initiatives. For example, *FQ Japan* is involved in a range of cooperative activities with other companies, which include activities such as hosting *ikumen* events. The best example for this is the *ikumen* festival *(ikufes)*, which attracted over 8000 visitors to Odaiba, Tokyo when it was held for a successive fourth time in September 2013. Next to an extensive workshop program with courses covering topics from baby yoga to toilet training, the *ikufes* also included celebrity appearances and booths by fifty-three companies from the children and childcare goods industry (FQ JAPAN 12.2013: 54–57). Another example is the childcare goods chain Akachan Honpo, which started to offer a Pre-Papa Night Tour in stores all over Japan in 2010. At each of the regularly held events, a group of 5–8 men who pre-register online is shown around the store by employees, and taught basic information about childcare goods, such as differences between several types of diapers. After becoming a weekly event in all stores of the chain nationwide, the tour was conducted about 3000 times between June 2014 and February 2015, up from 365 times in 2013. The event's title derives from it being held in the evening, often from 7 to 8 p.m., to allow (soon-to-be) fathers to participate after work (Akachan Honpo 2014). While the possibilities of fathering practices are often determined by men's work duties, companies, as market actors, are aware of these limitations and adjust their marketing activities to reach working fathers.

However, just as the *ikumen* market cannot be reduced to childcare goods, companies hosting father-/*ikumen*-targeting events are not limited to publishers of fathering magazines and businesses specializing in childcare goods. Department stores such as those of the chains Isetan, Hankyu and Takashimaya are regular venues for photo shoots held in cooperation with *FQ Japan*. Those photographed, customers of the store, are mostly young families. A selection of photographs is later published in *FQ* (FQ JAPAN 09.2013: 87, 90–97). Sometimes, the photo shoots are given a special theme. For example, during a photo shoot in the Hankyu department store in Nishinomiya, which was held as part of a local "parenting fair", families were photographed together with self-designed *ikumen sengen* posters (*ikumen* declaration) which carried slogans such as "papa is the best *ikumen*" *(papa ha ikumen no.1)*. Another example is an event organized by the department store chain Takashimaya, during which participating *ikumen* were given the chance to discuss father-friendly products with Fathering Japan founder Andō Tetsuya. With the help of the NPO, Takashimaya also created a website listing items that are "easy to use by both men and women". The product recommendations were accompanied by reviews written by anonymous fathers and were each marked with an *ikumen osusume* (recommendation for *ikumen*) logo, thus actively linking *ikumen* identity and consumer role. The department store chain also designed a logo in which the first two letters of the word *ikumen* resemble a man who is pushing a shopping cart (or a stroller?), thus further emphasizing the links between father identity and consumer role (Illustration 1).

The desire to target fathers as customers is also visible in evoking images of involved fathering in branding and advertisement strategies. Shiseido decided in 2006 to demarcate its Super Mild Shampoo, first sold in 1988, from the competition through rebranding it as a family-friendly product (Senden Kaigi 15.08.2012). Drawing on the public discussion of changing father ideals, Shiseido created *papa furo* (Bathing with Daddy), thereby striving to position the product as a crucial element of a Japanese family ritual – father and offspring taking a bath together. Not only are all shampoo bottles furnished with a *papa furo* sticker but cooperation with a creative agency also led to the design of a *papa furo* song and *papa furo* cards. These illustrated collector cards, available with the product or as a download on the product homepage, depict a number of activities such as soaping each other's backs or bathtub karaoke and thusly encourage father-child-bonding in the bath (Illustration 2).

Illustration 1: *Ikumen* logo of the Takashimaya department store chain

Source: ƒ ƒ•Š‹ ƒ›ƒ ƒ ƒ•Š‹ ƒ›ƒ Takashimaya Co., Ltd.

Illustration 2: Downloadable papa furo collector cards

Source: Shiseido Co., Ltd.

2011 TV advertisements for Nissan and Toyota cars also featured pictures of involved fathering (Ishii-Kuntz 2013: 60). While the presentation of family cars was traditionally mainly directed at women and focused on the good drivability of the car, the car is now depicted as a tool for a more diverse set of family practices. The use of *ikumen* ideals in advertisements shows that a culture of involved fathering has taken root in contemporary Japan (Ishii-Kuntz 2013: 61). Advertising campaigns and events hosted by recognized institutions such as department store chains can further be seen as examples of sanctioning acts that are offering socio-cultural legitimacy to involved fathers, thus improving the public perception of fathers who want to prioritize family over work (Ishii-Kuntz 2013: 62). Accordingly, companies not only have the potential to strengthen the position of involved fathers in their workforce, but also in wider society.

5. Conclusion

In recent years, fatherhood has become a topic of intense public discussion in Japan. While absent fathers who devote most of their time to their work were once the norm, today more and more fathers express the will to be more involved with their families. However, for a majority of Japanese men, this desire is thwarted by work-related concerns. Humberd, Ladge and Harrington's (2015) argument that work environment and support by direct superiors are crucial in determining fathers' possibilities of childcare and parenting involvement can thus be seen as applicable in the Japanese case. Increasingly, the importance of organizational culture is being recognized by public and private bodies. Aiming to rejuvenate Japan's childcare culture and empower working fathers, they have started several initiatives. The Ikumen Company Award and the Ikuboss Award are commending companies' attempts to modernize their approach to working fathers. In 2015, enterprises of all sizes have begun to implement policies advancing fathers' abilities to integrate family and work life. Furthermore, campaigns such as the Ikuboss Project help create company networks that can be used to share knowledge related to relevant organizational policies. Still, these very initiatives also illustrate the difficulties fathers encounter in their work life: A manager being lauded for not pressuring staff into overtime work in a national contest is a very clear indicator of the importance awarded to family and private life in Japanese companies.

Companies' attention to *ikumen* is not limited to fathers in their workforce. Instead, it also extends to involved fathers in wider society, who are considered as an important new group of customers. More likely to engage in a wide range of consumption activities, they are targeted as consumers with new products, marketing campaigns and company events.

In conclusion, we find that companies in Japan are increasingly turning to involved fathers in and outside of their workforce. Next to the public conversation about ideal fatherhood practices triggered by the *ikumen* phenomenon, this shift has been encouraged by government initiatives on both national and prefectural levels as well as by private campaigns. Further, it is also influenced by companies' business interests and their desire to be perceived as a modern company. Likely to continue, this trend will enhance working fathers' options to engage in parenting activities. Additionally, through offering socio-cultural legitimacy to involved fathers in general, these company initiatives could also contribute to the public recognition of fathers involved in childcare.

References

ADK Kids Marketing Research Institute (2013) *ADK Chichioya Shōhi Shiryō [Father and Consumption', ADK internal documents]*: ADK

Aichi Prefecture (2015) Ikumen ōen saito [Ikumen support website], Available at: http://famifure.pref.aichi.jp/ikumen/kokoroe/. Accessed August 9, 2015

Akachan Honpo. (2010) 2010 nen CSR katsudō torikumi repōto [2010 CSR Report]. Available at: http://www.akachan.jp/company/csr/pdf/2010/csr 2010_01.pdf. Accessed August 9, 2015

――― (2014) 2014 nen CSR katsudō torikumi repōto [2014 CSR Report], http://www.akachan.jp/company/csr/pdf/2014/csr2014.pdf. Accessed August 9, 2015

BERI (Benesse Educational Research Institute) (2011) *Di 2 Kai Nyūyōji no Chichioya ni Tsuite no Chōsa Hōkokusho [Report about the Second Survey of Fathers of Infants and Babies]*. Tokyo: Benesse Corporation

――― (2012) *Di 2 Kai Ninshin Shussan Kosodate Kihonchōsa 2006–2011 Sokuhōban [Second Survey about Pregnancy, Birth and Childcare 2006–2011]*. Tokyo: Benesse Corporation

Bettany, S. M., Kerrane, B. and Hogg, M. K. (2014) 'The Material-Semiotics of Fatherhood: The Co-Emergence of Technology and Contemporary Fatherhood'. *Journal of Business Research,* 67, pp. 1544–1551

CAO (Cabinet Office) (2012) Danjo Kyōdō Sankaku Shakai ni Kan Suru Yoron Chōsa [Public Opinion Poll Regarding the Gender-Equal Society]. Available at: http://survey.gov-online.go.jp/h24/h24-danjo/index.html. Accessed March 22, 2015

Coskuner-Balli, G, and Thompson, C. J. (2013) 'The Status Costs of Subordinate Cultural Capital: At-Home Fathers' Collective Pursuit of Cultural Legitimacy through Capitalizing Consumption Practices'. *Journal of Consumer Research,* 40 (1) pp. 19–41

Coulmas, F. (2007) *Population Decline and Ageing in Japan – The Social Consequences.* London, New York: Routledge

Duyvendak, J. W. and Stavenuiter, M. (eds.) (2004) *Working Fathers, Caring Men: Reconciliation of working life and family life.* The Hague: Ministry of Social Affairs and Employment

Eerola, P. and Huttunen, J. (2011) 'Metanarrative of the "New Father" and Narratives of Young Finnish First-Time Fathers', *Fathering: A Journal of Theory, Research, and Practice about Men as Fathers,* 9 (3) pp. 211–231

Fathering Japan (2014a) Ikuboss Project, http://fathering.jp/ikuboss/. Accessed August 9, 2015.

―――. 2014b, Ikubosu kigyō dōmei hassoku! [Ikumen Company Allianced founded]. Available at: http://ikuboss.com/ikuboss-alliance.html. Accessed August 9, 2015

――― (2015) Ikubosu chūshō kigyō dōmei wo setsuritsu shimasu! [Establishment of the Ikuboss Company Alliance for Small and Medium Enterprises]. Available at: http://ikuboss.com/ikuboss-chusho-alliance.html. Accessed August 9, 2015

FQ JAPAN. 01.2013. *Spring Issue* (2013/26)

———. 06.2013. *Summer Issue* (2013/27)

———. 09.2013. *Autumn Issue* (2013/28)

———. 12.2013. *Winter Issue* (2013/29)

Hakuhōdō (2013) Kosodate Josei, Kazoku no Kizuna ya Mirai Jūshi [Child-Rearing Women Put Special Focus on Family Bonds and the Future]. Available at: www.hakuhodo.co.jp/archives/reporttopics/10061. Accessed March 22, 2015

Hiroshima Prefecture (2014) Ikumen kigyō dōmei to ha [What is the Ikumen Company Alliance?]. Available at: http://www.pref.hiroshima.lg.jp/site/ikumen/about.html. Accessed August 9, 2015.

Holloway, Susan D. and Ayumi Nagase. 2014. 'Child Rearing in Japan'. In *Parenting Across Cultures,* ed. Helaine Selin. Dordrecht: Springer Netherlands: 59–76

Hook, J. L. and Wolfe, C. M. (2012) 'New Fathers?: Residential Fathers' Time With Children in Four Countries', *Journal of Family Issues*, 33 (4) pp. 415–450

Humberd, B., Ladge, J. J. and Harrington, B. (2015) 'The "New" Dad: Navigating Fathering Identity Within Organizational Contexts'. *Journal of Business and Psychology*, 30 (2) pp. 249–266

Ikumen Project (2013) Ikumen kigyō awādo 2013. Jushō kigyō no torikumi [Ikumen Company Award 2013. Initiatives of winning companies]. Accessed August 9, 2015

———(2014) Ikumen kigyō awādo 2014. Jushō kigyō no torikumiIkumen kigyō awādo 2013. Jushō kigyō no torikumi [Ikumen Company Award 2014. Initiatives of winning companies]. Available at: https://ikumen-project.jp/pdf/award_cases_2014.pdf. Accessed August 9, 2015

Ishii-Kuntz, Masako (1992) 'Are Japanese Families Fatherless?', *Sociology and Social Research,* 76, pp. 105–110

———(1994) 'Paternal Involvement and Perception Toward Fathers' Roles:: A Comparison Between Japan and the United States', *Journal of Family Issues,* 15 (1) pp. 30–48

———(2013) *Ikumen Genshō no Shakaigaku. The Sociology of Child-Rearing Dads.* Tokyo: Minerva Shobō

Kao Corporation (2014) Sustainability Report 2014. Available at: http://www.kao.com/jp/corp_csr/reports_01_10.html. Accessed August 9, 2015

Kingston, Jeff (2012) *Contemporary Japan. History, Politics, and Social Change since the 1980s.* Wiley-Blackwell: Oxford

Kohlbacher, F. and Mizukoshi, K. (2013) 'Papa Shōhi no Kōsatsu. Pure Papa no Aidentiti no Kōchiku.: [Inquiry into father's consumption. Identity construction of becoming fathers]', 132, pp. 1–13

Kohlbacher, F. and Schimkowsky, C. (2014) 'The Rise of Modern Dads: Support from Government, Media and Firms'. *BCCJ ACUMEN, Magazine of the British Chamber of Commerce in Japan,* (September): 30–31

Makino, K., Watanabe, H., Funabashi, K. and Nakano, H. (2010) *Kokusai Hikaku ni Miru Sekai no Kazoku to Kosodate [International comparison of Family and Child-rearing].* Kyoto: Minerva Shobō

Marsiglio, W., Amato, P., Day, R. D. and Lamb, M. E. (2000) 'Scholarship on Fatherhood in the 1990s and Beyond'. *Journal of Marriage and Family,* 62(4), pp. 1173–1191

Marsiglio, W. and Roy, K. (2012) *Nurturing dads: Social initiatives for contemporary fatherhood.* New York: Russell Sage

Meuser, M. (2011) 'Die Entdeckung der "neuen Väter" [The Discovery of "New Fathers"]', in: Hahn, K. and Koppetsch, C. (eds) *Soziologie des Privaten,* ed. Wiesbaden: VS Verlag für Sozialwissenschaften, pp. 71–82

MHLW (Ministry of Health, Labor and Welfare) (2012) *Heisei 23 Ikuji Kyūgyō Seido nado ni Kan suru Jittai Hāku no tame no Chōsa Kenkyū Jigyō [2011 Survey about the true understanding of parental leave and other care systems]*

———(2013) *Heisei 24 Nendo Koyō Kintō Kihon Chōsa no Gaikyō [2013 Survey regarding equality at the workplace – general tendencies]*

———(2014) *Heisei 25 Nendo Koyō Kintō Kihon Chōsa no Gaikyō [2014 Survey regarding equality at the workplace – general tendencies]*

Minahan, S. and Huddleston, P. (2013) 'Shopping with my Mother: Reminiscences of Adult Daughters'. *International Journal of Consumer Studies,* 37(4) pp. 373–378

Mizukoshi, K., Kohlbacher, F. and Schimkowsky, C. (2016) 'Japan's *ikumen* discourse: macro and micro perspectives on modern fatherhood'. *Japan Forum,* 28(2) pp. 212–232

Nakatani, A. (2006) 'The Emergence of 'Nurturing Fathers': Discourses and Practices of Fatherhood in Contemporary Japan', in: Rebick, R. and Takenaka, A. (eds.) *The Changing Japanese Family.* London: Routledge: 94–108

Nakazawa, J. and Shwalb, D. W. (2013) 'Fathering in Japan: Entering an Era of Involvement with Children'. In *Fathers in Cultural Context,* ed. David W. Shwalb, Barbara J. Shwalb and Michael E. Lamb. New York: Psychology Press, pp. 42–67

North, S. (2009) 'Negotiating What's 'Natural': Persistent Domestic Gender Role Inequality in Japan'. *Social Science Japan Journal,* 12(1) pp. 23–44

Rebick, M. (2006) 'Changes in the Workplace and their Impact on the Family', in: Rebick, R. and Takenaka, A. (eds.) *The Changing Japanese Family.* London: Routledge, pp. 75–93

Rebick, R. and Takenaka, A. (eds.) (2006) *The Changing Japanese Family.* London: Routledge

Schimkowsky, C. and Kohlbacher, F. (2016) 'Better deal at work for parents: Support for new HR policies'. *BCCJ ACUMEN, Magazine of the British Chamber of Commerce in Japan,* (April), pp. 28–29

Senden Kaigi (2012). 'Ikumen Shijō. Chūmoku Māketto Kenkyūkai Di 4 Kai: [Ikumen Market. 4. "Paying attention to markets" Workshop.]', 15.08.2012 (843) pp. 85–94

Shinsei Bank (2014) *2014 Nen Sararīman no Okozukai Chōsa [Salariman Pocketmoney Survey 2014].*

tadaima! 2013. *Kaji Shiea Hakusho [White Book about the Sharing of Domestic Chores].* Tôkyô: tadaima!

Taga, F. (2011) *Yuragu Sararīman Seikatsu [Salariman Lives becoming unstable].* Tôkyô: Minerva Shobô.

Yasuike, Akiko. 2011. 'The Impact of Japanese Corporate Transnationalism on Men's Involvement in Family Life and Relationships', *Journal of Family Issues,* 32(12) pp. 1700–1725

Yeung, W-J. J. (2013) 'Asian Fatherhood', *Journal of Family Issues,* 34(2) pp. 141–158

Yoshida, A. (2012) 'Dads Who Do Diapers: Factors Affecting Care of Young Children by Fathers', *Journal of Family Issues,* 33(4) pp. 451–477

4. Policies and Politics of Fatherhood

Constructing Male Employees as Carers Through the Norwegian Fathers' Quota

Elin Kvande and Berit Brandth

1. Introduction

In this chapter we take as our point of departure the classic article by Joan Acker: *Hierarchies, Jobs, Bodies: A theory of gendered organizations* (Acker 1990). She contributes to developing an understanding of gendered structures and processes in organizations and she discusses how working life's apparently gender-neutral ideas and routines build on unwritten implicit ideas about gender. Organizations seek employees without particular gender or ethnic backgrounds; abstract workers in a neutral hierarchy. Terms such as "worker", "leader" or "manager" are abstract constructions until filled with people. The physical absence of the human body highlights the abstraction in the construction. This is also why we understand the worker as just a worker, without acknowledging for instance that a worker is often also a parent. These abstract workers are without commitments and obligations that might disrupt their concentration on work. The assumption is also that there is "someone else" to take care of necessary reproduction work.

This is why the introduction of a special non-transferable quota for fathers in the Norwegian parental leave system represents a rupture with the disembodied thinking about gender in organizations (Kvande 2009). Firstly because it is a legitimization of the fact that employees have bodies which produce babies. Secondly because it focuses explicitly on embodying male employees as carers by giving them leave from work for this reason.

The father's quota has existed since 1993 and has become a mature institution in Norway. The great majority of fathers use their leave, and it is widely supported by parents (Lappegård and Bringedal 2013). In this chapter we will explore how the norms in working life have been affected by the introduction of the father's quota. How has the embodying of male employees as carers by this type of welfare state provision affected the thinking in work organizations? Do fathers experience that their long periods of leave are accepted or opposed by their work organizations? The chapter will start with a review of the development of the father's quota in the Norwegian parental leave system, focusing on how the principles of individualization have been strengthened in order to get more fathers to use the father's quota. We then discuss the research which has been done in the field of work and father's uptake of parental leave. In our empirical analyzes we firstly explore how fathers using their father's quota are received in different work organizations. Secondly we explore how the design elements of the father's quota function in relation to work.

2. Research and theory

2.1 Embodying male employees

When the special quota for fathers was introduced as part of the Norwegian parental leave system the explicit aim was to encourage gender equality in working life and caring (St.meld. 4, 1988–89). Through the introduction of the father's quota, male employees are given the right and duty to provide care in the child's first year of life (NOU 1995:27). Since its introduction the father's quota has been adjusted several times in order to strengthen fathers' rights in this field, building on the principles of individualization, the main component being that it is statutory and non-transferable – which means leave days are lost if not used. The fathers also receive full compensation of their individual wages.

Moves toward increased individualization of leave rights for fathers have also taken place through other changes implemented over the years. First, the quota has been lengthened from the original four weeks (1993) to ten weeks (2015), hence enabling men to stay home longer and women to return to work earlier. Second, the right to leave has been expanded to make more fathers eligible, e.g. by defining participation in the introductory program for immigrants and disability benefits as equivalent to paid employment. Whereas the father's rights to the quota were initially dependent on the mother's working hours, and excluded fathers when the mothers worked less than fifty percent, the rules now only demand her to be employed during six of the last ten weeks before birth. Thus from 2010, the eligibility rules for the father's quota have been made less dependent on the mother's employment. Making more fathers eligible can be seen as a development towards greater universality.

Parental leave given to the family without reserving an individualized right for fathers, does not have the same effect on constructing male employees as carers. When parental leave is a family-based entitlement, it has been argued that it *enables* gender equality by making it easier for men to engage in caregiving and women to combine employment with having children. On the other hand, it is only individual entitlements that *promote* gender equality in sharing child care according to Brighthouse and Wright (2008).

The fathers' quota in the Norwegian parental leave system is an example of this type of individual entitlement. Research based on the Nordic experience has documented that ensuring parental leave rights to individuals, rather than to families, is more effective when it comes to getting fathers to take leave (Duvander and Lammi Taskula 2011; Brandth and Kvande 2001, 2012; Kvande and Brandth 2016; Haas and Rostgaard 2011; Eydal and Gislason 2013). The presence of the father's quota in Nordic countries has had a very positive effect on fathers' leave take-up, and has been described as a success in involving fathers in caring for their young babies (Brandth and Kvande 2013; Haas and Rostgaard 2011).

In the case of Norway the use of the father's quota over the years shows that it has worked as a measure to get fathers to take parental leave. Family-based rights which encourage voluntary sharing between mothers and fathers has not had the same effect on father's take-up. After the father's quota was introduced, there was a dramatic increase in the proportion of fathers who took leave, from four percent in 1993 to eigthy five percent in 2000 (Brandth and Kvande 2013). Over the past decade, the take-up rate has stabilized at the ninety percent plus level. Survey data shows that as the available length has increased, fathers have taken leave corresponding to what is available (Grambo and Myklebø 2009). It is estimated that fathers take eigtheen percent of the total available parental leave days (NOU 2012:15).

2.2 Hindrances and opportunities at work

In Nordic research on the relationship between parental leave and work, there has been two strands of research; one has emphasized how workplaces and organizational cultures represent obstacles for fathers when it comes to being home doing care work. Taking leave may have long-term negative effects on men's careers, particularly for managers and elite professionals in which the career logic is strong (Allart, Haas and Hwang 2007; Halrynjo and Lyng 2013). Men's fear of being replaceable at work, as well as in terms of masculine identity being tied to work, have been described as hindrances on the individual level. Low take-up of parental leave among men has been explained insofar as they find it difficult to be absent from work (Brandth and Kvande 2001; Haas, Allart and Hwang 2002). Difficulties arranging at work may keep fathers from taking leave (Lammi-Taskula 2007). If the leave is associated with high costs for the workplace, and if their co-workers are seriously affected by the leave, fathers are also reported to take shorter parental leave (Bygren and Duvander 2006).

Men's use of parental leave is further found to be seriously affected by cultural factors at the organizational level, such as support from employers and work group norms (Haas and Hwang 2009). Fathers working in particularly male-dominated areas seem to meet the least positive attitudes (Almqvist and Dahlgren 2013). As a result, work demands and informal norms at work may oblige employees to minimize family commitments in order to not be regarded as uncommitted employees. Men have tended to feel less entitled than women in asserting family needs because this is less in accordance with gender expectations at work (Lewis 1997: 15).

In Denmark, there is no statutory, earmarked leave for fathers as in Norway, so fathers have to share the voluntary/family entitled leave with the mother. In addition to this legislated family entitlement, collective agreements and companies may offer fathers some weeks of income-compensated leave as part of their family-friendly policy. This results in Danish fathers having various leave rights. A study by Bloksgaard (2013) reports serious difficulties for fathers in negotiating optional leave with employers. Workplace culture and norms may hinder their very attempts at negotiations in fear of sanctioning. Bloksgaard attributes weak norms for parental leave use by men to the lack of statutory leave.

A second strand of research claims that there may not be such serious hindrances in work organizations after all. It has been argued that men are met with positive attitudes when taking parental leave to a greater extent than women, and that this may be seen in connection with the strong support for gender equality in the Nordic countries (Bekkengen 2002). A Finnish study also finds that attitudes toward men's paternity leave are predominantly positive, as only ten percent of fathers who take paternity leave get negative reactions from colleagues and managers (Lammi-Taskula 2007: 135). The study reports no difference between public and private sectors in this respect. Paternity leave in Finland is short, and it may therefore be easier to organize than a longer leave.

Several workplace aspects that stimulate fathers' use of leave are stressed in a study of men's parental leave use in four companies in Denmark (Olsen 2005). These are, for example, a modern, family-friendly management, role-models among colleagues who are also fathers, and organization of the work so that the individual father becomes less indispensable. In Swedish companies Haas and Hwang (2009) find that corporate support for fathers taking parental leave has increased considerably. They attribute this to the larger cultural environment and institutions in which the companies are embedded, including a father's quota which was introduced in Sweden in 1995 as part of the parental leave system.

Because the father's quota has existed for over twenty years in Norway, it seems to be well-known, and as stated the great majority of Norwegian fathers use all or part of the quota. Against this background, we will explore how fathers experience the way the father's quota works in relation to their different workplaces.

3. Data

The analysis in this chapter is based on a project, in which thirty-seven cohabiting or married heterosexual fathers who had been home on leave with the father's quota were interviewed, mainly in 2012 and 2013. The criteria for selection were that they had become fathers after the father's quota was extended to ten weeks in 2009. The fathers were recruited by contact with a university and various other firms, in addition to snowballing. After establishing contact with the potential respondents, we sent them information about the study and made interview appointments. The interviews were semi-structured, lasted from one to two hours, and for the most part the fathers were interviewed in their homes. At the time of the interview, their leave experiences were quite recent. Most fathers normally take their leave after the mother, i.e. starting when the child is from nine to twelve months old, and at the time of the interview the oldest child was two and a half years old. The quotations used in this chapter have been translated from Norwegian to English by the authors, and all the respondents are given pseudonyms to keep their identities anonymous.

As has become common in interview studies, people with a higher education more easily accept being interviewed, so an extra effort was put into finding interviewees with lower educational backgrounds. This was only a partial success, as two thirds of the sample have higher education. The occupational composition of the sample is, however, varied. Considering the Norwegian eligibility rules, in which the right to parental leave is earned through employment, the fathers and mothers had been permanently employed previous to the birth of the child. A majority of the sample was employed in private companies, and 10% were self-employed. All the fathers were employed full time, and none held precarious or temporary work. Most of the fathers were in their thirties, the age range being between 27 and 43 years. About a third of the sample were originally from another country, mostly European countries.

4. General acceptance from employers and managers

In this section we will explore how fathers' involvement in childcare is received in work organizations, by analyzing workplace attitudes when fathers want to make use of the father's quota.

None of the fathers in the sample had experienced any problems with their employers when taking their leave. Martin, who worked as an architect, explained how he experienced applying for parental leave for sixteen weeks at his workplace:

> I just asked, how do we do this in practice? Should I send in the paperwork or should you do it? I didn't feel that I had to negotiate about this. I knew that it was a right I had, and I just informed them (employer) quite early about when I planned to take leave. Because we are so few people working in this office, we need a bit of organizing when one of us is on leave a few months, so I let them know as soon as I could. That was that! There were no negative reactions.

Fathers taking leave has become common at Martin's work organization. His story illustrates that there were no negotiations or negative reactions. He just informed the employer about his plans, and this was accepted. In this sense leave-taking seems to have become normal at Martin's workplace. There were not many people working in the firm, which might have represented a problem when one of the employees went on leave because of having less people available to replace fathers on leave. In spite of this there were no negative reactions.

Peter took his father's quota when his child was nine months old. He worked as a housepainter, and was self-employed and married to a kindergarten teacher. Concerning the decision to take parental leave for 10 weeks, he explained that it was quite difficult to reconcile with his work because it was his own company, and he had to be there: *"So, I looked at the calendar and tried to fit it in with projects, but it was complicated. In the end, I just decided on a date and tried to act in accordance with that."* He tried to put together a time puzzle and find the right period to go on leave, but ended up just deciding on a random date.

Due to managing his own firm and having to organize all the job assignments, Peter's work situation was complicated. Nevertheless, he managed to take all the 10 weeks of his father's quota. This is contrary to the general pattern of self-employed fathers in Norway, and it demonstrates that even in this type of difficult work situation fathers are able to find openings for taking leave. His effort may be due to the embodying of employees as fathers, leading to strong moral obligations of involved fathering aided by the father's quota during its existence.

Generally, both mothers and fathers take longer leave with their first child (Halrynjo and Kitterød 2016). Eskil, who worked as a welder, represented an exception to this pattern as he wanted to take more than the father's quota when he had his second child. This was because he enjoyed staying at home with his first child, and because his wife also wanted to return early to work. He described his boss as being very positive towards his plans: *"He understood me very well. Fortunately, he is not 70 years old. I suppose he is 50, so he is very up-to-date."* He explained how his boss was very keen to help him figure out the regulations concerning the parental leave system and particularly the father's quota. Eskil appreciated this, and told us that he could have been unfortunate and had a boss who wanted him to use as little as possible of the parental leave days.

Eskil considered his boss to be a "modern" man with kids himself. He said the following: *"His kids are grown up, but maybe he was not so much at home. Maybe he regrets not being there. Maybe he sees the need for fathers to be there."* Here we see how being "a modern man" was constructed as being a caring father. Eskil defined himself and his boss as "modern men", who understood that fathers wanted to take parental leave and be together with their children. Tore, who worked as a medical doctor at a large hospital, also illustrated these "modern" attitudes to fathering when he told how his leave-taking was received by his director, a chief physician in his 60s: *"He is updated on the father's quota. He has got young children himself, and I am not the first father to have leave."* This case indicates how fathers' care obligations in the course of one generation seem to have created a general acceptance of male employees having obligations other than those to the job.

The fact that many fathers before have used the quota and paved the way makes it easier for contemporary fathers. The hospital where Tore worked had adapted to the fact that fathers, like mothers, have the right to parental leave:

> With us, at this hospital, this is no big problem. I believe that employers understand that this is part of life, society has decided that this is the way to organize; therefore, I believe that employers just adjust. It might be that they experience a lot of organizing. People stay at home without anyone grumbling. It's part of life.

Calling fathers' leave-taking a "part of life" is illustrative of the change that has taken place in Norwegian society concerning fathers' caretaking. It has become what we do in Norwegian society, as Tore says, and figures show that it has become a "majority practice" for fathers (Brandth and Kvande 2013). Daniel, who worked as a research scientist in a large, private organization, confirmed this, saying: *"In my job everybody has full understanding – I felt that my colleagues supported it. I feel that there is total acceptance for taking leave and staying at home with children."* When talking about the support he had registered at his workplace he also included his colleagues. This generally positive attitude towards fathers and family involvement also comes into view in his story about sending an e-mail to his manager on a Sunday and getting the following response: "Dani, it's Sunday, and you must take time off." This illustrates that the manager was highly conscious about respecting the fact that employees have a life outside of work.

Because the father's quota has become a mature institution in Norway, it seems to be well known, and as stated in the introduction the great majority of Norwegian fathers use the quota. It has been a widely used practice for Norwegian fathers from the early days of its existence, and might have led to what can be called a "normalization process" or institutionalized practices in most workplaces.

5. The importance of parental leave design

As emphasized above, it is an essential design characteristic of the father's quota that it is given to the fathers and not both parents. This part of the analyses explores how workplace support of the father's quota can be explained. Focus is on how the design elements of the father's quota function in relation to work.

5.1 Statutory right for all eligible fathers

The fathers we interviewed focused on the importance of the quota being based on national legislation. The Norwegian father's quota is a legal right given by the welfare state to all eligible fathers in working life. The universalistic nature of the quota stands in contrast to family- friendly programs given by the work organization or collective agreements that would be conducive to different leave rights between fathers. It is against this background Johannes explained:

> *I can easily envision that there are jobs where it's not so simple to just say, "Yes, I'll take half of the parental leave" if there are no state regulations. Because it's a different situation if you say, "I'll take the father's quota." If the man must take it or leave it, then it's very difficult for your employer to say, "No, you can't take it," which, incidentally, I can envision happening. Or 100% happen, because it's a market-oriented society.*

Because the quota is a state regulation, he believed that it secured the right of all eligible fathers. He saw the advantage of having a "pre-negotiated" right, in which the father did not have to negotiate with the employer, but which he decided upon himself. Considering the uneven power balance between employer and employee, negotiations in "a market-oriented society" would most likely lead to the employer determining the possibility to take leave. It is a right that is paid for by the state and designed for fathers. It is a regulation decided upon by a third party which has a neutralizing and legitimating effect. This is important when it comes to encouraging the majority of fathers using the right.

For example, a statutory father's quota with job security being given to individual fathers is understood as being of particular importance for its implementation process in working life. Daniel said:

> I knew we were not supposed to have problems at work, but I was a little concerned whether that was actually true. Because sometimes things look good on paper, but it may be that you get some problems. But I had no problems.

He emphasized the fact that the father's quota was an established right in working life. The fathers recognize the importance of a statutory quota as an important bargaining chip. If it disappeared, taking leave would be more difficult. Cristoffer, a craftsman, also illustrated the importance of the father's quota being a statutory right reserved for fathers when it came to creating bargaining power in the meeting with employers:

> The fact that it's statutory, which is very important, it is the most important thing! Because if it, for instance, had been like the Conservative party says that it should not be statutory, but optional, it would have created huge problems for men, very many men would have had problems with their employers when wanting to have parental leave. I am absolutely sure about this. I think it is important within other types of work as well, finance and all that.

If fathers had to negotiate individually in order to take leave, their willingness and availability to work would be decisive. In a gendered organization where parental leave often is regarded to be for mothers and therefore unnecessary for fathers, there are greater chances that men who would like to take leave would be met with scepticism, as is the case in Denmark (Bloksgaard 2013).

The quota is paid by the state, and Steinar, a graduate engineer with two daughters, agreed that a special quota for fathers is an advantage in relation to working life. He stressed the economic aspect and argued as follows:

> The employer may put pressure on you and suggest you to postpone or drop it, but if you say: 'Yes, you recommend that I drop it but that means I give away three months of vacation. Are you willing to pay me? That's what it's worth, a quarter of a year with pay. Will you give that to me?' I don't think

many employers would, so then you have quite a strong argument that is directly translatable into money, and employers would understand it.

To translate the value of the father's quota into money might work in negotiations with employers. It might have worked better than arguing about his relationship to his child, he thought, but it would depend on the attitude of the employer. His own bosses had always been positive to his leave even if it necessitated some reorganization of the job.

In short, the fathers reflected on how the statutory universalistic principle worked – that it created respect in working life and became the normal thing to do for male employees who are fathers. This supported its use by fathers, as they can take leave without fear of losing their jobs. They clearly saw the importance of the father's quota being a statutory leave for fathers, and not dependent on the employers' good will.

5.2 Earmarked and non-transferable leave – empowering fathers

The father's quota is earmarked for fathers, and in addition it is not transferable to mothers. These principles work together and put strong pressure on fathers to use it. Declining to use the quota creates a much shorter time period for parents to care for their baby in the home. It also makes it easier to obtain approval in working life. Daniel said: *"I believe that it is the fact that it is reserved for fathers that makes people in Norway respect it, because this is just the way it is, right? You have to take the leave, so there's no discussion about it."* Andreas, who originally came from Germany, had some similar thoughts about the leave being "compulsory", when compared with practices in his homeland:

> *If something is customary, and the employer is used to it, then it will work. I don't quite know how it is in Norway, but in Germany it is obvious that if it isn't compulsory and you don't have to do it, it is much easier to pressure an employee to do as much as possible at work.*

Several of the fathers recognized the compulsory nature of the father's quota as an advantage, because of the empowering effect it had on fathers in relation to employers.

The fathers also appreciated the fact that the earmarked father's quota did not have to be negotiated with the mother. If parental leave for fathers had been defined as a family entitlement instead of an individual entitlement, negotiations with the mother would have been more likely, and many would probably have regarded it as a considerable obstacle for taking leave. Another of the fathers read the non-transferability and its possible implications in a similar way: *"I think it's important that we have some time reserved for the father, and which lapses if it isn't used. I think this will give fathers not the option, but more the obligation to take leave."* If there was no obligation like this, he imagined that the mother would take the entire leave. Hence, he saw how the earmarked leave created room for him to care for his baby.

Being an individual, non-transferable right, the father's quota might also have an effect on gender equality in working life:

> *The obligation to take leave ensures that there is no difference according to your employer. With no obligation to take the father's quota, then it'll be the mother who stays at home with the child, and then an employer will be more sceptical about hiring a young woman who might become a mother and it will lead to differential treatment if there's no father's quota.*

Fabio, originally from Italy, saw earmarking as a contribution that might help employers to stop thinking differently about female and male employees, because it would define men as both employees and caregivers in the same way as women. Martin, who worked as a research scientist, expressed this advantage in the following manner:

> *I think it is important that we have one part of the leave that is reserved for fathers and that is taken away if it isn't used. I think it will support the gender equality aspect that the father does not only have the possibility, but that he must take his leave!*

His perception is that the obligation to take leave, issued by legislation, reduces differential treatment of mothers and fathers by employers. It is the non-transferability of the father's quota which generates an obligation and not just a possibility for fathers to take on childcare. It demonstrates that fathers, and not only mothers, have become "replaceable workers" (Halrynjo and Lyng, 2009), and consequently it stimulates gender equality in working life. Equality is defined here as the transformation of men into workers embodied with childcare obligations.

6. Conclusions

In this chapter we have explored how the embodying of fathers as carers through the introduction of the fathers' quota in the Norwegian parental leave system has been received in different work organizations. The quota was introduced in order to encourage gender equality in working life and caring. The analysis confirms that father's care obligations seem to be accepted in working life. Hence, our findings back other studies in the Nordic countries that report of organizational support for fathers' parental leave-taking (Haas and Hwang 2009) indicating that work and childcare can be reconciled for employees who are fathers with caring commitments. To make use of the father's quota has become normative, something which supports the dual-carer model in the family, as well as in working life.

In addition to the elements already pinpointed in the research literature our data show that the nature of fathers' quota being a statutory right is perceived as important, because it ensures the same rights to all eligible fathers and prevents them from losing their jobs when they are on leave. Being a statutory right which is paid by the state and not dependent on the employers' good will constructs the leave as a universal right. The principle of earmarking and non-transferability is important since it relates fathers' care responsibility to their role as employees. It is a right that is connected to being an employee and a father, and not something they obtain by negotiating with the employer. This is an important aspect of the father's quota, thereby making it a pre-negotiated, collective right that applies to all eligible employees. In sum we can state that the individualization of fathers' caring rights within the Norwegian parental leave system has contributed to constructing male employees as fathers with caring commitments (Kvande and Brandth 2016). It has been a widely used practice for Norwegian fathers from the early days of the father's quota, and might have led to what can be called a "normalization process" or institutionalized practices at most workplaces.

Through embodying male employees as potential fathers with caring responsibilities, the fathers' quota might also have an equalizing effect on working life. Both male and female employees are constructed as employees who will take parental leave. The construction of the male employee as a parent with caring commitments represents a rupture with abstract disembodied thinking about employees. According to Acker (1990) working life's apparently gender-neutral ideas and routines builds on implicit ideas about gender. The earmarking of parental leave embodies male employees as fathers that in turn may promote the development of a dual carer model in working life. This may also have an equality effect because care responsibility is no longer seen as falling upon the mother only.

References

Acker, J. (1990) 'Hierarchies, Jobs, Bodies: A Theory of Gendered Organizations', *Gender & Society*, 4(2), pp. 139–158

Adkins, L. (1995) *Gendered Work*. Buckingham: Open University Press

Allart, K., Haas L. and Hwang P.H. (2007) 'Exploring the paradox: Experiences of flexible working arrangements and work-family conflict among managerial fathers in Sweden', *Community, Work and Family*, 10(4), pp. 475–494

Almqvist, A-L. and Dahlgren, L. (2013) Swedish fathers' motives for parental leave take-up in different scenarios, in: Oinonen, E. and Repo, K. (eds.) *Women, men and childcare in families: Private troubles and public issues.* Tampere: University of Tampere Press, pp. 91–112

Bekkengen, L. (2002) *Man får välja – om föräldraskap och föräldraledighet i arbeidsliv och familjeliv.* Malmö: Liber

Blair-Loy, M. (2003) *Competing Devotions.* Cambridge, Mass: Harvard University Press

Bloksgaard, L. (2013) Uten fedrekvote i lovgivningen: Danske fedres forhandlinger om permisjon fra arbeidet, in: Brandth, B. and Kvande, E. (eds.) *Fedrekvoten og den farsvennlige velferdsstaten.* Oslo: Universitetsforlaget, pp. 194–210

Brandth, B. and Kvande, E. (2001) 'Flexible work and flexible fathers', *Work, Employment and Society,* 15(2), pp. 251–267

Brandth, B. and Kvande, E. (2012) Free choice or gentle force? How can parental leave change gender practices? in: Kjørholt, A. T. and Qvortrup, J. (eds.) *The Modern Child and the Flexible Labour Market: Early childhood education and care. Houndsmills.* Basingstoke: Palgrave Macmillan, pp. 56–70

Brandth, B. and Kvande, E. (2013) Innledning: Velferdsstatens fedrepolitikk, in: Brandth, B. and Kvande, E. (eds.) *Fedrekvoten og den farsvennlige velferdsstaten. Oslo: Universitetsforlaget,* pp. 13–28

Brandth, B. and Kvande, E. (2016) Fedrekvoten som en del av likestillingspolitikken: Er jobben gjort?, in: Halrynjo, S. and Teigen, M. (eds.) *U/Likestilling i arbeidslivet.* Oslo: Gyldendal Akademisk

Brighthouse, H. and Wright, E. O. (2008) 'Strong Gender Egalitarianism', *Politics & Society,* 36(3), pp. 360–372

Bygren, M. and Duvander, A-Z. (2006) 'Parents workplace situation and fathers' parental leave use', *Journal of Marriage and Family,* 68, pp. 363–372

Duvander, A-Z. and Lammi-Taskula, J. (2011) Parental Leave, in Gíslason, I,V. and Eydal, G. B. (eds.) *Parental Leave, Childcare and Gender Equality in the Nordic countries.* København: Nordisk Ministerråd, pp. 31–64

Eydal, G. B. and Gíslason, I. V. (2013) Tredelt permisjon og lang fedrekvote. Erfaringer fra Island, in: Brandth, B. and Kvande, E. (eds.) *Fedrekvoten og den farsvennlige velferdsstaten.* Oslo: Universitetsforlaget, pp. 222–237

Fougner, E. (2012) 'Fedre tar ut hele fedrekvoten – også etter at den ble utvidet til ti uker', *Arbeid og velferd,* 2, pp. 71–77

Gornick, J. C. and Meyers, M. K. (eds.) (2009) Gender Equality: transforming family divisions of labor. London: Verso

Grambo, A-C. and Myklebø, S. (2009) *Moderne familier – tradisjonelle valg: En studie av mors og fars uttak av foreldrepermisjon.* Report. Oslo: Nav

Haas, L., Allart, K., and Hwang, P. H. (2002) 'The impact of organizational culture on men's use of parental leave in Sweden', *Community, Work and Family,* 5 (3), pp. 319–342

Haas, L. and Hwang, P. H. (2009) 'Is fatherhood becoming more visible at work? Trends in corporate support for fathers taking parental leave in Sweden', *Fathering,* 7(3), pp. 303–321

Haas, L. and Rostgaard, T. (2011) 'Father's right to paid parental leave in the Nordic countries: Consequences for the gendered division of care', *Community, Work and Family,* 14(2), pp. 177–195

Halrynjo, S. and Lyng, S. (2009) 'Preferences: Constraints or Schemas of Devotion? Exploring Norwegian mothers' withdrawals from high-commitment careers', *British Journal of Sociology,* 60 (2), pp. 321–343

Halrynjo, S. and Lyng, S. (2013) Fedrepermisjon i karriereyrker, in: Brandth, B. and Kvande, E. (eds.) *Fedrekvoten og den farsvennlige velferdsstaten.* Oslo: Universitetsforlaget, pp. 222–237

Halrynjo, S. and Kitterød, R. H. (2016) *Fedrekvoten – norm for fedres permisjonsbruk i Norge og Norden: En litteraturstudie.* Report 2016:06. Oslo: Institute for Social Research

Kitterød, R. H. (2013) Mer familiearbeid og mindre jobb blant småbarnsfedre in: Brandth, B. and Kvande, E. (eds.) *Fedrekvoten og den farsvennlige velferdsstaten.* Oslo: Universitetsforlaget, pp. 42–59

Kvande, E. (2009) 'Work/Life Balance for Fathers in Globalized Knowledge Work. Some insights from the Norwegian context', *Gender, Work and Organization,* 16 (1), pp. 58–72

Kvande, E. and Brandth, B. (2016) Fathering alone in Norway: Changes and continuities, in: O'Brien, M. and Wall, K. (eds.) *Fathers on Leave Alone: Comparative Perspectives on Work-Life Balance and Gender.* London: Springer

Lammi-Taskula, J. (2007) Parental Leave for Fathers? Helsinki: Stakes

Lappegård, T. and Bringedal, K. H. (2013) Stor oppslutning om fedrekvoten in: Brandth, B. and Kvande, E. (eds.) *Fedrekvoten og den farsvennlige velferdsstaten.* Oslo: Universitetsforlaget, pp. 29–41

Lewis, S. (1997) '"Family friendly" employment policies: A route to changing organizational culture or playing about at the margins?', *Gender, Work and Organization,* 4, pp. 13–23

Moss, P. and Deven, F.(eds.) (1999) *Parental Leave: progress or pitfall.* Brussels: NIDI/CBGS Publications

NOU (1995: 27) *Pappa kom hjem. Oslo: Departementenes servicesenter,* Informasjonsforvaltningen

NOU (2012:15) *Politikk for likestilling.* Oslo: Departementenes servicesenter, Informasjonsforvaltningen

Ray, R., Gornick, J. C. and Schmitt, J. (2010) 'Who cares? Assessing generosity and gender equality in parental leave policy designs in 21 countries', *Journal of European Social Policy,* 20, 196–216

St.meld. 4 (1988–89) *Langtidsprogrammet 1990–1993.* Oslo: Finans- og tolldepartementet

The 'Daddy Months' in the German Fatherhood Regime: A Step Towards an Equal Share of Work and Care?

Johanna Possinger

1. Fathers – a new target group for family policy

Over the last decade, a remarkable social change has taken place in many European countries. Fathers – the once 'neglected sex' in family research (Toelke and Hank 2005) – have moved towards the center of many family and gender policies. Nordic countries, such as Norway, Sweden and Iceland, have been at the vanguard of this movement, successfully introducing father's quotas in the 1990s, which reserved a part of the parental leave period for fathers (Bergman and Hobson 2002; O'Brien et al. 2007). Following the Scandinavian example, political instruments which support 'active fatherhood', have been strengthened, thus boosting gender equality. Slovenia gradually added 90 days of paternity leave to its maternity leave between 2003 and 2005. Since 2014 each parent in Slovenia has the right to half of the parental leave days, with 130 days belonging to the mother and 130 days to the father (Stropnik and Humer 2016). Taking the Swedish leave scheme as a role model, Germany introduced its parental allowance in 2007, explicitly encouraging fathers to stay at home for a period of at least two months during the first fourteen months of their child's life. Austria followed suit in 2011, implementing a new leave scheme that included a 'daddy month' for fathers. In 2002, France expanded its paternity leave from three days to a maximum of two paid weeks, leading to a higher presence of fathers at home after the birth of a child (Milner and Gregory 2015: 200). In 2014, France also reformed its parental leave scheme offering families with one child, who are already entitled to six months parental leave, an additional six months for the father. In the UK, employed fathers are entitled to at least two weeks of paternity leave, and since 2015, fathers have been eligible for up to six months of additional paternity leave if the mother transfers her entitlements to six months leave to the father (Dermott and Miller 2015).

These political instruments signal significant changes in cultural ideals, attitudes, gender roles, family structures and the labor market, which have occurred in many European countries within the last decades. The 1950s were still characterised by an idealized family model in which fathers specialised in their role as breadwinners, while mothers, most of whom did not have paid jobs, bore sole responsibility for the children and the household. Even by the 1960s, this family structure, widely regarded as being the 'classic' model, had started to crumble, since other family forms, such as single-parent families and families in which both parents were employed, became increasingly significant. Moreover the labour market, which had hitherto been characterised by stable employment conditions and incomes that were adequate to support a family, shifted from manufacturing to the service industry. Whereas just a few decades ago young men could plan a career of employment as a matter of course, nowadays they increasingly find themselves confronted with a difficult transition from training to work, including fixed-term employment contracts and joblessness (Bertram and Deuflhard 2015). At the same time, the ratio of women in the labour market has risen as the result of an unparalleled increase in female education. For most young women today, motherhood and the pursuit of a career in the labour market no longer exclude each other (Allmendinger 2009). Moreover, there is a growing number of women who are the family breadwinners, earning the bulk of the family income (Ben-Galim and Thompson 2013). The disappearing qualifications gap between men and women, second-wave feminism and the structural changes within the labour market have contributed to the decline of the traditional breadwinner model. At the same time, they have given way to a more equal division of unpaid caring work and paid employment between men and women. The attitudes of men have also changed in response to women's increased expectations that their partners should be more involved in the task of caring for the family. As numerous studies in recent years have shown, men also wish for a more active participation in childcare. 75% of men in Germany approve of the idea that care work should be shared equally in constellations where both partners work full-time (Institut fuer Demoskopie Allensbach 2013). 79% favour the ideal of an 'active father' who is involved in the caring and nurturing of the children. However, in Germany, as well as in other European countries, breadwinning remains a key component of the concept of 'good' fatherhood (Dermott and Miller 2015). For most fathers it continues to be very important to be professionally successful and the main breadwinner in the family. Thus, the model of the father as breadwinner has not been completely superseded by a new image, but has merely opened up to create space for a more nurturing concept of fatherhood.

This chapter sets out to examine active fatherhood in Germany, drawing on the concepts of fatherhood regimes (Hobson and Morgan 2002), agency inequalities (Hobson and Fahlén 2009), and paternal involvement (Adler and Lenz 2016). It illustrates the effects of the German parental allowance and sheds light on the gap between the egalitarian discourse of fatherhood and the traditional practice of fathering. Furthermore, the chapter demonstrates how fathers themselves characterize the areas of work and childcare by ambivalence and conflicts. The German fatherhood regime has started to actively support an ideal of nurturing fatherhood. However, this change is still very contradictory. Thus, at the end of the chapter future policy steps towards a more gender-equal share of work and care will be outlined.

2. The concept of fatherhood regimes

The concept of *fatherhood regimes* is a useful framework for the analysis of policies that are directed towards supporting active fatherhood. The concept was originally introduced by Hobson and Morgan (2002), who extended the well established idea of *gender regimes* to fathers. *Fatherhood* is defined as the "cultural coding of men as fathers" (2002: 11). It implies rights and responsibilities, as well as the conferring of status. It covers the rhetoric terrain around 'good' and 'bad' fathering. The fatherhood regime denotes a bundle of rights defining fathers, fathering and fatherhood in the following clusters (Milner and Gregory 2015: 2):

- Rights and obligations of fathers after couple separation
- Family benefits and the tax-welfare nexus
- Parenting support targeting fathers only
- Measures to support working fathers (such as paternity leave)

These rights and benefits will vary by degree (strong, moderate and weak) among the different European welfare states in accordance with the particular intentions of the political legislators. As Hobson and Morgan (2002) point out, in order to analyse the fatherhood regime of a certain state it is necessary to view the position of men in the context of the triangular relationships between father, mother and child, as well as between the state, the family, and the market. This second institutional triangle allows us to see differences between welfare states with regard to rights, duties and obligations associated with fatherhood, but also to see differences with regards to the varying practices of fathering (Morgan 2002). Within these triangles contradictory elements can often be found. Gregory and Milner (2005) expanded Hobson and Morgan's concept of the fatherhood regime along three vectors: the specific rights and obligations placed on fathers by the state; state family and employment policies; and the national working time regime. Thus, the fatherhood regime shows how national policies, legislation, the labour market and the cultural ideology of fatherhood play a pivotal role in shaping modern fatherhood. The fatherhood regime offers a suitable framework for the analysis of *agency inequalities* – a term introduced by Hobson and Fahlén describing "a sense of entitlement to make a claim in the family and in workplace cultures" (2009: 35). Since studies continue to show a gap between men's discourse of active fatherhood and their actual practice, the two researchers present a concept that aims at integrating institutional contexts (such as the fatherhood regime) and individual micro-levels of agency and practice, building on Sen's capability approach. Hobson and Fahlén differentiate between capabilities (e.g. the capability to exercise family-friendly working-hours) and agency (actual working hours) in order to "capture tensions and contradictions between expectations, norms and practices, between rights and the ability to exercise them" (ibid.: 10). Thus, the concepts of fatherhood regime and agency inequalities are useful when it comes to combining the structural macro-level of policy and institutions with micro-levels of individual 'doing'.

The concept of the fatherhood regime also adds nicely to other typologies of welfare and gender regimes as Adler and Lenz have demonstrated (2016). Building on Esping-Andersen's classic typology of welfare regimes (1990) and Leitner's further refinement in her four 'varieties in familialism' (2003), Haas presents five types of gender regimes: the traditional breadwinner model, the modified breadwinner model, the egalitarian employment model, the universal carer model and the reversed role model (2005). More recently, Adler and Lenz developed a new conceptual model linking gender regime, policy and agency in terms of father involvement (2016). Comparing six different countries, they found a significant agency gap between fathers' entitlements and their uptake of provisions in all of them. This led them to develop the model of *fatherhood involvement* (meaning fathers' agency in everyday practice) that combines Hobson and Fahlén's ideas about agency inequalities with Hobson and Morgan's concept of the fatherhood regime (2002), as well as with Haas' gender regimes (2005), family policy instruments and workplace cultures.

Figure 1: Conceptual model of father involvement (Adler and Lenz 2016: 244)

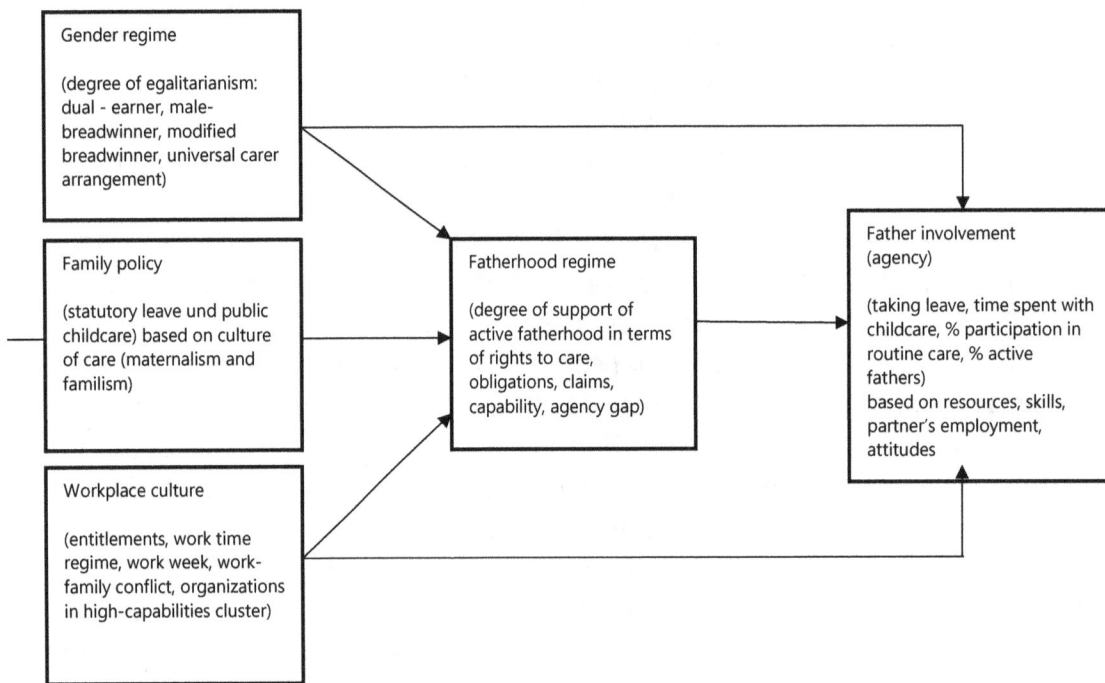

Adler and Lenz's conceptualization of father involvement offers an adequate framework for the analysis of the German fatherhood regime and its agency inequalities. Germany's gender regime has long been characterized by a strong male-breadwinner model especially in the Western part of the country (Pfau-Effinger 2003). As a conservative welfare state, Germany directed its family policies in the past to a large extent towards mothers. In addition to a tax system and a labour market which are underpinned by a male-breadwinner paradigm, a long standing lack of institutional childcare services in Western Germany has contributed to a situation where mothers are typically the primary caretakers. In the Eastern part of the country, the former German Democratic Republic (GDR), mothers were supported in their endeavours to reconcile work and family. Since unification, the German gender regime has been dominated by a modified breadwinner model in the West, with mothers usually working part-time, and by an egalitarian employment model in the East, with both parents working full-time (Toelke 2012). In both parts of the country, a gendered division of labour in the private sphere is still in place, leaving the lion's share of child and elder care to women. The introduction of parental allowance *(Elterngeld)* in 2007 marked a paradigm shift in German family policy. The 'use it or lose it' strategy of the new 'daddy months' was explicitly directed towards encouraging fathers to take on an active part in the child's care. Since most German fathers are unhappy with the little time they have for their family during the week and would prefer to be more present at home (Li and Zerle-Elsaeßer 2015), the parental allowance struck a chord with German fathers. However, the gendered division of labour in the household has in most parts remained untouched. Even though polls show that 60% of parents would favour an equal share of work and care between the sexes, only 14% translate this notion into practice (Müller, Neumann and Wrohlich 2013). A recent German time-budget study illustrates the gap between intent and practice even further: while fathers devote 2:51 hours per day to childcare and household tasks, mothers dedicate 5:08 hours of their daily time to unpaid care work (Meier-Graewe and Kluender 2015: 9). The following sections will therefore take a closer look at the German fatherhood regime and its agency inequalities concerning the uptake of parental allowance and the 'daddy months'.

3. Method

The data used for this book chapter draws on a qualitative study with twenty-four employed fathers in Germany (Possinger 2013a). In 2009 and 2010, fathers from Eastern and Western Germany were interviewed through biographical interviews in Berlin with respect to their past and current experiences regarding career and family life. Half of the fathers had taken the 'daddy months' for varying periods of two to nine months. The other half had had not. In order to analyse in detail the extent to which working conditions can influence fathers' decision to take parental leave, only men who worked at the same company were interviewed. The company that opened its sacred halls for the research was the *Hetektro* corporation – an internationally operating heat and energy enterprise with more than 30,000 jobholders within Europe (note: the name *Hetektro* is a pseudonym in order to maintain the anonymity of the company). The respondents worked in different business divisions of the company (heat, energy, marketing, human resources, communications). In order to grasp a wide range of the experiences of fathers with different hierarchical positions within the company, interviews were conducted with trained workers of power stations, technical instructors, managers in low-level and mid-level positions, as well as managing directors. The interviews were analyzed based on the paradigm of Grounded Theory (Strauss and Corbin 1998), sequence analysis and a reconstructive approach introduced by Kruse (2014).

Hetektro was an interesting case for this research. As a company in a predominantly male industrial sector it strived to improve its family-friendly personnel policy. The upper management praised the company as a family-friendly workplace. The company had even been given an award for its family-friendliness by a renowned German foundation. However, as the research brought to light, the corporation turned out to be a major obstacle to involved fatherhood.

4. The 'daddy months' and their effects in Germany

Parental allowance *(Elterngeld)* in Germany entitles parents to about 65% of their average net income up to a maximum of €1,800 per month in compensation for the loss of earnings when parents interrupt or reduce their employment after the birth of a child. One parent can claim the parental allowance for a maximum of 12 months, and the period of eligibility is extended for a further two months (the so-called partner months or 'daddy months') if the partner also applies for the allowance. In a country in which family policy has traditionally focused on mothers, the introduction of parental allowance represented a clear cut. It was harshly criticized and ridiculed as a 'nappy changing internship' ('Wickelvolontariat') by some conservative politicians. Nevertheless, since its introduction this instrument has proved very popular among German families. Since 2007, there has been a continuous rise in uptake from fathers, currently reaching a nationwide average of 33%. In some areas of Saxony and Bavaria almost 50% of fathers use their 'partner months' of leave (Destatis 2015). However, almost 80% of the fathers who claim the parental allowance only use it for a period of two months – even though they would be entitled for a longer break from their place of employment. But what exactly happens to the division of labour when fathers take the leave?

4.1 Intermezzo or prelude? The parental leave phase

At first sight, those fathers who had taken the parental leave practiced a more equal share of caretaking with mothers than the fathers who had refrained from claiming the 'daddy months'.

For all the respondents who had taken the leave it was very important to experience their child's development first hand. Their main motifs were to establish a close relationship with the child and at the same time support the mother with caretaking tasks. Furthermore, the parental leave period also meant an important timeout in their professional careers. Many respondents stated that it not only improved their ties with the child, but also the relationship with their partner, since they developed a greater appreciation of the mother's everyday caring work.

During the parental leave some fathers actually did share the work of caring for the children and the household equally with the mother. Some even reversed the traditional role model by completely taking on the lion's share of care work during their 'daddy months'. This was especially the case when the fathers were home alone in that time because the mother had returned to her place of employment. The less the mother was co-present during the father's leave, the more likely it was that he did all the chores. That means, during fathers' parental leave the employment of the mother and her related limited availability seemed to have a significant positive influence on the father's caregiving. Moreover, the 'daddy months' could be seen as providing the initial spark for a long-term equal division of labour, which continued after the parental leave for both parents had come to an end. However, in most cases the 'daddy months' were by no means a guarantee for a more equal share of work and care. Again, the co-presence of the mother made all the difference: since it was very popular among the respondents to use the parental allowance to stay at home right after the child was born, the mothers were usually still on maternity leave. With both parents at home, most fathers adopted only a traditional role during their parental leave. They left the main responsibility for the childcare in the hands of their partner and restricted their own participation to providing assistance. Instead of switching roles, they took on the status of their partner's helpful 'intern'. Hence, if the mother was present during the father's parental leave, in most cases the caring tasks were not re-distributed between the sexes. Thus, the use of the 'daddy months' in itself cannot represent a suitable indicator for active fathering.

Furthermore, even in the case of the fathers who switched roles with the mother in order to take on the burden of childcare and household, a re-traditionalisation of work and care started creeping in after both parents had returned to work. The fathers predominantly focused their attention on their job, while the mothers had to balance most of the childcare with their part-time employment. In conclusion, while for some fathers parental leave provided a prelude for a long-term arrangement in which both partners shared care and domestic tasks to a similar extent, for others it meant no or only a short intermezzo of equally sharing work and care.

4.2 Mother's little intern? Fathers and the family routine

In addition to analysing father's involvement in childcare during parental leave, it is instructive to also take a look at what happens to the gendered division of labour *after* this period. Three patterns of father engagement could be identified amongst the interviewees: first, the traditional caring father, second, the partnership-focused father and third, the egalitarian caring father

(Possinger 2013a). In all three patterns, fathers actively took on some of the caring tasks which went beyond purely pleasurable activities, such as taking physical care of the child (e.g. nappy-changing) as well as tasks related to the education of older siblings. All of them had a 'second shift' of care (Hochschild 1989) when they came home after work. Many fathers of school-aged children spent a lot of time checking homework, helping with studies, going to parents' meetings and driving their children to various activities. However, the main difference among the three types of fathers revolved around their levels of participation in the care of sick children and the household.

Most fathers belonged to the type 'traditional caring' and mainly focused on their careers. As 'after-work dads' they did not feel responsible for staying at home when their child got sick. This task was entirely left to the mothers who usually worked part-time in order to manage the care workload. This was also true for household tasks, such as cleaning, doing the laundry and cooking. The fathers restricted themselves to stereotypically male chores that required physical strength, technical skills or taking out the garbage. Most of them argued that this gendered division of labour was rooted in 'natural female caring talents' and 'male inabilities', which in combination with the mothers' demand for perceived high standards in domestic work lead to a reluctance to take over any 'female' chores – unless mothers specifically requested it. Thus, the fathers saw themselves as the main family breadwinner, who only had an 'internship status' regarding care work. The second type comprised fathers who belonged to a partnership-focused pattern. For them it was very important to share work and care equally with their partner. They felt more responsible for the care of sick children and the household. However, traditional gender stereotypes could still be traced in the interviews with the fathers. They too saw the household as the true area of maternal responsibility and regarded their active involvement as a special courtesy towards their wives. Only the fathers who fit into the third egalitarian pattern shared the care work symmetrically. These fathers did not only equally share the burden of staying at home for sick child, but also participated in all the household chores. Since their wives were more involved in the labour market, they felt equally responsible for the children's caregiving. As they emphasized in the interviews, for them as a couple, it was important to get the chores done and it didn't matter who did what. The only relict of a gendered division of labour that could be found among these men was in the field of shopping for children's clothes. They saw clothes shopping as a female sphere for which they as men lacked 'talent'. Thus, only fathers of the two last groups, which were both a minority in the sample, truly practiced an involved fathering and lived up to their own expectations of being an 'active father' to their children.

5. Barriers to paternal involvement

So why are traditional arrangements in the division of labour so persistent? Why is it that fathers often fail to put their aspirations to be an active caregiver into practice? The interviews demonstrated that fathers' involvement in childcare is highly context specific. Three main barriers to active fathering practices could be identified within the interviews: income-related and economic factors, 'maternal gatekeeping' and cultural gender stereotypes, as well as workplace-related obstacles.

5.1 Money rules the world

As research has shown, the biggest obstacle to the realisation of an equally shared division of labour is constituted by the economic conditions of a family (Vogt 2010; Fthenakis and Minsel 2002). Even though the number of female breadwinners in Germany is on the rise, in most couples men earn more than women. The economic disadvantages suffered by women lead to higher costs for families when men take parental leave. Unsurprisingly, a lot of fathers stated in the interviews that due to their breadwinner position they could not afford the reduced income associated with the parental allowance. For them, refraining from parental leave was simply a matter of economic rationality. Nevertheless, the instrument of the parental allowance has changed the way couples talk about parental leave, because all of the non-users I interviewed had at least seriously considered its uptake. The financial "logic of the pocketbook" (Hochschild 1989: 221) thus seems to be a powerful barrier to involved fatherhood. Nonetheless, economic considerations are not the only important factor; there are two more obstacles that prevent fathers from interrupting their employment in favour of looking after their children.

5.2 Mother knows best?

Traditional gender norms within the family can be identified as another barrier. These include, for example, the conviction held by both parents that it is more conducive to the child's wellbeing if the mother assumes the main caring responsibility. Care is regarded as a skill which women 'naturally' possess, while men can only learn it by dint of hard work. The interviews also demonstrated the interplay between the quality of a couple's relationship and the father's care involvement (Fthenakis and Minsel 2002). The better the relationship, the more actively the father usually participated in caring tasks. Another obstacle that could be identified was 'maternal gatekeeping' (Pleck and Masciadrelli 2004). According to the interviewed fathers, in these cases the mothers regarded childcare and housework first and foremost as their 'preserve'. They kept a close eye on the father's involvement in childcare. Some of the fathers complained that their wives only accepted them as 'assistants' while preferring to take on the main responsibility for care work themselves. High – and for some fathers unreachable – performance standards in childcare and housework (e.g. cleaning), represented another form of 'maternal gatekeeping' and encouraged fathers to further withdraw from active caring activities.

5.3 The employer, the 'greedy child'

The third main obstacle mentioned by fathers related to their working-conditions. Employers and workplaces determine to a large extent the quantity and daily timing of hours parents have to work. They also play a crucial role in the employees' claims of their entitlements, such as flexible working hours or parental leaves. As research has proven, most workplaces remain deeply rooted in traditional gender norms discouraging men from taking parental leave (see Holter et al. 2005; Pfahl and Reuyß 2009; Oechsle 2014). For this reason, particular attention was paid during the interviews to the role of the *Hetektro* company – the employer of the respondents. As mentioned above, *Hetektro* was an interesting case of company policies and actual practices being in conflict with each other. It offered various family-friendly measures, including flexible working hours, different part-time working arrangements and leave of absence at short notice, in order to facilitate the reconciliation of family and career for its employees. The respondents all praised the instruments that were available to them. However, hardly anyone had claimed them for themselves. As it turned out, fathers had to face a severe agency gap between their rights to take parental leave and their actual ability to claim these rights within the *Hetektro* corporation.

5.3.1 The 'career setback' – more nightmare than reality?

A predominant fear of a 'career setback' kept many men from claiming the parental allowance. Concerns about a career disadvantage represented a decisive obstacle for young fathers in particular, whose career start at *Hetektro* had been increasingly determined by insecure employment conditions and fixed-term contracts. They frequently shelved their plans to use the parental leave in favour of their equally strong desire to offer their family financial security. The fathers feared career sanctions which would also be to the family's detriment, such as a failure to renew an employment contract. Most of them worried that their 'daddy months' would lead to a loss of status within the company:

How will my boss see me? My workmates? Will I lose my status here at the company? Will I be seen as a sissy? My boss might think that I'm no longer focused on my career. (Mr. Berger)

Nevertheless, the fear of a 'career setback' might in many cases be more nightmare than reality. In fact, formal job sanctions due to the uptake of parental leave, such as the loss of a job, salary reductions or the withdrawal of responsibilities did not occur on a single occasion among the respondents. Other research has also shown that the anticipated fear of professional disadvantages is often much greater than corporate reality (Pfahl and Reuyß 2009). However, it was not just the fear of formal sanctions that kept men from taking the leave; they generally worried about breaking the 'hidden rules' (Oechsle 2014) of the company. Such rules and internal norms play a pivotal role in fathers' involvement at home by signalling to staff informally what is expected of them as 'good employees'. At *Hetektro,* the 'hidden rules' were so powerful that they abrogated the family-friendly programs of the corporation that existed on paper.

5.3.2 Performance pressure, face-time and availability

The work culture of *Hetektro* was characterised by high performance requirements, competition and constant time pressure. In order to manage the large work load, most fathers worked overtime on a regular basis. Regardless of their position within the corporate hierarchy, many respondents complained about the large agency gap between their working hours as stipulated in their contract and the actual amount of time spent at work. The high performance pressure was further exacerbated by a restructuring of the company which was associated with increased competition between the business areas. Most fathers characterized the atmosphere within the company as 'hostile', since a lot of them had the impression that their superiors were fuelling the staff's fears of job cuts in order to increase their performances. The claim of *Hetektro* to be a family-friendly company collapsed in the face of the reality of day-to-day operations, which demanded a high degree of work commitment and left little space for family life.

Face-time is crucial for Hetektro. If you want to succeed you have to be present and show your face. (Mr. Timm)

There's a lot of pressure to get things done. And there's a huge difference between the family friendly policies of the company and its reality. Hetektro doesn't practice what it preaches. (Mr. Golz)

Within the company, physical presence was seen as a sign of hard work and productivity. Moreover, this also meant showing your face at the 'right time'. While technically-oriented areas of the company were characterized by a 'lark culture' with an early start to the working day – before 8 am – in other departments like marketing, controlling and human resources it was essential to be present at the office during the evening hours in line with an 'owl culture'. Despite their informal character, both attendance cultures were so dominant that they overrode the flexible working hours which officially existed. Employees who deviated from this pattern for family reasons had to deal with critical remarks by their workmates. The 'hidden rules' were applied to all employees, but they were particularly strict with managers and executives. Men and women with managerial responsibilities were to be available at all times, even during holidays, in the evenings and during weekends.

> I believe that the company really wants to be family friendly, but in reality the pressure in our business is extremely high. It's simply no option to take the parental leave, to work part-time or to avoid overtime. Of course this highly depends on your position in the hierarchy. It's a no-go for me as a manager to leave the office at 5.30pm, even if it's my daughter's birthday. (Mr. Jansen)

This ideal of the constantly available employee (Sennett 1998), as communicated by the company, also contributed to the conviction of many that top positions at *Hetektro* were per se 'indispensible'. Job sharing or part-time work was simply no option for managers. Some managers who had dared to take two 'daddy months' started to spend more time at work than even before the birth of their child just to demonstrate their availability and career motivation.

> Parental leave in itself is something we can handle as a company. We hire a substitute for the father or split the work among his co-workers for a few months. However, after this period, if the father or the mother decided to reduce his or her regular working hours to part-time, then we'd have a problem. (Mr. Albrecht)

5.3.3 Caring competition between company and family

Male employees found it so difficult to distance themselves from these ideals because the culture of being present and available was directly linked to an implicit model of traditional masculinity. Within the *Hetektro* corporation masculinity was synonymous with continuous full-time employment, family breadwinning and a striving for success in one's career. If fathers wanted to spend more time with their families they were faced with a dilemma because they had to break two 'hidden rules' (Oechsle 2014) at the same time: firstly, they were deviating from the hegemonic image of the father as breadwinner and were thus running the risk of being seen as 'unmanly'. Secondly, they were dropping out of the dominant culture of face-time and therefore risked acquiring the reputation of being a 'bad' and 'unproductive' staff member.

> *The corporation definitely has its family friendly policies, but men are expected to devote all their time and energy to the company. For women, it's easier. It's more socially accepted when a mother stays at home when the child is sick or when she has to leave the office early to pick up the kids. Because it's simply not normal for a father to leave the office early at 4pm. It's not normal.* (Mr. Jansen)

From the company's point of view male employees were expected to be 'caring' for the company rather than for the family. They had to be available for their co-workers, their bosses, their customers and their projects. One of the respondents described *Hetektro* as a 'greedy child', which felt that it never got enough attention from its employees. The firm and everything that went with it was not to be 'left in the lurch'. Since the workload was so high, using family-friendly instruments was seen as equivalent to violating a code of honour towards other staff members. The *Hetektro* corporation competed with the families at home over fathers' time, attention, energy and care – a competition that discouraged many fathers from putting their aspirations to be an active father into practice.

> *So imagine, my staff members have to talk to me and I'm not available because I have already gone home to spend time with my family. I have to be there for them. They expect me to be there for them. Because in return I also expect from them to be available at all times.* (Mr. Jansen)

6. Changes in Germany's fatherhood regime – contradictory, yet promising

To summarize, what conclusions can we draw from these findings with regard to Germany's fatherhood regime? As stated above, Hobson and Morgan use triangles as heuristic devices for conceptualizing fatherhood regimes, such as the triangle of "family-market-state" (2002: 9). They emphasize that these triangles can be contradictory in themselves. This is exactly the case with the German fatherhood regime: on the one hand, the state – the first dimension of the triangle – with its parental allowance and parental leave regulations sets a strong incentive for fathers to claim these rights and to take responsibility for caregiving activities. On the other hand, German family policy can only be seen as semi-supportive towards active fatherhood and is in itself very contradictory (Adler and Lenz 2016: 241). It has promoted the male breadwinner regime for decades, enforcing today's strong prevalence of a gendered division of labour. In addition to a lack of public childcare facilities, the German tax system for married couples *(Ehegattensplitting)* also contributes to keeping mothers at home or in part-time jobs, while rewarding fathers' uninterrupted full-time work because it tends to penalize parents who receive similar earnings while rewarding those who have a high gender income gap. In the 'logic of the pocketbook' (Hochschild 1989) it is simply not affordable for most parents to share family tasks equally.

Ambivalent change can also be found in the second dimension of the 'family'. Parenting ideals of equally sharing the burden of work and care are on the rise among mothers and fathers in Germany. As the growing take-up rates of the 'daddy months' have demonstrated, more and more fathers want to be actively involved in the care at home. All of the interviewed fathers of the *Hetektro* corporation aspired to be active and nurturing caregivers to their children. They felt that spending time together as a family after the birth of a child is of great benefit for their relationship to the mother and the child. They did not want to pick and choose the more pleasant aspects of care work (such as playing with the children). Rather, they all tried to participate in routine care work like housework, personal care, tasks related to school and education, or chauffeur duties between childcare facilities, leisure activities and doctor's appointments. Even in families who shared work and care in a traditional pattern, new areas of 'active fathering' could often be observed. Nevertheless, within the dimension of 'family' the shift towards active fatherhood is a contradictory one due to traditional gender norms, financial considerations and firm-related barriers. Despite the fathers' desire to be involved caregivers, most of them could not manage to put their aspirations into practice. The majority of German fathers still do not make use of their entitlements for parental leave. If fathers claim the 'daddy months' most of them only use two months. Usually, they spend those two months in the co-presence of their partner, often limiting themselves to be the mother's 'assistant'. Furthermore, while the 'daddy months' provided an initial spark for a long-term care involvement for some fathers, the majority either maintained or fell back into a gendered division of labour after this period had passed. As the interviews showed, it is crucial for fathers to spend time alone with their children, if we want to change the gendered division of work and family in the long run.

Looking at the third dimension of Hobson's and Morgan's triangle – the 'market' – the *Hetektro* corporation with its informally established norms, proved to be one of the main obstacles to an equal share of work and care. The globalised labour market with its high time pressure, work load and international competitiveness left little time for the respondents' families. Thus, the fathers faced a dilemma: they wanted to be successful at work and at home, but they found themselves struggling to combine the traditional workplace culture of *Hetektro* with their caregiving aspirations. The pressure of 'having it all' – this 'New Male Mystique' as Aumann, Galinsky and Matos call it (2011) – came at the price of a constant lack of time, feelings of guilt and exhaustion. Many fathers tried to solve these work-family conflicts through 'boundary management' (Jurczyk et al. 2009) creating time slots of 'quality time' for their children, avoiding overtime, and reducing hours of sleep. However, in many cases, these measurements led to stress-related diseases and other chronic fatigue syndromes (Possinger 2013a).

As the case of the *Hetektro* corporation indicates, in Germany's workplace culture taking care of children is usually seen as 'the mother's job'. Male employees are being encouraged to concentrate on breadwinning and to constrain themselves to a role as 'after-work dads'. Thus, Germany's fatherhood regime has remarkable 'agency inequalities' (Hobson and Fahlén 2009) between entitlements for fathers and uptake rates.

Thus, more change is needed in order to strengthen father involvement (Adler and Lenz 2016) in Germany – a change in government policies, workplace cultures and the families themselves that clearly moves away from male breadwinning and instead points in the direction of egalitarian sharing arrangements. This would imply several bold steps (Possinger 2013b) – the German Federal Ministry for Family Affairs, Senior Citizens, Women and Youth is indeed already working on some of them:

- First, a reform of the German family tax system which rewards the employment of mothers instead of penalizing it.
- Second, an extension of the 'daddy months' within the current framework of the parental allowance scheme, moving from a 12+2 months-model to a 12+4 months or 12+6 months-model. This would encourage fathers to spend a longer period of time home alone with the children.
- Third, an increase in state investments in childcare facilities and early education, which would allow both parents to participate in the labour market.
- Fourth, an entitlement to be able to return to full-time working hours after a certain period of part-time work. This might keep mothers from being stuck in dead end part-time jobs, while at the same time making temporary part-time employment more attractive for fathers.
- Fifth, an introduction of a new state subsidized family working time model (Mueller et al. 2013) which would allow both parents to reduce their working hours to 80% (28–32 hours) in order to equally share work and care. According to the Secretary of Family Affairs, this model would also imply a flat rate payment for the resulting loss of income of 250 Euro, which would be provided by the German government (Bullion, 11.11.2015)
- Parallel to these measures, the German workplace culture will have to change if we want to promote active fatherhood. Companies will have to

realize that letting go of face-time and availability is not only beneficiary for their employees, but also for their own economic success. Since breadwinning remains a key component of 'good' fatherhood, it is necessary to better integrate career *and* care in the lives of women *and* men.

References

Adler, M. A. and Lenz, K. (2016) Comparative Father Involvement: The dynamics of gender culture, policy and practice, in: Adler, M. A. and Lenz, K. (eds.) *Father Involvement in the Early Years: an international comparison of policy and practice.* Chicago: Polity Press, pp. 231–252

Allmendinger, J. (2009) *Frauen auf dem Sprung. Wie junge Frauen heute leben wollen.* Die Brigitte-Studie. München: Pantheon

Aumann, K., Galinsky, E., and Matos, K. (2011) *The New Male Mystique: national study of the changing workforce.* New York: Families and Work Institute

Ben-Galim, D. and Thompson, S. (2013) *Who's breadwinning? Working mothers and the new face of family support.* London: Institute for Public Policy Research

Bergman, H. and Hobson, B. (2002) Compulsory fatherhood: the coding of fatherhood in the Swedish welfare state, in: Hobson, B. (ed.) *Making Men into Fathers: men, masculinities and the social politics of fatherhood.* Cambridge: Cambridge University Press, pp. 92–124

Bertram, H. and Deuflhard, C. (2015) *Die überforderte Generation. Arbeit und Familie in der Wissensgesellschaft.* Opladen: Barbara Budrich Publishers

Bullion, C. von (2015) ,Nur 28 bis 32 Stunden. Familienarbeitszeit', Süddeutsche Zeitung, 11.11.2015. Available at: http://www.sueddeutsche.de/politik/familienarbeitszeit-nur-bis-stunden-1.2732424 (download 04.27.2016)

Dermott, E. and Miller, T. (2015) More than the sum of its parts? 'Contemporary fatherhood policy, practice and discourse', *Families, Relationships and Societies,* 4 (2), pp. 183–195

Destatis (2015) ,Rund 80% der Väter in Elternzeit beziehen Elterngeld für 2 Monate.' Statistisches Bundesamt: Pressemitteilung, 25.03.2015. Available at: https://www.destatis.de/DE/PresseService/Presse/Pressemitteilungen/2015/03/PD15_109_22922.html (download 10.14.2016)

Esping-Andersen, G. (1990) *The Three Worlds of Welfare Capitalism.* Cambridge: Polity Press

Fthenakis, W. E. and Minsel, B. (2002) *Die Rolle des Vaters in der Familie.* Stuttgart, Berlin, Cologne: Kohlhammer

Gregory, A. and Milner, S. (2005) *'Fatherhood: Comparative Western Perspectives'. Sloan Work and Family Encyclopedia Entry.* Available at: http://wfnetwork.bc.edu/encyclopedia_entry.php?id=368&area=academics. (download 04.27.2016)

Haas, B. (2005) 'The Work-Care Balance: is it possible to identify typologies for cross-national comparisons?, *Current Sociology,* 53 (3), pp. 487–508

Hobson, B. and Fahlén, S. (2009) *Applying Sen's Capabilities Framework to Work Family Balance within a European Context: theoretical and empirical challenges. Working Papers on the Reconciliation of Work and Welfare in Europe,* REC-WP 03-2009

Hobson, B. and Morgan, D. (2002) Introduction, in: Hobson, B. (ed.) *Making Men into Fathers: men, masculinities and the social politics of fatherhood.* Cambridge: Cambridge University Press, pp. 1–21

Hochschild, A. (1989) *The Second Shift: working parents and the revolution at home.* New York: Viking Penguin.

Holter, Ø. G., Riesenfeld, V. and Scambor, E. (2005) "We don't have anything like that here!" Organisations, Men and Gender Equality, in: Puchert, R., Gärtner, M. and Höyng, S. (eds.) *Work Changes Gender: men and equality in the transition of labour forms.* Opladen: Barbara Budrich Publishers, pp. 73–103

Institut für Demoskopie Allensbach (2013) *Vorwerk Familienstudie 2013. Ergebnisse einer repräsentativen Bevölkerungsumfrage zur Familienarbeit in Deutschland,* Wiesbaden: Vorwerk & Co.

Jurczyk, K., Schier, M., Szymenderski, P., Lange, A, and Voß, G. G. (2009) *Entgrenzte Arbeit – entgrenzte Familie. Grenzmanagement im Alltag als neue Herausforderung.* Berlin: Ed. Sigma

Kruse, J. (2014) *Qualitative Interviewforschung. Ein integrativer Ansatz.* Weinheim: Beltz Juventa

Leitner, S. (2003) 'Varieties of Familialism: the caring function of the family in a comparative perspective'. *European Societies,* 4, pp. 160–177

Li, X. and Zerle-Elsäßer, C. (2015): Können Väter alles unter einen Hut bringen? Das Vereinbarkeitsdilemma engagierter Väter, in: Walper S., Bien,W. and Rauschenbach, T. (eds.) *Aufwachsen in Deutschland heute. Erste Befunde aus dem DJI-Survey AID:A 2015.* München: Deutsches Jugendinstitut, pp. 16–20

Meier-Graewe, U. and Kluender, N. (2015) *'Ausgewählte Ergebnisse der Zeitbudgeterhebungen 1991/92, 2001/02 und 2012/13',* Study for the Heinrich-Boell-Stiftung. Gießen, Juli 2015

Milner, S. and Gregory, A. (2015) 'Fathers, Care and Family Policy in France: an unfinished revolution?', *Families, Relationships and Societies,* 4 (2), pp. 197–208

Müller, K. U., Neumann, M. and Wrohlich, K. (2013) *Bessere Vereinbarkeit von Familie und Beruf durch eine neue Lohnersatzleistung bei Familienarbeitszeit.* Deutsches Institut für Wirtschaftsforschung. Berlin. (DIW Wochenbericht, 46)

O'Brien, M., Brandth, B. and Kvande, E. (2007) 'Fathers, Work and Family Life: global perspectives and new insights', *Community, Work & Family,* 10 (4), pp. 375–386

Oechsle, M. (2014): *Hidden Rules and a Sense of Entitlement: working fathers within organizations.* Unpublished Paper presented at the Work and Family Researchers Network Conference. New York City

Pfahl, S. and Reuyß, S. (2009) *Das neue Elterngeld. Erfahrungen und betriebliche Nutzungsbedingungen von Vätern.* Düsseldorf: Hans-Böckler-Stiftung

Pfau-Effinger, B. (2003) *Development Paths of Care Arrangements and New Forms of Social Integration.* Paper presented at the ESPANET conference 13.-15.11.2003. Copenhagen

Pleck, J. H. and Masciadrelli, B. P. (2004) Paternal Involvement by U.S. Residential Fathers: levels, sources, consequences, in: Lamb, M. E. *The Role of the Father in Child Development.* Hoboken, NJ: Wiley, pp. 222–271

Possinger, J. (2013a) *Fürsorgliche Vaterschaft im Spannungsfeld von Erwerbs- und Familienleben. Neuen Vätern 'auf der Spur'.* Wiesbaden: Springer VS Verlag

Possinger, J. (2013b) Wie neu sind die neuen Väter? Eine Klärung. Freiburg im Breisgau: Lambertus

Sennett, R. (1998) *The Corrosion of Character.* New York: W. & W. Norton and Company

Strauss, A. L. and Corbin, J. M. (1998) *Basics of Qualitative Research: Techniques and procedures for developing grounded theory.* Thousand Oaks: SAGE Publications

Stropnik, N. and Humer, Z. (2016) Slovenia, in: Adler, M. A. and Lenz, K. (eds.) *Father Involvement in the Early Years: an international comparison of policy and practice.* Chicago: Polity Press, pp. 127–156

Toelke, A. (2012) Erwerbsarrangements. Wie Paare und Familien ihre Erwerbstätigkeit arrangieren, in: Rauschenbach, T. and Bien, W. (eds.) *Aufwachsen in Deutschland. AID:A – der neue DJI-Survey.* Weinheim: Beltz Juventa, pp. 201–214

Toelke, A. and Hank, K. (2005) *Männer – das „vernachlässigte" Geschlecht in der Familienforschung.* Wiesbaden: VS Verlag für Sozialwissenschaft

Vogt, A.-C. (2010) *Warum Väter ihre Erwerbstätigkeit (nicht) unterbrechen. Ökonomische versus sozialpsychologische Determinanten der Inanspruchnahme von Elternzeit durch Väter.* Dissertation. Universität München: Rainer Hampp Verlag

Reconciliation: The Different Political Goals of Organizations, Governments and Lobbies for Fathers and Children in Germany

Stephan Höyng

1. Introduction

The increase of the active participation rate of fathers in childcare has been a policy demand of the women's and men's movements since the 1980s in Germany. Since then, family research also has documented that fathers increasingly want to take care of children. Indeed mostly young fathers (of young children) want to contribute to family life and childcare instead of solely having a breadwinner role (Fthenakis and Minsel 2001; Walbiner 2006).

Since the beginning of the new millennium, the image of caring fathers has been strengthened by government policies, and supported by the media as well as men's and women's organizations, and it has become an important economic issue in Germany. Nevertheless, a shift away from the role of men as family breadwinner, or at least as the main earner still has to be made. Up until now, men who are involved in paid and unpaid labour ('earning and caring') are affected by a double burden and face the same risks as women face in the "rush hour of life" (Bundesministerium für Familie, Senioren, Frauen und Jugend 2006b). However, fathers have also start to seek for reconciliation measures and changes in working conditions today.

In this chapter, the author intends to look at current German policies for fathers from two different angles: a) the perspective of a social researcher, focussing on work and education, and b) the perspective of a political actor for men's interests towards caring masculinities. Most of the arguments will be based on my own research of male bonding culture in the realm of work (Höyng and Puchert 1998a), on men practicing unusual working patterns (Puchert, Höyng and Gärtner 2005), and on studies about the reconciliation of work and private life (Höyng 2012).

2. Government family policy provides the framework

The field of family policy in Germany is represented by different actors: important stakeholders for fathers' policies are work organizations, trade unions and governmental institutions. Furthermore, education and care facilities, usually representing the interests of children, fathers, mothers and partners are relevant actors as well.

State family policies provide an important framework for balancing the interests of work organizations, fathers, children and partners. Current examples of these policies are parental benefits and parental leave regulations, or the guarantee of childcare facilities for children from three to six years. However, tax splitting for married couples or registered civil partnerships that fosters single-earner couples, and a maintenance law based on the dual-earner couple, also make clear that state frameworks influence decisions concerning the share of labour in partnerships, and strengthen different models of (un) equal gender balance.

The income-based parental benefit, in place since 2007, convinced a growing number of employed fathers to make use of it: an average of 29% (in individual cities and counties like Jena and Main-Spessart it is about 50%) of entitled fathers took the parental benefit (Statistisches Bundesamt 2014: 7–8). Nevertheless, the number of parental benefit months taken by fathers in Germany is only about 7.7% of all months taken (WSI Gender Datenportal 2015d). Since 2015 the *Elterngeld Plus* (a new model of parental benefit) supports the dual-earner/dual-carer model, within which both partners work part-time, and both care for children.

Since 2013 the guarantee for institutional childcare has been offered for parents in different family forms, but statistics show that it seems especially to meet the needs of single parents and dual-earners. As in other western federal states, the legal claim for institutional childcare for children up to three years was related to the parents' employment, training or studies until 2013 in Germany. But the guarantee itself did not (yet) change reality. A great demand for more care facilities still exists, especially in the western part of Germany.

Currently it seems quite difficult to picture governmental messages concerning active fatherhood: state campaigns provide a new caring image of paternity, the creation of a maintenance law based on the dual-earner model, and measures such as parental benefit focus on an active role for men in childcare duties. But at the same time, an even more important legal framework sends contradicting messages to all unmarried fathers-to-be through the first legal steps they have to take: The recognition of paternity, child custody and maintenance obligations primarily emphasizes the assumption of financial responsibility and neglects the social responsibility of fatherhood. The legal framework therefore encourages men to take responsibility for children only in a particular way. Simultaneously, the fact that child custody is given to all unmarried mothers without questioning the right and duties of care and education also illustrates a traditional image of motherhood in society, in which children are ('naturally') associated to women. The difference between messages of campaigns and laws illustrate the conflicting incentives in state activity.

3. Family policy is challenged

Over the last few years family policy in Germany has been challenged, especially by two mega-trends: the formation of more diverse lifestyles (individualisation) and a declining birth rate (cf. Wissenschaftlicher Beirat für Familienfragen 2010).The first trend is characterized by an increase of diverse lifestyles, models of relationships and ways of life (cf. Wippermann, Calmbach and Wippermann 2009). Family models are becoming more and more diverse; and the numbers of separated parents and dual-earner families are increasing. Particularly men's fear of insecure social and economic conditions leads to less interest in having children (cf. Huber 2015). Secondly, as a consequence of the declining birth rate, a shortage of skilled workers is emerging in some regions and economic sectors (Scambor et al. 2013). Executives and policy makers are looking for labour force reserves, and support women's and mothers' employment as well as a later retirement age and lifelong learning.

Within this context family policy supports and strengthens certain images of the family. It takes position in an area of political conflict around images of family between traditional and progressive ideals (cf. Schneider et al. 2015). And current government policy is still trying to adapt to the interest of traditional voters. It still picks up on the interest of most employers to take advantage of their male workers as much as possible, for example by means of income splitting and care benefits at home.

Today, family policy is facing the challenge of stopping the declining birth rate, while at the same time supporting the integration of more women into the labour market as a result of a growing skill shortage. Government family policy also intends to strengthen dual earner/dual-carer-families, and fathers' family work. Parental benefits can be seen as an instrument for this:

> *In retrospect, it can therefore be stated that supporting active fatherhood in the context of 'sustainable family policy' is created as a by-product of the political agenda, while originally it was to increase the birth rate and not*

primarily to produce justice with respect to the division of labour between the sexes (Baronsky et al. 2012: 35, translation by the author).

The political measure of an income-based parental benefit simultaneously reflects social tensions. These politics are based on the assumption of employed parents, and particularly high-earners, who avoid having children because they fear decreased standards of living as well as career disadvantages (ibid.). This is exactly the social group that is privileged by parental benefit. For low-earners, in contrast, wage replacement of about 67% of their income is not enough, and people without gainful employment will not feel supported by an income based welfare regulation; they come away with a fixed allowance or empty handed.

As we see different motives for and different ideals in family policy, it seems obvious that incentives are sometimes conflictive. A progressive diversity policy has to reflect on this situation and especially take notice of the needs and equality of all the groups involved in society.

4. Different needs of organizations, children, fathers and partners

In the above-mentioned area of conflicting interests, it can be helpful to work out the resources and needs of the groups concerned and the interests of the stakeholders. The following is an outline of the different interests and needs of organizations, fathers, children and partners in the context of fatherhood and reconciliation in Germany.

4.1 Organizations want to gain, bind and benefit from qualified specialists

Usually organizations are interested in growth and profits. This matches with a work culture based on male bonding in which employees in leadership positions experience payed work in the organization as the starting point of all activity and as the main focus of life (Acker 1992). In this dominant work culture, performance is defined by availability, commitment, physical capacity and participation in informal networks. Informal rules have to be accepted and personal loyalty has to be shown to the management (cf. Höyng and Puchert 1998a). One condition for being promoted is to demonstrate social homogeneity and similarity (Ohlendieck 2003). Long-term disadvantages of this work culture, for example impairments of health and the exclusion of personnel (those who do not bond), are often ignored (Höyng 2012).

In fact we do not see a general skills shortage in the labour market, but bottlenecks and labour market adjustments in individual regions, industries and professions (cf. Czepek et al. 2015). Reconciliation policy used to be an instrument to increase the labour market participation of women (cf. Czepek et al. 2015). Yet such a promotion of work roles for women is quite limited. In recent years it has become the norm for organizations to offer their reconciliation measures to both genders. Nowadays the management of organizations offers work-family balance measures (e.g. temporarily part-time work, flexible working models) for men (and women) in order to keep workers with high potential in their organization. Less attractive fields of work, like the defence industry or the military, polish up their image not only by certified family-friendliness, but also by special measures for fathers (cf. Liebig, Peitz and Kron 2016). It is *en vogue* for human resource departments to present attractive work-family balance measures like childcare and flexible worktime models for men in order to reach out to highly skilled workers. At the same time, organizations intend to profit from the labour of their employees as much as possible. The experiences of reconciliation measures for women usually show a glossy presentation and a poor daily practice.

4.2 Children need a family, healthy conditions and protection

Family policies reflect the relevance of ensuring every child is as qualified as possible for the future. Since it has attracted public attention that early childhood education is highly relevant for later achievement (Thole et al. 2008), there has been more attention given to quality in kindergartens and day care. Education deficits because of class, origin, gender or other socially relevant markers should be reduced. Taking the interests of children as a starting point, early childhood education has to be a place of informal learning and development.

The United Nations state that children's rights are protection, participation and promotion (United Nations 1989). The German children's lobby organization "Deutscher Kinderschutzbund" defines similar needs of children: protection from violence and from poverty, healthy food, family time and a child-friendly living environment are only some of the outlined needs (Deutscher Kinderschutzbund, 2014: 30–33, 16–17). Fulfilling these needs generates a huge responsibility for parents and for the whole society. Fathers and mothers have to provide the economic base, care for the children's safety and health, and be active in improving their environment in their favour. But there should also be time left to spend with the children. This sounds like an excessive demand for parents as long as the community takes little responsibility for a child-friendly environment or for the protection of children from poverty.

In recent years educational experts have assigned more importance to men with respect to the upbringing of children – at home and in institutions of care and education (cf. Hurrelmann 2012; Hüther 2008; Rohrmann 2012; Brandes et al. 2015). From a psychological perspective an active relationship between the child and the father is important for socialisation: the father provides a male identification figure and, according to bond research, is important for the development of social skills (Klinger 2015). Research on fathers shows, for example, that they play in a more rough, exploratory, stimulating and challenging manner than women. They seem to favor different types of interaction, making activities exciting and exploring dangerous areas (Brandes 2010). However, Brandes also illustrates that the positives for children are less due to a special 'male' nature or a gender-typical approach. Instead, he assumes systemic effects on children of two highly involved parents who are complementary in their educational qualities (ibid.). Children therefore do not benefit from a specific male education but from parents with their own attitudes, and men in professional child care as role models for caring men (Brandes 2015).

4.3 Fathers wish for more time for their children

Many fathers wish for less work in favour of spending more time with their children. Current research shows that fulltime working fathers would reduce paid working hours, and part-time working mothers would increase their paid work for about the same amount of time (Absenger et al. 2014). If there was no gender pay gap, many couples could turn these wishes into reality without financial losses.

Actually, most fathers do not reduce their work hours, but even work more than men without children. The average weekly working hours of fathers is 41–42 hours in Germany (cf. WSI Genderdatenportal 2015a). Only 5.6% of fathers work part-time, but 9.6% of employed men without children do (WSI Genderdatenportal 2015b). It seems too easy to conclude that fathers just pay lip service. There are a lot of fulltime employed fathers with other working-time preferences. 41% of working fathers fear that parental leave could have a negative impact on their careers (Burkhardt 2015: 37). They need security that their valuation and professional recognition does not depend on assumptions, but on their activities and abilities.

Many fathers do not want to gain negative attention in their organizations (Gärtner and Bessing 2015) as they still feel responsible as breadwinner and provider. Instead of special regulations for working fathers, organizational changes for all employees and changes in work culture would help fathers much better. But currently it is not likely that concerned fathers in different statuses of paternity, with a variety of social backgrounds, incomes, time and mobility requirements, will engage for change in the dominant patterns in their organizations.

Reconciliation measures such as shift work or telework will definitely suit some of the differing needs of fathers. Sustainable support could provide a culture of reconciliation (Gärtner 2005), in which it would be common for employees to make deals around working conditions that fit with private and/or family duties. If not only men, but also organizations wanted men to care for their children, a working culture could be expected in which a strong link is drawn between paid and unpaid labour (Höyng 2012). Measures would be more flexible, including not only shift work, but also reducing and increasing work hours without disadvantages for the employee. "Time sovereignty" (Mückenberger 2015: 2) would allow more time for and flexibility in the organization of family work, without sacrificing the job.

Fathers without permanent and full time contracts are not often reached by family policy; unusual forms of paternity and of work-care patterns are not even touched. There are many different needs of fathers who do not participate in the labour market, are unemployed or receive a precarious income, for example as trainees, students or freelancers (Halrynjo and Holter 2005). Most fathers without standard employment are highly interested in a more stable, secure and also responsible connection to the organization (cf. Höyng 2010: 255f). In order to spend more time with their children, fathers need working conditions which allow some time sovereignty.

Good working conditions are not enough; to be content, fathers also need a new self-image as a male carer. Most young fathers between 20 and 39 years of age see themselves in contradiction to society: their personal role models and overall strategies include egalitarian partnerships (Lück 2015); yet they believe that the majority of society follows the model of a complementary partnership with a breadwinning father and caring mother. If most young fathers do not represent this model, for whom is a complementary partnership relevant? Is it predominantly represented by older generations, the media or the elite, or is it just a tradition developing a life of its own (cf. ibid.)? Constructing themselves in contradiction to society seems to be important for these men. But these competing cultural models may also illustrate a role conflict: the ambiguity of reaching for both the care role and the provider role at the same time (ibid.: 230f). As long as the role of a male carer is not a masculine one, active fatherhood is setting men apart from hegemonic masculinity, and that makes it difficult to create a self-image as a man (cf. Scambor et al. 2005). By imagining themselves as courageous and avant-garde, young fathers can care and simultaneously see themselves as brave, which is a pattern of hegemonic masculinity (Seehaus 2015). They need "a new definition and public recognition of male sexual identity, including caring, child-oriented attitudes and behaviours of men" (Huber 2015: 135, translation by the author).

In order to spend more time with their children, fathers need a close cooperation with mothers. If mothers believe that dealing with children is an excessive demand for fathers, and do not share the responsibility, they are discouraging men (Seehaus 2015: 72), and many fathers will give up trying sooner or later. Seehaus (2015) concludes, based on research which concentrated on fathers, mothers and parents of the middle and upper classes, that mothers seem to be very ambivalent about the integration of their partners. These mothers wish to maintain the definition of power in regards to care work, which can be seen as similar to reserving sovereign rights. Fathers need mothers to have confidence and allow them to have access to the child.

4.4 Needs of partners

Most partners of fathers want a fair division of domestic work and care, but find limited conditions for combining paid and unpaid labour (Höyng 2009). In Germany 38% of employed women without children work part-time, while 70% of employed women with children do (WSI Gender Datenportal 2015b). Many of them want to increase their working hours.

As only 5.6% of employed fathers work part-time, mothers retain the main responsibility for domestic work and children (WSI Gender Datenportal 2015b). Regardless of the labour force participation of mothers, the division of responsibilities in families is traditional: family labour is still allocated to women (Wissenschaftlicher Beirat für Familienfragen 2010: 191). 82% of women in Western Germany, but only 53% in Eastern Germany, claim that familial care is the reason for their part-time work (cf. WSI Gender Datenportal 2015c). For a fair division of domestic work and care, both partners should be responsible; this includes the presence of fathers at home. Fathers should be available in special situations, in order to organise daily duties (for instance taking a free day in case of a child's illness). Until now, in such situations only a few fathers take over (Volz and Zulehner 2009).

5. Changing work cultures – overcoming obstacles

In regards to fathers' reconciliation of work and family life, there have to be improvements on the level of the employers, the institutional childcare and – in a more personal sense – at home. Some of the most important aspects shall be pointed out below.

5.1 Changing work culture in organizations

In order to solve the problem of skills shortage, in the last decade the recruitment of women for STEM[1]-occupations was fostered by state-funded campaigns. As that is not enough, employers have to devise new recruitment strategies. Now companies and organizations want to recruit young men by attracting them through their needs; the support of active fatherhood as one among others. This is provided for by economic and governmental policy campaigns, including meetings and conferences with the German chancellor Angela Merkel (Bundesforum Männer 2014a, 2014b).

Obviously, organizations and businesses competing for skilled workers are about twice as active in fostering reconciliation measures: "Companies are considerably more active in the area of reconciliation if they expect difficulties in finding skilled workers" (Czepek et. al. 2015: 4, translation by the author).

Analysing the list of certificated family-friendly organizations in Germany we find a lot of organizations with mainly female employees, or organizations with highly specialised jobs (Audit Beruf und Familie 2015). But a few technical measures like telework or working time accounts will not reduce the stress for parents. A certification has to be only the beginning of a change in working culture. The cultural change needed in politics and business, and in the minds of employers and employees, is much deeper: we need a culture of reconciliation (Gärtner 2011; Höyng 2012).

Organizations could develop a new work culture which fosters satisfied, healthy and committed employees. They would perform better with open networks instead of male bonding. Active fathers, and of course women, would participate. Such family-friendly working conditions and sustainable products can provide satisfaction and success. Some small community orientated organizations no longer reward a permanent presence or an overload of tasks. They already benefit from a new understanding of performance and working time (Oya 2015).

Trade unions request that employers take responsibility for common welfare. The 'Confederation of German Trade Unions' is agitating for the hu-

---

1   STEM: Science, Technology, Engineering and Mathematics

manisation of work (Magazin Mitbestimmung 12/2014 and 1+2/2015), for gender equality and for a general shortening of working time (Wirtschafts- und Sozialwissenschaftliches Institut 2014, 2015). Some organizations do not count working time anymore, but rather performance. However, this is not a reconciliation measure, as performance-only orientated work does not solve parents' problems. If wages are only performance related, this also places a very heavy burden on workers (Lott 2014). Therefore, time should still be relevant for the measurement of wages. On the one hand the organizations usually expect far too much from their employees. On the other hand, many employees have internalized responsibility for their job such that they engage themselves until self-exploitation. Protecting workers from self-exploitation and consequences like burnout and other serious illnesses is in the responsibility of themselves as well as the organizations.

5.2 Changing work culture in education and care facilities

The educational system in Germany seems to be outdated with respect to working culture. Educational institutions and care facilities still seem based on structures of the industrial age, while trying to prepare children for the digital age. For example, the daily time-frame of day care centres and schools is related to the industrial workers' time structure of former times: from eight o'clock am to four o'clock pm and with collective annual holidays. But a decreasing number of parents work in this way. The inflexible time structure of care and education hinders fathers and mothers with different work patterns. In the field of tension between adaptation to current employment, (de-)regulation and parents' and children's needs, new modular structures have to be generated (cf. Frühe Chancen 2015). Modular structures imply various learning offers for pupils at different stages of learning. Educators and teachers have developed adapted models serving different interests and different approaches to learning (Debus 2014: 116).

Some children's institutions seek closer ties with fathers. For instance, fathers are often in kindergarten during the acclimatisation process, but then somehow disappear. Experts assume that more male educators could improve this situation (Rohrmann 2013). Many child care institutions are looking for ways to recruit more male educators (Koordinationsstelle 2012). New family education programmes address fathers in order to keep them close to their child's development (Mikoleit 2013). A gender reflective development of institutional childcare will also bring female educators into better cooperation with fathers (Koordinationsstelle 2014).

5.3 Changing culture and overcoming obstacles at home

Many fathers do not follow their wish to care personally for their children. Sometimes they abandon their claim of work reduction in fear of career disadvantages. In some organizations this fear is superfluous. Fathers could represent and bargain for their requirements with more self-confidence (Gärtner 2012). As employers need skilled workers, the coming generation of employed parents will have an increasing chance to make their wishes for equal division of labour come true. The skills shortage gives skilled fathers the chance to choose an employer with real family-friendly conditions. A researcher of Generation Y (today's 20–35 year-olds) put it in these words: "We have the privilege to claim and put into practice our wishes and needs, for that was already fought for in the generation of '68" (Burkhart 2015: 36, translation by the author).

But even when well designed working conditions exist, an equal division of domestic work and childcare has still to be negotiated. Fathers have to increase their domestic work. That means giving up privileges and getting involved equally in family-work and housework. Taking full responsibility means, furthermore, to be available for their children – even in special care situations. In such a change, mothers have to transfer their part in the field of childcare to fathers. For a trusting cooperation with fathers, a new division of care work has to go hand in hand with dividing responsibility and definitions of power.

After separation and divorce, especially in partnerships based on the housewife-breadwinner model, men suddenly become aware of the costs of limited familial commitment. Children then often go to live mainly with their mothers. Some mothers and judges do not comply with fathers' demands to spend as much time with their children as mothers do. Therefore, some lobbies of fathers in separation and divorce claim that mothers are supported by law and fathers are not treated equally (Bundesforum Männer 2014c). Those groups often complain of general social disadvantages for men, and claim feminist control, but they ignore the social privileges and disadvantages for other groups (Scambor et al. 2014). It is not easy, but care of children has to be negotiated on the basis of equality and respect.

The social acknowledgement of the 'masculinity' of male carers is a socially relevant phenomenon, but has to be negotiated in relations as well. This would protect against men's temptations to valorise themselves by referring to hegemonic masculinity (Seehaus 2015). There are hints that a caring masculinity is starting to become a norm in European societies, although with big variations all over Europe (Scambor et al. 2013). This upcoming caring masculinity has to be promoted and explained to men and fathers who fear changes and uncertain gender roles. It also has to be defended against men who react with extreme traditionalism to these transformations, or who fight against gender equality.

The ideal case for children would be family time with both parents and an educational cooperation and partnership between parents and care-institutions (Deutscher Kinderschutzbund 2014). What promotes children's development really needs to be considered. For example, for some parents children's time needs to create "a qua natural predetermined childlike time structure; this proves in practice to be unable to be circumvented and therefore socially not a modifiable setting" (Seehaus 2015: 71, translation by the author). An educational cooperation between parents and care-institutions could be a frame for reflecting these very high expectations aimed at parents and parents' self-expectations.

6. Conclusion for government policy

Current family policy follows the goals of increasing birth rates and human capital for the labour force. Economic arguments lead to the aim of a balanced division of work between men and women. Therefore, female labour market participation and the balanced division of family care between parents is supported. This means to support male care participation. The risks of too much paid/unpaid work in the "rush hour of life" have to be reduced by reconciliation measures, while not limiting the economy too much. Early childhood education improves educational success. Such an economically guided social and family policy is not only reacting to new forms of living and working and the increasing relevance of a dual-earner model, it is part of their creation. A policy like this considers the needs of fathers, mothers and children only as far as they correspond with its economic goals.

For parents the changes in work and employment increase the possibilities of modernizing the reconciliation of work and family and gender, but also make it necessary to negotiate the conditions (Wissenschaftlicher Beirat für Familienfragen 2010). "But as much as parents endeavour to cope with these structural fragmentations and differentiations of modern societies, these challenges are best handled by families with the appropriate resources. The structural problems cannot be solved at the individual level of the family" (Bundesministerium für Familie, Senioren, Frauen und Jugend 2006b: 261, translation by the author). It seems that families need more and other kinds of attention and support from government policy.

Organizational and governmental time-use policy has to create measures that fit for the different life situations of families, and to consider the needs of fathers, mothers and children. It has to find measures supporting patterns as different as the breadwinner model and the dual-earner model. More or less, actual reconciliation measures such as the guarantee of kindergarten places may help dual-earner couples. But even those couples need another kind of freedom: "It takes both opportunities and conditions to adjust working hours in the course of life according to respective living conditions" (Nelles 2015: 27, translation by the author). Government policies have to give incentives for a change in work culture and the division of responsibility in the family. In organizations this would be reflected in a culture of reconciliation.

Further, general work-related measures can improve conditions for most parents. The Deutscher Frauenrat and the Bundesforum Männer (German Council of Women and the Federal Forum for Men) are demanding, in a joint declaration, a general reduction of work hours and more income equality. This is seen as an opportunity for fathers, organizations, children and partners. A general reduction of work hours and more fulltime jobs would be useful for many parents, in order to spend more time on child care without being disadvantaged. Parents would be able to have family time and community involvement in a child-friendly environment. They might sometimes be less available for their employer, but for a longer period of time they would be more satisfied and presumably healthier (cf. Deutscher Frauenrat und Bundesforum Männer 2015).

Family formation behaviour could be polarised in terms of existing resources (Wissenschaftlicher Beirat für Familienfragen 2010). The living conditions for fathers and mothers with low or precarious income security, few professional opportunities and little acknowledgement should be increased. A general reduction of income differences and more equal wages regardless of the position in the hierarchy and working areas could also improve the conditions for care in many families (cf. Deutscher Frauenrat und Bundesforum Männer 2015). It must be possible to gain an income which is high enough to secure subsistence and retirement, even with reduced general workhours.

Government family policy does not focus enough on the needs of children, as yet. But children need care and education possibilities regardless of the work situations of their parents – and policies have to be developed to guarantee this. Overall, the best way to foster children's development is to reduce children's poverty. Children's needs may be responded to by addressing and securing a basic income directly to every child (Bündnis Kindergrundsicherung 2015).

A fathers' policy that is based on gender equality and social justice should address the limits of policies which are related only to economic goals. It has to acknowledge that the far-reaching perspective of gender equality goes hand in hand with measures for social justice. The more equal the living conditions of a population, the higher their health and wellbeing (Pickett and Wilkinson 2010). Øystein Holter argues, in his transnational macro study on gender equality, well-being and health: "The combined new evidence, as a whole, points to gender equality as a benefit for men as well as for women" (Holter 2014: 541). Fathers policy should be directed towards fathers', mother's and children's well-being. It should locate itself as a part of an integrated agenda for a social strategywith the aim of a better quality of life for families and in general. Therefore it has to demand systematic attention to gender related questions, innovative social solutions and the adaption to different requirements of families (Wissenschaftlicher Beirat für Familienfragen 2010). It would set the reduction of children's poverty, income differences and work hours as generally basic measures at the top of the political aims.

References

Absenger, N. et al. (2014) *Arbeitszeiten in Deutschland. Entwicklungstendenzen und Herausforderungen für eine moderne Arbeitszeitpolitik.* WSI Report Nr. 19 November 2014. Düsseldorf

Acker, J. (1992) Gendering Organizational Theory, in: Mills, A. J. and Tancred, P. (eds.) *Gendering Organizational Analysis.* London: SAGE Publications, pp. 248–260

Aktionsrat Bildung der Vereinigung der Bayerischen Wirtschaft e.V. (ed.) (2009) *Geschlechterdifferenzen im Bildungssystem.* Jahresgutachten 2009. Wiesbaden: VS Verlag für Sozialwissenschaften

Baronsky, A., Gerlach, I. and Schneider, A. K. (2012) 'Väter in der Familienpolitik', *Aus Politik und Zeitgeschichte,* 40, Bonn: Bundeszentrale für politische Bildung, pp. 31–36

Brandes, H. (2010) Ersatzmuttis oder tolle Spielkameraden: Was bringen Männer in die Erziehung ein?, *Erziehung & Unterricht. Österreichische Pädagogische Zeitschrift,* 5–6, pp. 484–496

Brandes, H., Andrä, M. Rösler, W. and Scheider-Andrich, P. (2015) *Spielt das Geschlecht eine Rolle? Erziehungsverhalten männlicher und weiblicher Fachkräfte in Kindertagesstätten.* Kurzfassung der Ergebnisse der „Tandem-Studie". Rostock: BMFSFJ

Bundesministerium für Familie, Senioren, Frauen und Jugend (ed.) (2006a) *Facetten der Vaterschaft. Perspektiven einer innovativen Väterpolitik.* Berlin: BMFSFJ

Bundesministerium für Familie, Senioren, Frauen und Jugend (ed.) (2006b) Familie zwischen Flexibilität und Verlässlichkeit Perspektiven für eine lebenslaufbezogene Familienpolitik. Siebter Familienbericht. Berlin: BMFSFJ

Burkhardt, S. (2015) 'Die Generation why ist wer?' danmag. Das inspirierende Business Magazin. *Arbeit,* 2, pp. 34–40

Czepek, J., Dummert, S. K., Leber, U., Müller, A. and Stegmaier, J. (2015) Betriebe im Wettbewerb um Arbeitskräfte : Bedarf, Engpässe und Rekrutierungsprozesse in Deutschland. Bericht 5/2015. Bielefeld. Institut für Arbeitsmarkt- und Berufsforschung

Debus, K. (2014) Aktuelle Berichte. Geschlechterbilder als Ausgangspunkt von Pädagogik, in: Debus, K.and Laumann, V. (eds.) *Rechtsextremismus, Prävention und Geschlecht. Vielfalt – Macht – Pädagogik.* Düsseldorf. Hans Böckler Stiftung, pp. 105–122

Fthenakis, W. E. and Minsel, B. (2001) *Die Rolle des Vaters in der Familie.* Zusammenfassung des Forschungsberichtes im Auftrag des BMFSFJ. Berlin/Bonn

Gärtner, M. (2012) *Männer und Familienvereinbarkeit. Betriebliche Personalpolitik, Akteurskonstellationen und Organisationskulturen.* Opladen: Budrich University Press

Gärtner, M., Atanassova, M., Riesenfeld, V., Scambor, C. and Schwerma, K. (2005) Men are Gendered, not Standard: scientific and political implications of the results, in: Puchert, R., Höyng, S. and Gärtner, M. (eds.) *Work Changes Gender: men and equality in the transition of labour forms.* Opladen: Verlag Barbara Budrich, pp. 175–192

Gärtner, M. and Bessing, N. (due to be published 2016) Zwischen Verfügbarkeit und Vereinbarkeit: Wie Organisationskulturen die Inanspruchnahme von Elternzeiten prägen, in: Nelles, H.-G. (ed.) *Partnerschaftliche Arbeitsteilung in Familien.* Berlin: BMFSFJ, pp. 188–194

Halrynjo, S. and Holter, Ø. (2005) Male Job and Life Patterns: A Correspondence Analysis, in: Puchert, R., Höyng, S. and Gärtner, M. (eds.) *Work Changes Gender: men and equality in the transition of labour forms.* Opladen: Verlag Barbara Budrich, pp. 105–115

Holter, Ø. (2014) '"What is in it for Men?": Old Question, New Data', *Men and Masculinities,* 17(5) pp. 515–548

Höyng, S. (2009) Männer: Arbeit, privates Leben und Zufriedenheit, in: Volz, R. and Zulehner, P. M., *Männer in Bewegung. Zehn Jahre Männerentwicklung in Deutschland.* BMFSFJ Forschungsreihe Band 6. Baden-Baden: Nomos Verlag, pp. 343–356

Höyng, S. (2010) Exkurs: Männer zwischen Beruf und privatem Leben, in: Projektgruppe GIB (ed.) *Geschlechterungleichheiten im Betrieb. Arbeit, Entlohnung und Gleichstellung in der Privatwirtschaft.* Berlin: Edition Sigma, pp. 240–256

Höyng, S. (2012) Getriebene – zu wenig Zeit für Beruf und Familie, in: Prömper, H., Jansen, M. and Ruffing, A. (eds.) *Männer unter Druck. Ein Themenbuch.* Opladen: Verlag Barbara Budrich, pp. 275–307

Höyng, S. and Puchert, R. (1998b) „Die nicht angenommene Herausforderung: Patriarchale Arbeitskultur, Maskulinitäten und berufliche Gleichstellung", *Zeitschrift für Frauenforschung,* 3, pp. 59–75

Höyng, S. and Puchert, R. (1998a) *Die Verhinderung der beruflichen Gleichstellung.* Bielefeld: Kleine Verlag

Hurrelmann, K. (2012) Pädagogische Arbeit braucht gemischte Fachkollegien, in: Hurrelmann, K. and Schultz, T. (eds.) *Jungen als Bildungsverlierer: Brauchen wir eine Männerquote in Kitas und Schulen.* Weinheim: Beltz/Juventa Verlag, pp. 47–64

Hüther, G. (2008) 'Angeboren oder erworben? Über männliche und weibliche Gehirne', TPS. *Leben Lernen und Arbeiten in der Kita,* 2, pp. 8–11

Jurczyk, K. and Lange, A. (2009) Vom „ewigen Praktikanten" zum „reflexiven Vater"? Eine Einführung in aktuelle Debatten um Väter, in: Jurczyk, K. and Lange, A. (eds.) *Vater-werden und Vatersein heute. Neue Wege – neue Chancen!* Gütersloh: Bertelsmann Stiftung, pp. 13–39

Klenner, C. and Pfahl, S. (2008) *'Jenseits von Zeitnot und Karriereverzicht – Wege aus dem Arbeitsmarktdilemma', Arbeitszeiten von Müttern, Vätern und Pflegenden.* WSI-Diskussionspapier Nr. 158. Januar 2008: Düsseldorf

Klinger, L-M. (2015) Der Papa der macht alles, was sonst keiner gerne tut? Deutungsmuster von Vaterschaft aus der Perspektive von Fachkräften im Jugendamt, in: Seehaus, R. and Rose, L. and Günther, M. (eds.) *Mutter, Vater, Kind – Geschlechterpraxen in der Elternschaft.* Opladen: Verlag Barbara Budrich, pp. 223–241

Koordinationsstelle „Männer in Kitas" (ed.) (2012) *Männer in Kitas.* Opladen: Verlag Barbara Budrich

Le Camus, J. (2001) *Väter. Die Bedeutung des Vaters für die psychische Entwicklung des Kindes.* Weinheim und Basel: Beltz

Liebig, B., Peitz, M. and Kron, C. (eds.) (2016) *Väterorientierte Massnahmen in Unternehmen und Verwaltungen in der Schweiz. Ein Handbuch.* Meiring: Rainer Hampp Verlag

Lott, Y. (2014) *Working Time Autonomy and Time Adequacy: What if performance is all that counts?* WSI-Diskussionspapier Nr. 188. Juni 2014: Düsseldorf

Lück, D. (2015) Vaterleitbilder: Ernährer und Erzieher?, in: Schneider, N. F., Diabaté, S. and Ruckdeschel, K. (eds.) *Familienleitbilder in Deutschland. Kulturelle Vorstellungen zu Partnerschaft, Elternschaft und Familienleben.* Opladen: Verlag Barbara Budrich, pp. 227–245

Mikoleit, D. (2013) Pädagogische Fachkräfte als Multiplikatorinnen und Multiplikatoren für Väterarbeit. In: *Koordinationsstelle „Männer in Kitas" (ed.) Vielfältige Väterarbeit in Kindertagesstätten. Handreichung für die Praxis.* Berlin, pp. 41–46

Nelles, H.-G. (2015) *ElterngeldPlus. Ein Plus für Väter?* Eine Expertise zum ElterngeldPlus und eine Dokumentation einer Fachveranstaltung des Bundesforum Männer. Berlin: Bundesforum Männer

Ohlendieck, L. (2003) Gender Trouble in Organisationen und Netzwerken, in: Pasero, U. and Weinbach, C. (eds.) *Frauen, Männer, Gender Trouble. Systemtheoretische Essays.* Frankfurt a. Main: Suhrkamp, pp. 171–185

Pickett, K. and Wilkinson, R. (2010) *Gleichheit ist Glück: Warum gerechte Gesellschaften für alle besser sind.* Berlin: Tolkemit

Rohrmann, T. (2012) Warum mehr Männer?, in: Rohrmann, T. (ed.) *Koordinationsstelle „Männer in Kitas".* Opladen, Berlin & Toronto: Verlag Barbara Budrich, pp. 115–129

Rohrmann, T. (2013) Die Bedeutung männlicher Fachkräfte für die Zusammenarbeit mit Vätern in der Kita, in: Rohrmann, T. (ed.) *Koordinationsstelle „Männer in Kitas" Vielfältige Väterarbeit in Kindertagesstätten. Handreichung für die Praxis.* Berlin, pp. 29–34

Scambor, C., Schwerma, K. and Abril, P.(2005) Towards a New Positioning of Men, in: Puchert, R., Gärtner, M. and Höyng, S. (eds.) *Work Changes Gender: Men and Equality in the Transition of Labour Forms.* Opladen: Barbara Burdrich Verlag, pp. 117–173

Schneider, N. F., Diabaté, S. and Ruckdeschel, K. (eds.) (2015) *Familienleitbilder in Deutschland. Kulturelle Vorstellungen zu Partnerschaft, Elternschaft und Familienleben.* Opladen, Berlin & Toronto: Barbara Budrich Verlag.

Seehaus, R. (2015) Vergeschlechtlichte Sorge um das Kind, in: Seehaus, R., Rose, L. and Günther, M. (eds.) *Mutter, Vater, Kind – Geschlechterpraxen in der Elternschaft.* Opladen, Berlin, Toronto: Barbara Budrich Verlag. pp. 65–77

Seehaus, R., Rose, L. and Günther, M. (eds.) (2015) *Mutter, Vater, Kind – Geschlechterpraxen in der Elternschaft.* Opladen, Berlin, Toronto: Barbara Budrich Verlag.

Sievers, S. and Kröhnert, S. (2015) *Schwach im Abschluss: Warum Jungen in der Bildung hinter Mädchen zurückfallen – und was dagegen zu tun wäre.* Berlin: Institut für Bevölkerung und Entwicklung

Thole, W., Rossbach, H-G., Fölling-Albers, M. and Tippelt, R. (eds.) (2008) *Bildung und Kindheit: Pädagogik der Frühen Kindheit in Wissenschaft und Lehre.* Opladen/Farmington Hills, MI: Barbara Budrich Verlag

Volz, R. and Zulehner, P. M. (2009) *Männer in Bewegung. Zehn Jahre Männerentwicklung in Deutschland.* BMFSFJ Forschungsreihe Band 6. Baden-Baden: Nomos Verlag

Walbiner, W. (2006) Mehr als (nur) Brotverdiener: Neue Konzepte von Vaterschaft, in: Walbiner, W. (ed.) Bundesministerium für Familie, Senioren, Frauen und Jugend *,Facetten der Vaterschaft. Perspektiven einer innovativen Väterpolitik.* Berlin: BMFSFJ, pp. 16–28

Wippermann, C., Calmbach, M. and Wippermann, K. (2009) *Männer: Rolle vorwärts, Rolle rückwärts? Identitäten und Verhalten von traditionellen, modernen und postmodernen Männern.* Opladen/Farmington Hills, MI: Barbara Budrich Verlag

Wissenschaftlicher Beirat für Familienfragen beim Bundesministerium für Familie, Senioren, Frauen und Jugend (ed.) (2010) Familie, Wissenschaft, Politik: Ein Kompendium der Familienpolitik. Berlin: BMFSFJ.

Online resources

Audit Beruf und Familie (2015) Available at: http://www.beruf-und-familie.de/files/frdata/Veranstaltungen/Zertifikatsempfaenger_2015_PLZ.pdf 10.02.2016

Bosch, Gerhard (2015) 'Warum nicht mal 30 Stunden?', in: *Magazin Mitbestimmung (1+2/2015) Arbeitszeit: Warum wie eine neue Debatte brauchen.* Available at: http://www.boeckler.de/53014_53035.htm 10.02.2016

Bundesforum Männer (2014a) Bundesforum Männer im Gespräch mit der Bundeskanzlerin. Available at: https://bundesforum-maenner.de/2014/09/3279/ 10.02.2016

Bundesforum Männer (2014b) *Vereinbarkeit für Väter – ein Erfolgsfaktor für Unternehmen?!* Available at: https://bundesforum-maenner.de/2014/10/vereinbarkeit-fuer-vaeter-ein-erfolgsfaktor-fuer-unternehmen/ 10.02.2016

Bundesforum Männer (2014c) Michael Kimmel: "Angry White Men. American Masculinity at the End of an Era". Available at: https://bundesforum-maenner.de/2014/06/zu-michael-kimmel-angry-white-men-american-masculinity-at-the-end-of-an-era/ 10.02.2016

Bündnis Kindergrundsicherung (2015) Available at: http://www.zukunftsforum-familie.de/themen/kinderarmut/ 10.02.2016

Deutscher Frauenrat und Bundesforum Männer (2015) Pressemitteilung zum Internationalen Frauentag. Available at: https://bundesforum-maenner.de/2015/03/mehr-zeit-fuer-ein-gutes-leben-arbeitszeitverkuerzung-weiterdenken/ 10.02.2016

Deutscher Kinderschutzbund (ed.) (2014) Kinderpolitisches Programm des Deutschen Kinderschutzbundes. Berlin. Available at: http://www.dksb.de/Content/E-Paper-Kinderpolitisches-Programm/ 10.02.2016

Hexel, D. (2013) Kapitalbesitzer tragen zum Gemeinwohl nur wenig bei, in: *Mitbestimmung 01+02/2013. Wirtschaften für das Gemeinwohl.* Stiftung, Genossenschaft & Co. Available at: http://www.boeckler.de/42171_42215.htm 10.02.2016

Institut für Demoskopie Allensbach (2015) *Weichenstellungen für die Aufgabenteilung in Familie und Beruf.* Untersuchungsbericht zu einer repräsentativen Befragung von Elternpaaren im Auftrag des Bundesministeriums für Familie, Senioren, Frauen und Jugend. Allensbach. Available at: https://www.demografie-portal.de/SharedDocs/Informieren/DE/Studien/Aufgabenteilung_Familie_Beruf.html 10.02.2016

Koordinationsstelle Männer in Kitas (ed.) (2014) G*eschlechtersensibel pädagogisch arbeiten.* Berlin. Available at: http://mika.koordination-maennerinkitas.de/unsere-themen/gender-in-der-paed-arbeit

Liebig, B., Peitz, M. and Kron, C. (2013-2016) *Projekt: Familienfreundliche Organisationen und Vaterschaft.* Available at: http://www.fhnw.ch/aps/ifk/projekte/aktuelle-projekte/familienfreundliche-organisationen 10.02.2016

Mückenberger, U. (2015) 'German Society for Time Policy', Deutsche Gesellschaft für Zeitpolitik (ed.): 2015: Zeitpolitisches Magazin Nr. 26 Juli 2015. Available at: http://www.zeitpolitik.de/pdfs/zpm_26_0715.pdf#page=3&zoom=auto

Nelhiebel, N. (2013) *Kleine Jungen ohne männliche Vorbilder. Ein Gespräch mit Gerald Hüther.* Available at: http://www.vaeter.nrw.de/Aktiv_Vater_sein/Vater_sein/radio-interview-mit-professor-gerald-huether-warum-jungen-maennliche-vorbilder-brauchen/mitschrift-nordwestradio-interview-huether.php 10.02.2016

Oya (2015) *Anders denken. Anders leben.* Oya Ausgabe 34. Oya Medien eG, Lassan. Available at: http://www.oya-online.de/article/issue/34-2015.html 10.02.2016

Portal Frühe Chancen (2015) Bundesministerium für Familie, Senioren, Frauen und Jugend. Available at: http://www.fruehe-chancen.de/themen/kinderbetreuung-international/bildungs-und-betreuungssysteme/bildung-und-betreuung-international/aus-politik-praxis/kindertagespflege-in-norwegen/ 10.02.2016

Scambor, E., Wojnicka, K. and Bergmann, N. (eds.) (2013) *The Role of Men in Gender Equality – European strategies & insights.* Luxembourg: Publications Office of the European Union. Available at: http://ec.europa.eu/justice/events/role-of-men 10.05.2016

Scambor, E. and Kirchengast, A. (2014) *Zwischen Geschlechterdemokratie und Männerrechtsbewegung. Geschlechterpolitische Zugänge in der österreichischen Männerarbeit.* Institut für Männer- und Geschlechterforschung. Available at: http://vmg-steiermark.at/de/forschung/publikation/zwischen-geschlechterdemokratie-und-maennerrechtsbewegung 10.06.2016

Statistisches Bundesamt (2014) *Elterngeld für Geburten 2012. Nach Kreisen.* Available at: https://www.destatis.de/DE/Publikationen/Thematisch/Soziales/Elterngeld/ElterngeldGeburtenKreise5229204127004.pdf?__blob=publicationFile 10.02.2016

United Nations (1989) *Kinderrechtskonvention. Übereinkommen über die Rechte des Kindes.* Available at: http://www.kinderrechtskonvention.info 10.02.2016

Wirtschafts- und Sozialwissenschaftliches Institut (2014) WSI-Herbstforum. Available at: http://www.boeckler.de/wsi_52319.htm 10.02.2016

Wirtschafts- und Sozialwissenschaftliches Institut (WSI) (2015) WSI-Gleichstellungstagung. Available at: http://www.boeckler.de/cps/rde/xchg/hbs/hs.xsl/veranstaltung_wsi_53930.htm 10.02.2016

WSI GenderDatenPortal (2015a) *Themenbereich Arbeitszeiten. Arbeitszeit und Elternschaft. Mütter arbeiten deutlich kürzer – Väter aber nicht.* Available at: http://www.boeckler.de/51975.htm 10.02.2016

WSI GenderDatenPortal (2015b) *Themenbereich Arbeitszeiten. Arbeitszeit und Elternschaft. Teilzeitquoten von Müttern liegen deutlich über dem allgemeinen Durchschnitt.* Available at: http://www.boeckler.de/51974.htm 10.02.2016

WSI GenderDatenPortal (2015c) *Themenbereich Arbeitszeiten. Arbeitszeit und Elternschaft. Unterschiedliche Gründe für die Teilzeitbeschäftigung von Frauen und Männern.* Available at: http://www.boeckler.de/51973.htm 10.02.2016

WSI GenderDatenPortal (2015d) *Themenbereich familienpolitische Leistungen. Mütter nehmen über 90 Prozent der Elterngeldmonate.* Available at: http://boeckler.de/51834.htm 10.02.2016

5. Issues and Challenges in Research

Research on Work and Family: Some Issues and Challenges

Suzan Lewis and Bianca Stumbitz

1. Introduction

The work-family field began half a century ago with the seminal publications of Rhona and Robert Rapoport (Rapoport and Rapoport 1965). Although they considered the role of fathers (Rapoport et al. 1979), subsequently research tended to focus more on women, especially mothers. However, as this volume illustrates, norms and expectations of fathering have shifted in many contexts and the importance of understanding work-family issues of fathers as well as mothers in organizations is increasingly recognised as crucial to gender equality. Nevertheless, as with most areas of research, the more we learn about men and women in families and workplaces, the more challenges and issues emerge. In this chapter we select and discuss four specific ongoing and emerging research challenges and illustrate these with case studies and other research. Unlike other chapters in this volume we base our discussion on the wider work and family field, but also consider implications for fathers.

The first, fundamental challenge for work and family researchers that we discuss below is the ongoing need to better understand and confront deeply embedded and change-resistant gendered workplace practices and cultures that can undermine active fatherhood and reinforce gendered sense of entitlement to support for parenting and employment. Although we focus here on the workplace, organizations do not exist in a vacuum and wider context is important, so a second research challenge is how to capture the impact of complex intersecting layers of societal, community, organizational and family contexts on experiences of work and family. A third challenge is to broaden the range of contexts studied. Most research takes place in large organizations within western, high income countries, neglecting other experiences in smaller organizations and in the developing world. Finally there is the question of how research can progress beyond describing and analysing challenges towards contributing to systemic change in workplaces and families.

2. Gendered organizations and sense of entitlement to support for work and family

Organizations are rarely if ever gender neutral. It is widely acknowledged by gender scholars that workplace structures, cultures and practices that are perceived as gender neutral tend to be based on, reinforce and reproduce gendered assumptions of separate spheres with women as primary carers and men as work-primary and breadwinners (Acker 1990, 1998; Bailyn 1993, 2006; Holt and Lewis 2011; Williams et al. 2012). Consequently ideals of competence and value in the workplace tend to be conflated with hegemonic masculinity (Bailyn 2006); that is, ideal employees according to the traditional male model, who can work as though they have no social or caring obligations outside work, can be constantly visible, always available to work full time and often work long hours with no 'concessions' for family (Acker 1990; Holt and Lewis 2011). Moreover, an uninterrupted full time work trajectory with progress tied to normative age (coinciding with family formation phases) is also idealised (Guerrier et al. 2009). Hegemonic masculine workplace cultures and ideal worker norms can make it difficult for women's achievements to be recognised unless they perform traditional masculinity via their working practices (Cahusac and Kanji 2014). Ideal worker assumptions conflict with societal assumptions about the ideal mother (Herman and Lewis 2012; Christopher 2012) which, although shifting to some extent, remain strong in most cultures and sustain inequalities at work and at home (Crompton et al. 2007). However, the male model of work and traditional ways of doing masculinity in the workplace also impacts on fathers. Although it is increasingly recognised that there are a diversity of masculinities (Connell 2012), and some limited evidence of shifts in masculinity and men's ways of doing family towards a 'new' fatherhood in some contexts (e.g. Johannson and Ottemo 2015; Johansson 2011) the traditional ideology of fatherhood tends to be more congruent with traditional ideal worker norms. This can hold back ideological shifts relating to fatherhood.

As working hours in many occupations extend and/or intensify, it is increasingly recognised that full time occupations for two parents are difficult to sustain and in some societies a one and a half breadwinner family is normative (Hook 2014). Consequently a range of flexible and reduced hours working arrangements, variously termed 'family-friendly', 'work and family' or 'work-life balance' policies and practices, have been developed in many countries, particularly in large organizations and multinationals. Such policies tend to be positioned as providing mothers with 'choices' to meet their 'preferences' while a discourse of providing choice for fathers is less common, at least beyond paternity or parental leaves. Moreover, the choice narrative assumes the ability to make unconstrained choices and neglects other contextual constraints on agency and real freedom of choice, which shape capabilities and decision making about how to combine work and personal life (Nussbaum 2000; Sen 1999; Hobson 2013). The effects of working less than traditional full-time hours on women's and men's careers, and gender equity more broadly, remain contentious in the context of widespread gendered organizational values and practices (Haas and Hwang 2007; Guerrier et al. 2009). In this ideological context those who use such arrangements (mostly women with children) are often marginalised, perpetuating the organizational silent discourses associated with deeply embedded and virtually unconscious traditional male values (Schein, 2007). For many men, the loss of income and opportunities for advancement at work associated with non-traditional working patterns is a powerful deterrent, limiting decisions to work in ways that may be more congruent with active fatherhood.

A gendered organizational theoretical lens thus highlights organizational assumptions that systematically disadvantage women/mothers but also impact on fathers. Gender inequities persist in workplaces because they are embedded in and reinforced by everyday working practices, beliefs and knowledge structures that are taken for granted and therefore not acknowledged or scrutinised (Bailyn 2006; Myerson and Tompkins 2007; Holt and Lewis 2011). A major challenge in work-family research then, is not only to understand and challenge gendered workplace assumptions but particularly to identify the everyday practices and processes that reinforce and reproduce gendered prescriptions in the workplace.

There is also a need to understand more about how these practices impact on cognitive, affective and behavioural processes at the individual level, which sustain more traditional and inequitable parental and employment roles. So, while research on gendered organizations is crucial for drawing attention to social and organizational challenges in fatherhood and work-family research more generally, it is important not to neglect the link with individual issues and expectations. In this chapter we focus on the related concept of sense of entitlement. This denotes a set of beliefs and feelings about rights, entitlements, or legitimate expectations, based on what is perceived to be fair and equitable (Major 1993; Bylsma and Major 1994; Lewis and Smithson 2001). Sense of entitlement is influenced by assumptions about ideal workers and ideologies of motherhood and fatherhood as well as broader social ideology and practices and shapes the supports and outcomes that mothers and fathers feel entitled to expect in the workplace and elsewhere (Lewis and Smithson 2001; Herman and Lewis 2012). Subjective sense of entitlement is highly gendered. For example, there is evidence that women often feel less entitled to higher rates of pay or other rewards than men (Bylsma and Major

1994). Mothers also feel more entitled than fathers to ask to modify traditional working patterns for family, but less entitled to advance their careers if they do prioritise childcare for a period of time (Herman and Lewis 2012;Webber and Williams 2008; Walters and Whitehouse 2014). Conversely, fathers tend to feel less entitled to ask for workplace support for active fatherhood which deviates from notions of organizational masculinities, while conformity to the traditional male model of work creates a higher sense of entitlement to career progression.

Although the concept of subjective sense of entitlement is an individual cognitive and affective construct (Lewis and Smithson 2001; Herman and Lewis 2012; Peper et al. 2014), it derives from social justice theory and emphasizes the role of social processes, particularly social comparison (Lerner, 1987). This theoretical basis provides one useful framework for understanding the impacts of gendered expectations in the workplace and family. Sense of entitlement is theorised to be constructed on the basis of social, normative and feasibility social comparisons (Lewis and Smithson 2001; Lewis and Haas 2005). Judgements about what is fair or equitable are made on the basis of normative comparisons with social comparators, that is, those who are assumed to be similar to oneself (Major 1993; Bylsma and Major 1994). Thus fathers would be more likely to, for example, take up flexible working options if they could compare themselves with other fathers and realise that it is feasible to do so. Gender role models are important in providing social comparisons. If there are few, if any, organizational role models of fathers who modify work for family and sustain career progression (or mothers who do so and nevertheless advance in their careers) social comparisons result in perceptions that this would be neither normative nor feasible. However, this still does not explain why or under what conditions some fathers can become social comparative referents for deviating from normative male career patterns, and we need to know more about this. Wider national contexts, including social policies and the cultural values that they reflect, also impact on sense of entitlement to support for work and parenthood (Lewis and Smithson 2001; Lewis and Haas 2005). Conditions that encourage the perception that paternal active involvement in day to day parenting is both normative and feasible, or conversely undermine fathers' sense of entitlement to support for active fatherhood, are thus highly context specific. They are influenced by national, family and workplace structures, policies and cultures, as well as historical, political and economic factors. A further work-family research challenge is therefore to capture the impact of intersecting layers of societal, organizational and family contexts on fathers' sense of entitlement to, as well as expectations and capabilities for active fatherhood.

3. Capturing the impact of intersecting layers of context on work and family experiences

Despite calls for context sensitive research on work and family over many years (Lewis et al. 1992; Powell et al. 2009) most work-family research has neglected context or attends only to certain limited aspects of it, ignoring the complexity of contextual interconnections (Nilsen et al. 2012). Quantitative research in particular has often rendered context invisible, or fails to analyse its nature and significance, frequently using constructs that are treated as universal or context neutral. There has nevertheless been a growing focus on the importance of context in work and family research more recently (Ollier-Malaterre et al. 2013), including cross national comparisons (e.g. Allen et al. 2015; Lyness and Judiesch 2014), although exploration of layers of contextual influences and their intersections remain relatively limited (Lewis et al. 2009; Nilsen et al. 2012).

In this chapter we focus primarily on the organizational layer of context, in terms of workplace practices, culture, structures and discourses, while emphasising that this cannot be separated from wider socio-economic and cultural factors. Experiences and expectations at work are shaped not only by organizational cultures and practices but also by the specific national contexts in which workplaces are located (Nilsen et al. 2012; Granovetter 1985). It is useful to situate workplace processes within intersecting global, national and local layers of contexts. At the global layer, globalization, the spread of global capitalism and associated values, international regulations and directives, such as those set by the International Labour Organization (ILO) and the EU, global recessions and economic trends are all reflected to varying extents in organizational processes. At the national layer, most research focuses on public policies and whether or not these are enforced on institutional characteristics (e.g. Abendroth and Den Dulk 2011; Lyness and Judiesch 2014; Ruppaner and Huffman 2013). At the local layer the influence of rural and urban contexts has received some limited attention, as well as the influence of communities and neighbourhood (Voydanoff, 2014). The journal *Community, Work and Family* was developed to encourage research on the interface between the three domains, but it has taken time for these to be considered simultaneously. These contexts are important, but many other contextual factors such as economic context, employment relations, cultural values and practices, societal discourses and trends as well as the impact of particular time periods, and readiness for change merit more consideration (Nilsen et al. 2012). The interface of these contextual factors may all contribute to scope for agency to resist traditional gender norms and assumptions at work and at home, as well as to gendered sense of entitlement regarding parenting and employment.

How can work and family research do justice to these complexities? Different methodological approaches, both qualitative and quantitative have a role to play. It is not possible to explore all intersecting layers of context in all research but approaches which focus on several contextual layers, with an awareness of wider contextual influences, offer insights into processes for challenging gendered assumptions about work and family roles. A contextualised case study approach (e.g. Lewis et al. 2009; Nilsen et al. 2012) is particularly appropriate for foregrounding and exploring aspects of context and how they influence organizational processes, complementing other research approaches. Qualitative case studies, by definition, embed workplaces in context and can be combined with quantitative data collection. An issue for such research, however, is that aspects of context are not always articulated by interviewees or by survey respondents, as these are often taken for granted. Brannen and Nilsen (2005) discuss these as the 'silent discourse' – the taken for granted aspects of context. How to access these – and to bring them to bear in the research discussion – is a further challenge.

Below we discuss two case studies that illuminate the impact of sets of contextual factors and the interplay between them on working patterns that are considered normative and feasible, for fathers as well as mothers, and which we argue can potentially enhance sense of entitlement to active fatherhood. The first case concerns a 'four day week' initiative implemented in two different science, engineering and technology (SET) companies in France. Contextual factors that influenced expectations and sense of entitlement to support for work and parenting included national policy, working hours, cultural norms and values, economic context and role of the unions, as well as type of organization and specific occupational context. The second case brings in the notion of historical time, exploring flexible working arrangements in a specific place, country and sector (UK public sector organizations) and time (post 2008 global recession).

3.1 The impact of layers of context – place

The two SET case study organizations were multinationals, headquartered in France and, typical in this sector, were very male dominated, with a traditional masculine culture. However, there was a drive to enhance recruitment and retention of highly educated women scientists and engineers, who tended to drop out of their careers after becoming mothers. There was no discourse about supporting fathers in either workplace as turnover among men was not considered to be a problem.

The overall French national context was characterised firstly by a relatively short working week (at least formally). The 35 hour week was introduced to reduce unemployment rather than for gender equality reasons, and the discourse of working less was important at the time of the case studies. Secondly, the working mother model is the norm in France. Mothers are expected to be employed and this is supported by good public preschool childcare and other policies. Nevertheless the gendered assumption is that mothers will take the main responsibility for childcare (Fagnani and Letablier 2004).Thus, many mothers wished to reduce their working days because of a four and a half day school week in France, but fathers normally worked full time. This context facilitated the development of workplace four day week working policies, which were well established at the two companies, which we call Scienco and Innovco (Herman and Lewis 2012; Lewis 2009). In both cases this involved, in practice, an intensification of work rather than a 4 day workload, alongside reduced earnings (albeit differently structured in the two companies). The four day week was taken up only by mothers in Scienco but used by women and men, both with and without children, in Innovco. Why was this?

Pay was important. In Scienco the four day week involved the loss of 20% income and the discourse around this organizational social practice was about supporting mothers. Mothers who took up this practice tended to be marginalised, rather than recognised as more efficient. Although a few women had been promoted while working a four day week this was not common. Innovco, in contrast was a former public sector organization with a strong union and there was more general support for the government drive for shorter hours to reduce unemployment. The union negotiated an option of a 32 hour week (for a fixed number of years) with loss of only 3 hours pay per week, retaining all benefits and pensions contributions. The dominant discourse was about working less, rather than supporting mothers. At first women used the four day week mostly for childcare while men used it for other reasons, especially leisure. But as it became normative, in this context, and working practices adapted to this (for example, meetings were not held on Mondays or Fridays to take account of four day schedules), men started saying they wanted to work four days for childcare reasons. Thus a combination of intersecting contexts and factors influenced workplace social practices and culture. Social comparisons and perceptions that a four day working week was normative and feasible, enabled fathers to speak up and increased sense of entitlement to support for active fatherhood. The minimal financial costs (compared to Scienco) in this context may also have reduced threats to masculinity and breadwinner identity, especially as the company made specific efforts to ensure that women working four days were not disadvantaged in promotion terms (this had not yet been addressed for men). However, importantly, this result was very context specific even within the company. It was limited to only one section of the organization (research and development) and, noticeably, did not apply to heavy engineering. Thus the case illustrates how focusing on the broader benefits of working less (not just for women) and attention to issues of pay have the potential to shift workplace cultures and enhance fathers' sense of entitlement to make more time for family, but also cautions that specific policies are likely to need some adaptations beyond limited contexts.

3.2 The impact of layers of context – time

Aspects of historical and present time also form an important and often neglected context for work and family research (Nilsen et al. 2012; Gambles et al. 2006). This raises questions of how research can capture the impact of shifting economic contexts, such as recession or phases of economic development as well other dynamic trends. An example of the significance of time as well as place comes from a study of the impact of financial austerity on work-life balance (WLB) policies and practices in the UK public sector (Lewis et al. 2017). This qualitative study of public sector HR Directors carried out in 2011–12 examined the impact of austerity on flexible working arrangements. It illustrates the interplay of time and place by focusing on flexible working arrangements in a particular national and institutional context (the UK public sector) at a critical time; a period of financial austerity following the 2008 global recession which particularly hit the public sector.

The historical context included a history of commitment to family-friendliness in the public sector (Yeandle et al. 2002). This was reinforced when the Labour administrations of 1997–2010 carried out a prominent campaign on WLB. The development of legislation extending WLB initiatives such as the right to request flexible working (albeit, less progressive than some other European countries) was associated with discourses emphasizing the compatibility of social justice with economic prosperity (DTI 1998) – a mutual benefit discourse. Subsequently the public sector strove to be a 'model employer' in terms of diversity and WLB provisions (Corby and Symon 2011; Rubery and Rafferty 2013). Following the financial recession however, the public sector was faced with severe austerity budget cuts in the context of a Conservative led government that was ideologically committed to reducing the size of the public sector.

In an earlier recession, work-family policies were reduced (Dex and Smith 2002). However, since that time the public sector had developed a range of flexible working arrangements, including investing in an infrastructure of IT and other supports for flexible ways of working. There had also been an evolution of the WLB discourse and mutual benefit arguments. The findings of the study of HR directors after the 2008 recession revealed that, rather than the availability of flexible working arrangements being reduced at this time, they were being developed and used strategically to manage the financial crisis. The history of developments in flexible working and experiences of what were now very well established and embedded flexible practices, together with a public sector ethos of supporting employees provided a baseline from which employer-led cost cutting initiatives could be developed. These ranged from the positive encouragement of staff to reduce their hours to avoid redundancies, to a growth in remote work as employers cut down on estate and utilities costs to increase efficiency and transfer costs to workers. The discourses of work-life balance and mutual benefit to employer and employee, generated by earlier governments were appropriated to justify these cost cutting changes, implying employee choice. However, in some cases remote working was non-voluntary and meant than men and women were required to work away from the office. While this reduced employee autonomy in one sense, it also challenged the notion that ideal workers must be constantly visible, thus creating a situation where flexible working, including remote working became not only feasible but normative. The shifts in norms and perceptions of feasibility and entitlements may ultimately benefit some fathers and others by challenging gendered assumptions about ideal workers as constantly visible at work although further research will be needed to see how this plays out. This was an unanticipated consequence of the interface between economic recession, austerity and political factors on the one hand, occurring at a point in time when organizational factors (development of supports for flexible working arrangements) facilitated new ways of working. Qualitative case study research provided insights into the process whereby this was happening. However, further research would be needed to examine whether this actually enhances father friendliness, and men's sense of entitlement to support for active fathering, which were not the focus of this study.

4. The Way Forward

4.1 The need to broaden the organizations and national contexts studied

A further issue and challenge for work-family research is to expand the range of workplaces and national contexts that we study in order to understand the work and family experiences of wider populations. Despite the substantial research examining the impact of organizational support for employed parents, this mostly focuses on workers employed in large organizations, in affluent countries. In particular research currently neglects experiences in small or medium sized enterprises (SMEs) and workers in informal and developing economies (Lewis et al. 2014). The neglect of SMEs in work-family research is significant as, in the majority of countries across the world, more people work in SMEs than larger companies (de Kok et al. 2013). Research on large organizations cannot be applied uncritically to smaller firms which tend to differ from their larger counterparts in a number of respects. Despite the heterogeneity of SMEs, there are a number of key characteristics described in the literature which affect the availability and nature of work and family supports including father-friendly measures at the workplace. For example, resource constraints and high failure and turnover rates often result in antipathy to government intervention in the form of regulation and a focus on short-term planning and immediate outcomes. Unlike larger organizations, smaller firms rarely have a formal HR function and organizational work cultures are strongly related to (owner-) managers' attitudes (Lewis et al. 2014; Croucher et al. 2013). Typically SME owners prefer more informal approaches to labour management. Nevertheless, a recent international review of research on maternity protection in SMEs (Lewis et al. 2014) revealed that although gendered assumptions are often strong in SMEs, especially in male dominated sectors, it is often easier in practice to provide informal supports for parents in SMEs than in large, hierarchical organizations and that such support can have a number of positive outcomes for employees and for employers.

SMEs are also more strongly influenced by their local communities and environment than large firms (Edwards and Ram 2006). Societal views on the role of men as fathers and workers can be expected to influence strongly the level of support at the workplace (Carlier et al. 2012). Thus national context is important for understanding work and family supports in SMEs. For example, in a study of small and large organizations in Spain and Latin America, Carlier et al. (2012) found that although formal family-friendly *policies* are less common in Latin American than in Spanish firms, actual family-friendly *practices* were more readily available in SMEs than in larger firms in Latin America (but not in Spain). The authors propose that this may be a consequence of strong family-oriented cultural values which result in Latin American managers providing family-friendly working arrangements. However, their motivation to do so may be driven by the need to support women in their traditional roles as carers rather than with a view to address gendered career issues.

Research focusing on fathers in SMEs is rare. The limited evidence concerning the relationship between firm size and father friendliness is mixed and appears to vary according to national context (Lewis et al. 2014). Nevertheless, there is some indication that fathers may be more willing to take up family leave in smaller and less hierarchical firms where there are fewer opportunities for promotion and therefore less to lose than in larger organization. Illustrating the experiences of fathers in SMEs in a Japanese study, Ishii-Kuntz (2013) found that greater levels of reported autonomy at work, as well as companies' accommodation of parental needs (including parental leave and fathers' evaluation of these provisions) increase involvement in childcare for men working in SMEs, but not in larger companies where job stress reduces such involvement.

Thus the key characteristics of SMEs and emergent findings from the limited research on work and family issues in SMEs indicate the difficulties in generalising work family and fatherhood research findings from large to smaller organizations. Given the greater number of people working in smaller rather than larger organizations, this is a significant gap.

Another important challenge is to broaden the national contexts studied, not least because research in developing country contexts can draw attention to what we take for granted as western researchers. Most research on work and families, and on gendered organizational assumptions and practices, focuses on relatively privileged workers in developed countries. Research that examines work-family issues in the developing world overwhelmingly focuses on large, often multinational companies (MNCs) (Lewis et al. 2014). This may be because it is easier to gain access to MNCs than small indigenous businesses. However, the majority of the population in these counties work in small enterprises and in the informal economy. Research focusing on MNCs thus fails to provide a picture of the experiences of work and family and the support available to the majority of the country's workforce.

A qualitative study of workers with family responsibilities in both the formal and informal economy in Ghana (Stumbitz et al. 2015), illustrates the importance of work and family research in developing countries taking account of multiple layers of context – global, national, regional (rural or urban) organizational and cultural. At the global layer the ILO sets global standards for workplace support for pregnant women and workers with family responsibilities which are implemented to varying extents across national contexts. In Ghana, maternity entitlements are enacted through Labour Act 2003 (Act 651) and appear generous in international context, but cross-country comparisons of regulatory provisions can often be misleading. For example, according to Ghanaian law, new mothers are entitled to 12 weeks' maternity leave, paid at 100% of previous earnings. In practice, however, only a small percentage of women workers currently benefit from these entitlements, as more than 80% are self-employed or work in informal employment, where regulation is often not enforced (GSS 2013a; Osei-Boateng and Ampratwum 2011; Osei-Boateng 2011). In addition, maternity leave is expected to be paid fully by the employer, which is a substantial burden on small enterprises, often putting the firm's survival at risk, particularly in poverty-stricken remote rural areas and if employing more than one woman of childbearing age. Organizational size in diverse regions is therefore an important aspect of context in relation to supports available to parents. Stumbitz et al. (2014) found that MNCs and other large firms were most likely to offer statutory maternity provisions in the form of paid time off for antenatal visits, maternity leave (sometimes beyond statutory provisions) and paid breastfeeding breaks upon return to work. However, larger organizations were characterised by a more individualistic work culture and were often perceived by employees to be less family-friendly than smaller firms. New mothers in larger organizations were particularly concerned about childcare support and limited ability to combine work with breastfeeding. Experiences were not dissimilar to those reported in research in developed countries with relatively short maternity leave entitlements.

Small firms, on the other hand, tended to find it difficult to provide any paid maternity leave and, with little national emphasis on enforcement of regulations, the level of support provided, if any, also depended on whether the employee had already proven to be skilled and trustworthy. Consequently, the length of maternity leave for individual women and the rate at which it was paid was inconsistent and inequitable. While some women received some leave and pay, others received no paid leave. At the extreme, especially in very poor rural areas, women often return to work a few days after the birth with the baby strapped to their backs. Obviously there are considerable health risks to such circumstances, especially in a country with a very high level of maternal and child mortality (GSS 2013b). Yet in less extreme cases, it was much more common for small employers than larger ones to allow workers to bring children to work and also to breastfeed at the workplace. Workers with these informal work arrangements had a much lower sense of entitlement to formal support and were often more content with the level of support received than employees in large firms, who had access to formal but not informal supports.

The situation was very different for fathers. No ILO global standards currently exist concerning paternity and parental leave and there is currently no provision on paid or unpaid paternity or parental leave in Ghana. Nevertheless, Stumbitz et al. (2014) reported that paternity leave was often available in large firms and also offered by some small firms. However, the number of men taking up such provisions was minute. Gendered organizational culture can be a powerful obstacle to take up of family related leaves by men, but this also overlaps and intersects with wider cultural norms especially in small organizations (Carlier et al. 2012). For example, according to Stumbitz et al. (2014), social stigmatisation of what were labelled 'womanly' men, who become involved in childcare, remains an important barrier in Ghana, particularly in rural areas. The same applies in other developing countries such as Nepal

(Mullany 2005). Nevertheless, Stumbitz et al. (2014) also reported some evidence of changing norms of masculinity in Ghana, at least in urban areas and amongst highly educated parents. However, change was uneven and, again, context specific.

Equality of opportunities for women has been identified by the World Bank as the most important driver of economic development for low income countries. Father friendliness is important as a contributor to gender equality. Yet discourses of father involvement in families and policies and practices to support egalitarian parenting are often non-existent especially in subsistence, rural economies (Lewis et al. 2014). Challenging traditional views of masculinity will be particularly difficult in these contexts. Nevertheless, returning to the global layer of context, it may be timely to build on small pockets of shifting discourses and emerging practices of fatherhood as well as motherhood, and to link them to wider debates about gender, corporate social responsibility, and responsible and sustainable capitalism as well as sustainable societies.

4.2 How can research contribute to systemic change in gendered organizations?

The final challenge discussed here is how to progress beyond describing and analysing barriers to gender equity and involved fatherhood, towards finding ways of actively contributing to systemic change in workplaces and supporting change in families. How can gendered organizational assumptions, cultures, practices and discourses be challenged and sense of entitlement to gender equity at work and at home be enhanced in a range of contexts?

Research identifying organizational barriers and conditions for overcoming them, including evaluations of both public and workplace policies and practices are of course, important in this respect. To move things forward however, it is necessary to think about how research can be proactive in stimulating context specific changes. The tradition of action research addressing a dual agenda of gender equity and organizational effectiveness (Rapoport et al. 2002; Kim et al. 2016) which challenge gendered ideal worker assumptions, together with other successful programmes of organizational intervention research (Kossek et al. 2014) provide important models for challenging workplace cultures and practices. These programmes have largely been developed in large organizations in the USA. There is also emerging evidence that they can be effective in other industrialised country contexts (Kim et al. 2016). However, the processes involved in bringing about change in these studies are not necessarily easily transferable to all contexts, even within the USA and certainly beyond. For example, a dual agenda action research case study in an IT company in Malta, focusing on male workers, had limited success for a number of reasons, one of which was that the fathers in the study were very happy to work long hours and not be active caregivers (Borg, 2014). They had a high sense of entitlement for support from their partners to enable them to be absorbed in their work and perceived no problem to be addressed. The combination of a very traditionally gendered society, a male dominated industry, and workers who were highly involved in and enjoyed their work rendered the attempted action research irrelevant. It could be argued that in this context there was a lack of readiness to consider active fathering as an issue (Bailey 2015; Johansson and Klinth 2008) and that some changes in the cultural context would be needed before workplace interventions become appropriate. Extending intervention research to a wider range of organizational and national contexts, with different cultural norms and traditions, will thus present many new challenges.

While workplace interventions provide one promising strategy for challenging gendered assumptions in some contexts, there is also a need for intervention research to focus on how workplaces intersect with other layers of context. For example, research examining national parental leave policies with a fathers' quota and their impacts at the workplace level (e.g. Haas and Hwang 2008; Brandth and Kvande 2015) makes a significant contribution to knowledge about the intersection of specific national and workplace contexts. This has potential to influence policy making elsewhere. Nevertheless, there remains resistance to such policy developments in most industrialised countries and they are still largely irrelevant in the developing world. Challenging deeply held convictions about women and men and their reproductive and economic roles in wider society in many national contexts would be a huge challenge, potentially involving support from a range of key stakeholders, including government, employers, educational organizations and NGOs (Johansson 2011; Matzner-Heruti 2014). Nevertheless some pockets of change are occurring in gendered values even in some very traditional contexts (Stumbitz et al. 2014), implying that intervention research at some level may be valuable.

Research on work and family has made considerable strides in the half century since Rapoport and Rapoport first drew attention to the intersection between work and family, not least in terms of greater attention to men, especially fathers, as well as understanding of the impact of gendered assumptions in the workplace and, more recently, intervention studies to contribute to organizational change. Nevertheless, gendered organizations and related gendered sense of entitlement to support for active parenting persist. There is some evidence of shifts in workplaces and different ways of doing masculinity in work and families, within some contexts. A focus on intersections of various layers of context may help to identify combinations of conditions that could contribute to both mother and father-friendly workplaces for more than just Western and relatively privileged workers.

References

Abendroth, A. K. and Den Dulk, L. (2011) 'Support for the work-life balance in Europe: The impact of state, workplace and family support on work-life balance satisfaction', *Work, Employment & Society,* 25(2) pp. 234–256

Acker, J. (1990) 'Hierarchies, jobs, bodies: A theory of gendered organizations', *Gender & Society,* 4(2) pp. 139–158

Acker, J. (1998) 'The future of 'gender and organizations': connections and boundaries', *Gender, Work & Organization,* 5(4) pp 195–206

Allen, T. D., French, K. A., Dumani, S. and Shockley, K. M. (2015) 'Meta-analysis of work–family conflict mean differences: Does national context matter?', *Journal of Vocational Behavior,* 90, pp. 90–100

Bailey, J. (2015) 'Understanding contemporary fatherhood: masculine care and the patriarchal deficit', *Families, Relationships and Societies,* 4(1) pp. 3–17

Bailyn, L. (1993) *Breaking the mold: Women, men, and time in the new corporate world.* London: Simon and Schuster

Bailyn, L. (2006) *Breaking the mold: Redesigning work for productive and satisfying lives.* Ithaca (NY): Cornell University Press

Blickenstaff, J. (2005) 'Women and science careers: leaky pipeline or gender filter?', *Gender and Education,* 17(4) pp. 369–386

Borg, A. (2014) *A CIAR study in a male dominated ICT Company in Malta which looks at work-life issues through the masculine lens: A case of: if it ain't' broke, don't fix it?,* Unpublished PhD thesis . Middlesex University, London

Brandth, B. and Kvande, E. (2015) 'Fathers and flexible parental leave', *Work, Employment and Society,* 1–16

Brannen, J. and Nilsen, A. (2005). 'Individualisation, choice and structure: a discussion of current trends in sociological analysis', *The Sociological Review,* 53(3) pp. 412–428

Bylsma, W. H. and Major, B. (1994) 'Social Comparisons and Contentment Exploring the Psychological Costs of the Gender Wage Gap', *Psychology of Women Quarterly,* 18(2) pp. 241–249

Cahusac, E. and Kanji, S. (2014) 'Giving up: How gendered organizational cultures push mothers out', *Gender, Work & Organization,* 21(1) pp. 57–70

Carlier, S.I., Llorente, C.L. and Grau, M.G. (2012) 'Comparing work–life balance in Spanish and Latin-American countries', *European Journal of Training and Development,* 36, pp. 286–307

Christopher, K. (2012) 'Extensive Mothering Employed Mothers' Constructions of the Good Mother', *Gender & Society,* 26 (1) pp. 73–96

Connell, R. (2012) 'Masculinity research and global change', *Masculinities & Social Change,* 1(1) pp. 4–18

Corby, S. and Symon, G. (eds) (2011) *Working for the State.* Basingstoke: Palgrave Macmillan.

Crompton, R., Lewis, S. and Lyonette, C. (eds) (2007) *Women, Men, Work and Family in Europe.* Basingstoke: Palgrave

Croucher, R., Stumbitz, B., Vickers, I. and Quinlan, M. (2013) *Can better working conditions improve the performance of SMEs? – An international literature review,* Geneva: International Labour Organization

De Kok, J., Deijl, C. and Veldhuis-Van Essen, C. (2013) *Is small still beautiful? Literature review of recent empirical evidence on the contribution of SMEs to employment creation.* Geneva: International Labour Organization.

Dex, S. and Smith, C. (2002) *The Nature and Pattern of Family-friendly Employment Policies in Britain.* Bristol: Policy Press

Edwards, P. and Ram, M. (2006) ,Surviving on the margins of the economy: Working relationships in small, low-wage firms', *Journal of Management Studies,* 43, pp. 895–916

Fagnani, J. and Letablier, M. T. (2004) 'Work and family life balance: the effects of the 35 hour law in France Work', *Employment and Society,* 18(3) pp. 551–57

Gambles, R., Lewis, S. and Rapoport, R. (2006) *The Myth of Work-Life Balance: The Challenge of our Time. Men, Women, and Societies.* Chichester, John Wiley

Granovetter, M. (1985) 'Economic Action and Social Structure: 'The Problem of Embeddedness", *American Journal of Sociology,* 91(3) pp. 481–510

GSS (2013a) *Ghana Living Standards Survey 6 – With Labour Force Module (GLSS6/LFS) 2012/2013.* Accra: Ghana Statistical Service

GSS (2013b) *2010 Population and Housing Census – Millennium Development Goals in Ghana.* Accra: Ghana Statistical Service

Guillaume, C. and Pochic, S. (2009) 'What would you sacrifice? Access to top management and work-life balance', *Gender, Work and Organization,* 16(1) pp. 14–36

Haas, L. and Hwang, C. P. (2008) 'The Impact of Taking Parental Leave on Fathers' Participation In Childcare And Relationships With Children: Lessons from Sweden'. *Community, Work & Family,* 11(1) pp. 85–104

Herman, C. and Lewis, S. (2012) 'Entitled to a sustainable career? Motherhood in science, engineering and technology', *Journal of Social Issues,* 68(4) pp. 767–789

Hobson, B. (ed.) (2013) *Worklife Balance: the agency and capabilities gap.* Oxford: Oxford University Press

Holt, H. and Lewis, S. (2011) ''You Can Stand on Your Head and Still End Up with Lower Pay': Gliding Segregation and Gendered Work Practices in Danish 'Family-friendly'Workplaces', *Gender, Work & Organization,* 18 (s1) e202–e221

Hook, J. L. (2015) ,Incorporating 'class' into work–family arrangements: Insights from and for Three *Worlds', Journal of European Social Policy,* 25(1) pp. 14–31

Ishii-Kuntz, M. (2013) 'Work environment and Japanese fathers' involvement in child care', *Journal of Family Issues,* 34, pp. 250–269

Johansson, T. (2011) 'Fatherhood in Transition: Paternity Leave and Changing Masculinities', *Journal of Family Communication,* 11(3) pp. 165–180

Johansson, T. and Ottemo, A. (2015) 'Ruptures in hegemonic masculinity: the dialectic between ideology and utopia', *Journal of Gender Studies,* 24 (2), 192–206

Kim, H., Bailyn, L. and Kolb, D. (2016) 'Revisiting the Dual Agenda: Why companies miss the point when they retract flexible work arrangements during bad times', in S. Lewis, D. Anderson, C. Lyonette, N. Payne and S. Wood (eds) *Work-Work-Life Balance in Times of Recession, Austerity and Beyond: meeting the needs of employees, organizations and social justice.* New York: Routledge

Kossek, E. E., Hammer, L. B., Kelly, E. L. and Moen, P. (2014) 'Designing work, family & health organizational change initiatives', *Organizational dynamics,* 43(1) pp. 53–63

Lerner, M. J. (1987) 'Integrating societal and psychological rules of entitlement: The basic task of each social actor and fundamental problem for the social sciences', *Social Justice Research,* 1(1) pp. 107–125

Lewis, S (2009) 'Flexible working policies, gender and culture change', in: *Women in Science and Technology. Creating sustainable careers.* Brussels: European Commission

Lewis, S. and Haas, L. (2005) Work-life integration and social policy: a social justice theory and gender equity approach to work and family, in: Kossek, EE and Lambert, S (eds) *Work and Life Integration,* Lawrence Erlbaum Associates

Lewis, S. and Smithson, J. (2001) 'Sense of entitlement to support for the reconciliation of employment and family life', *Human Relations,* 55(11) pp. 1455–81

Lewis, S., Izraeli, D. N. and Hootsmans, H. (eds) (1992) *Dual-earner families: International perspectives.* London: Sage.

Lewis, S., Stumbitz, B., Miles, L. and Rouse, J. (2014) *Maternity protection in SMEs. An International Review.* Geneva: International Labour Organization

Lewis. S., Brannen, J. and Nilsen, A. (2009) *Work, Families and Organisations in Transition: European Perspectives.* London: Policy Press

Lyness, K. S. and Judiesch, M. K. (2014) 'Gender egalitarianism and work–life balance for managers: multisource perspectives in 36 countries', *Applied Psychology,* 63(1) pp. 96–129

Lewis, S., Anderson, D., Lyonette, C., Payne, N. and Wood, S. (2017) 'Public sector austerity cuts in Britain and the changing discourse of work–life balance', *Work, Employment & Society,* doi: 10.1177/0950017016638994

Major, B. (1993) 'Gender, entitlement, and the distribution of family labor, *Journal of Social Issues,* 49(3) pp. 141–159

Matzner-Heruti, I. (2014) 'All You Need Is Leave: Rethinking the concept of paternity leave', *Cardozo JL & Gender,* 21, p. 475.

Meyerson, D. and Tompkins, M. (2007) 'Tempered radicals as institutional change agents: The case of advancing gender equity at the University of Michigan', *Harvard Journal of Law and Gender,* 30, p. 303

Mullany, B. C., Hindin, M.J. and Becker, S. (2005) 'Can women's autonomy impede male involvement in pregnancy health in Katmandu, Nepal?', *Social Science and Medicine,* 6, pp. 1993–2006

Nilsen A., Brannen, J. and Lewis, S. (2012) *'Transitions to parenthood in Europe. A Comparative Life Course Perspective.'* Bristol: Policy Press

Nussbaum, M. (2000) 'Women's capabilities and social justice', *Journal of Human Development,* 1(2) pp. 219–247

Ollier-Malaterre, A., Valcour, M., Den Dulk, L. and Kossek, E. E. (2013) 'Theorizing national context to develop comparative work–life research: A review and research agenda', *European Management Journal*, 31(5) pp. 433–447

Osei-Boateng, C. (2011) 'The Informal Sector in Ghana: A Focus on Domestic Workers, Street Vendors and Head Porters (Kayayei)', Background Paper. Labour Research and Policy Institute, Ghana Trades Union Congress (TUC)

Osei-Boateng, C. and Ampratwum, E. (2011) *The informal sector in Ghana*. Ghana: Friedrich Ebert Stiftung.

Peper, B., den Dulk, L., Lewis, S., Cerigoj Sadar, N. and Smithson, J. (2013) 'Capabilities for work-life balance: Managerial attitudes and employee practices in the Dutch, British and Slovenian banking sector', in: Hobson, B. (ed.) (2013) *Work-life Balance: the agency and capabilities gap*. Oxford: Oxford University Press

Powell, G. N., Francesco, A. M. and Ling, Y. (2009) 'Toward culture – sensitive theories of the work-family interface', *Journal of Organizational Behavior*, 30(5) pp. 597–616

Rapoport, R. and Rapoport, R. (1965) 'Work and family in contemporary society', *American Sociological Review*, pp. 381–394

Rapoport, R., Bailyn, L., Fletcher, J. and Pruitt, B. (2002) *Beyond work-family balance: advancing gender equity and workplace performance*. San Francisco: Jossey-Bass

Rapoport, R., Rapoport, R. N. and Strelitz, Z. (1977) *Fathers, mothers and society: towards new alliances*. New York: Basic Books (AZ)

Rubery, J. and Rafferty, A. (2013) 'Women and recession revisited', *Work, Employment & Society*, 27(3) pp. 414–432

Schein, V. E. (2007) 'Women in management: reflections and projections', *Women in Management Review*, 22(1) pp. 6–18

Sen, A. (1999) *Development as Freedom*. Oxford: Oxford University Press

Stumbitz.B., Kyei, A., Lewis, S. and Lyon, F. (2014) *The Legal, Policy and Regulatory Environment Governing Maternity Protection and Workers with Family Responsibilities in the Formal and Informal Economy of Ghana including Practices, Gaps and Measures for Improvement*. Report submitted to the International Labour Organization, Geneva

Voydanoff, P. (2014) *Work, family, and community: Exploring interconnections*. London: Psychology Press

Walters, P. and Whitehouse, G. (2014) 'Mothers' perceptions of support in the workplace: A sense of entitlement or resignation?', *Journal of Sociology*, DOI: 1440783314536793

Webber, G. and Williams, C. (2008) 'Part-time work and the gender division of labor', *Qualitative Sociology*, 31(1) pp. 15–36

Williams, C. L., Muller, C. and Kilanski, K. (2012) 'Gendered organizations in the new economy', *Gender & Society*, 26(4) pp. 549–573

Yeandle, S., Crompton, R., Wigfield, A. and Dennett, J. (2002) *Employers, communities and family-friendly employment policies*. Chicago: Joseph Rowntree Foundation

6. Authors and Editors

About the Authors

Annette von Alemann, Dr., is a senior researcher at University of Cologne, Germany, developing young scientists in the field of educational research. In her research, she focuses on social and gender inequalities in organizations, both in work and educational contexts. Her study about patterns of interpretation in management was published in 2015. From 2011 to 2015, she was a research associate in the project 'Work Organizations and Life Conduct of Fathers' at Bielefeld University, Germany (Collaborative Research Center 882 *From Heterogeneities to Inequalities*).

Sandra Beaufaÿs, Dr., is a senior researcher at GESIS, Leibniz Institute for the Social Sciences in Cologne, Germany. Her main research interests are the academic profession, gender in higher education, and gender in work contexts and professions. From 2012 to 2015 she was a research associate in the project 'Work Organizations and Life Conduct of Fathers' at Bielefeld University, Germany, as part of the Collaborative Research Center 882 *From Heterogeneities to Inequalities.*

Mary Blair-Loy, PhD, is Associate Professor at the Department of Sociology, UC San Diego, and Director of the Center for Research on Gender in STEMM, USA. She uses multiple methods to study gender, the economy, work, and family. Her empirical research has examined business elites, call center workers, and professionals in science and technology. Her book, *Competing Devotions: career and family among executive women,* won the William J. Goode Award from the American Sociological Association and was listed as one of the 100 most-cited works in Sociology, 2008–2012.

Berit Brandth is Professor (em.) of Sociology at the Department of Sociology and Political Science, at the Norwegian University of Science and Technology (NTNU). Her research interests include work-family issues, gender and rural sociology. She has been working extensively on topics dealing with gender in rural industries such as agriculture, forestry and tourism. A second main topic is family policies, particularly fathers' use of parental leave. Recent publications include 'Rural masculinity and fathering practices (*Gender, Place and Culture* 2016).

Sigtona Halrynjo, PhD, is Senior Research Fellow at the Institute for Social Research, Oslo, Norway, and member of Center for Research on Gender Equality (CORE). Current research include interplay between family policies and work-family dynamics, career tracks and gender (im)balance in top management. She has authored and co-authored articles published in *British Journal of Sociology, Gender, Work and Organization and International Journal of Police Science & Management*. Halrynjo is co-editor of the book *Work-Family Dynamics: competing logics of regulation, economy and morals*, Routledge Advances in Sociology.

Stephan Höyng, Dr., is Professor for Social Work with boys and men at the Catholic University of Applied Social Sciences, Berlin, Germany, and Director of the Institute for Gender and Diversity in Social Practice Research. His current research focuses on masculinities in relation to employment and care, on men and employment equality, and on men in child care centers. He is also board member of the federal forum for men, an association for boys, husbands and fathers.

Florian Kohlbacher, Dr., is the North Asia Director of The Economist Corporate Network in Tokyo, where he manages the Networks in Japan and South-Korea. Prior to joining The Economist Group Florian was an Associate Professor of Marketing and Innovation in the International Business School Suzhou (IBSS) at Xi'an Jiaotong-Liverpool University (XJTLU) in China, and the Founding Director of the XJTLU Research Institute on Ageing and Society (RIAS).

Christian Kron, MA, is a Junior Research Fellow at the Institute for Research and Development of Collaborative Processes at the University of Applied Sciences, Northwestern Switzerland. Prior to this engagement he studied psychology at the University of Zurich with main interests in coaching, collaborative processes mediated by group goals and group efficacy, and general topics of social psychology.

Elin Kvande, Dr., is Professor of Sociology at the Department of Sociology and Political Science, Norwegian University of Science and Technology (NTNU). Her research focuses on gender relations in work organizations and work-family reconciliation. Recent publications include 'Masculinity and Fathering Alone during Parental Leave (*Men and Masculinities* 2016, with Berit Brandth). She is co-editor of *Work-Family Dynamics: competing logics of regulation, economy and morals*, Routledge Advances in Sociology.

Suzan Lewis, PhD, is Professor of Organizational Psychology at Middlesex University, London, United Kingdom. Her research focuses on work-personal life issues and workplace practice, culture and change in diverse national contexts. Her recent research includes a study of work-life balance in UK public sector organizations in a time of austerity. She is a founding editor of the international journal *Community, Work and Family* and currently Vice President of the international Work Family Researchers Network.

Selma Therese Lyng is a sociologist and senior researcher at the Work Research Institute, Oslo and Akershus University College of Applied Sciences in Norway. Her research focuses on mechanisms and dynamics of inclusion and exclusion in education and working life. She is currently finalizing her PhD dissertation on gender and work-family conflict in career jobs. She has authored and co-authored articles published in *British Journal of Sociology, Men and Masculinities* and *Gender and Education.*

Michael Meuser, Dr., is Professor for the Sociology of Gender Relations at the TU Dortmund University, Germany. His research interests include the sociology of gender relations, knowledge and the body, and qualitative research methods. Currently he is conducting a project on fathers in parental leave, which focuses on negotiation and decision-making processes in partnerships and work organizations.

Annalisa Murgia, PhD, teaches Human Resources Management at the Department of Sociology and Social Research at the University of Trento, Italy. She is currently the Scientific Coordinator of the FP7 project GARCIA: Gendering the Academy and Research: Combating Career Instability and Asymmetries. Her research interests focus on precariousness and on the social construction of gender in organisations. Her works on fatherhood and hegemonic masculinity have been published in the journals *Organization* and *Gender, Work and Organization.*

Benjamin Neumann, MA, is a research assistant at the institute for sociology at the TU Dortmund University, Germany. His research interests focus on Gender-/Queer Studies, Cultural Sociology, Family and Relationships, (Poststructural-)Discourse Analysis, Epistemology and Qualitative Methodology. Currently he is working within a research project on fathers in parental leave, which focuses on the negotiation and decision making processes of couples' and work organizations.

Barbara Poggio, PhD, is Vice-Rector for Equality and Diversity Policies at the University of Trento, Italy, where she also coordinates the Centre for Interdisciplinary Gender Studies. She teaches Sociology of Work and Sociology of Organisation at the Department of Sociology and Social Research. Her research interests mainly deal with social and narrative construction of gender in organisations, gender and entrepreneurship and work-life balance policies.

Johanna Possinger, Dr., is a Professor for Gender Studies and Social Work at the Protestant University of Applied Sciences Ludwigsburg, Germany. From 2012 to the summer of 2016 she was head of the research group *Family Policy and Family Support* at the German Youth Institute in Munich. Her major fields of research and publication are family policy, fatherhood, reconciliation of work and care, as well as child poverty.

Christoph Schimkowsky MA, studied Anthropological Research Methods at the School of Oriental and African Studies (SOAS), University of London. He is currently continuing his studies as a Japanese Government Scholarship student at the Graduate School of Asia-Pacific Studies, Waseda University, Tokyo and is working as a research associate at the Economist Corporate Network in Tokyo. His research interests include the social construction of cultural identities and nationalism in East Asia.

Bianca Stumbitz, Dr., is a Research Associate at Middlesex University in London, United Kingdom. In 2015, she concluded a study on workers with family responsibilities in Ghana, which examined the feasibility of innovative maternity and paternity supports at low or no cost. In collaboration with the Universiti Sains Malaysia, Bianca and her colleagues also develop local capacity with respect to maternity protection research, policy and practice in Malaysia. Recently Bianca has co-authored the ILO publication *Maternity protection in SMEs: an international review.*

Stacy J. Williams is a PhD candidate in sociology at the University of California, San Diego and a Visiting Scholar in Nutrition and Food Studies at New York University, USA. Her research on feminism and cooking demonstrates that the home is an important site of social movement activity. In a piece in *Advances in Gender Research,* Williams shows how feminists have advocated for cooking in ways that challenge patriarchal institutions.

About the Editors

Brigitte Liebig, Dr., is Professor for Organizational Science at the University of Applied Sciences, Northwestern Switzerland and lecturer for the Sociology of Gender at the University of Basel, Switzerland. Her research interests include various issues on gender, work and organization, on science and education, and on female entrepreneurship. She directed the national research program on 'Gender Equality' (2008–2015) of the Swiss National Science Foundation. Besides other publications she recently co-edited the book *Gender Equality in Context: Policies and Practices in Switzerland.*

Mechtild Oechsle, Dr., is Professor (em.) of Social Sciences at University of Bielefeld, Germany. Her publications and research focus on gender and work, work life balance, professional orientation and career guidance, sociology of youth, social and cultural change. She has led research projects on life planning of young women, professional and career orientation of young people, and organizations and life conduct of fathers. She has published many books and articles on these issues and is co-editor of a German book series, *Gender and Society.*

Index

www.ingramcontent.com/pod-product-compliance
Lightning Source LLC
Chambersburg PA
CBHW080526220326
41599CB00032B/6220